D0051692

"A good book . . . should help to demystify psychotherapy . . ." *Thomas Szasz*

". . . a service to all of us who are trying to make psychology useful to people." *Leona Tyler, former president, American Psychological Association*

"Fascinating . . . amassed a good deal of dynamite!" *Melitta Schmideberg, psychiatrist*

". . . an important service in showing up the iniquities of so-called 'dynamic' psychotherapy . . . deserves to be widely read." *Joseph Wolpe, M.D., Professor of Psychiatry, Temple University School of Medicine*

". . . should be mandatory reading for anyone who is about to seek mental help for themselves or their loved ones." *Marvin Harris, Department of Anthropology, Columbia University*

Psychotherapy:

THE HAZARDOUS CURE

Dorothy Tennov

ANCHOR BOOKS
ANCHOR PRESS/DOUBLEDAY
GARDEN CITY, NEW YORK
1976

This book was originally published in a hardcover edition by Abelard-Schuman, New York in 1975

Anchor Books Edition: 1976

ISBN: 0-385-11657-8
Copyright © 1975 by Dorothy Tennov
All rights reserved
Printed in the United States

for my aunt, Ann Nystrom

DOROTHY TENNOV, PH.D., is a practicing behavioral consultant and Professor of Psychology at the University of Bridgeport, Connecticut. She is the author of numerous articles on psychological topics published in scientific and educational periodicals and of essays on aspects of woman's condition for feminist publications. She is a member of the American Psychological Association, the British Psychological Society, the Society for Psychotherapy Research, the Association for Women in Psychology, and the National Organization for Women (NOW).

Contents

2 / PSYCHOTHERAPY AND SCIENTIFIC RESEARCH

3 / SOMATOPSYCHIC ILLNESS

7 / ALTERNATIVES TO PSYCHODYNAMIC INSIGHT THERAPY

Preface

As a research psychologist I have long been aware of the weakness of the data upon which assertions of the effectiveness of psychotherapy are based. As a behavioral consultant, I have often worked with clients after years of expensive psychotherapies had failed to help. As a feminist and as a psychologist, I have been forced to recognize that psychodynamic psychotherapy is not yet a footnote on the pages of cultural history but is currently being promoted by an aggressive group of professionals far from ready to concede the defeat implied by doubts and qualifications expressed within their own journals. It was at Women's Movement conferences that I first listened to former patients tell about their personal lives and about the role that therapy and therapists had played in them. Tales of long, traumatic, futile, and expensive psychotherapy shocked and dismayed me. When I tried to describe the status of psychotherapy within science, I was not believed. When I spoke before groups on the subject, I was "controversial"—cheered by some, literally cursed by others. I found that I could not explain it all in a two-hour talk; hence, this book.

I have written with restraint. With few exceptions, only points that are well documented and enjoy widespread agreement within the profession or among scientific psychologists have been included. I have emphasized commonly used, standard, professionally acceptable psychotherapy techniques and practices, not therapist behaviors that would be condemned by the professionals themselves. My emphasis is not on psychotherapy malpractice.

Nor is this a personal vendetta. I have not been directly and personally harmed by psychotherapy. My one three-month experience with psychotherapy was undertaken in my college days with a view toward personal improvement. It turned out to be disappointingly dull and too expensive, but not otherwise harmful. On two subsequent occasions I was subjected to a "psychiatric interview," once as part of a general medical diagnostic workup and once in connection with the therapy of a family member. In both instances I was declared to be essentially sound psychiatrically and not in need of treatment.

On the other hand, I cannot say that I have been totally unaffected in my personal life by the nature of psychotherapy practices as they exist. I have often wished that there were counseling services available in which one could be safe fron insult and damaging disrespect. If there had been, I would have sought them out over the years, for myself once or twice, and many times for others. Because I was aware of the dangers of interpretation and consequent entrapment, I did not seek therapy services nor refer my students, clients, friends, or family members to them. It is unfortunate that the kind of help my clients in behavioral practice receive today was not available during those years.

Because my focus, although not my exclusive concern, is on females who are psychotherapy patients, and because we do not yet have a satisfactory substitute for male pronouns used as if generic, I use the female pronouns to refer to patients and clients avoiding use of male terms even in material quoted from others. Unless a specific male patient is being referred to, I substitute female pronouns in brackets. Because psychotherapy is largely based on patriarchal assumptions and because most therapists are male, psychotherapists are designated by male terms. This solution to the problem of pronouns is entirely ad hoc. I invite others not to copy my example, but rather to adopt a new pronoun system in which the generic is expressed by neutral terms. On the subject of psychotherapy, however, there is some value in continually reminding the reader that the field consists largely of men behind the desk and women in front of it, or on the couch.

The women I visualize as I write are composites of women I have known, interviewed, or read of. Mostly, they began private, individual, "talking" psychotherapy in their twenties, thirties, or forties because they felt depressed, anxious for inexplicable reasons, or worried about a marital or family problem. Some of them began therapy in a clinic or hospital, sometimes as children or adolescents. A few had drug or sexual problems. For many of them, whatever their initial reason for involvement, therapy came eventually to function partly as a kind of religion in that responsibility for both well-being and for life's decisions were given over to another agent (the therapist). For others, it was a welcome distraction from everyday tedium. Neither the appearance nor the behavior of the woman in my mind's eye differs from women of her age and background who are not psychiatry patients. I believe that the bulk of women "patients" are not mentally ill but particularly afflicted by the "woman's situation."

Acknowledgments

I want to express my great appreciation to the many persons who helped me in one way or another, either directly or indirectly.

For the encouragement they gave me as a person and as a writer, I am grateful to Elane Rehr, Pat Ginoni, Nancy Henley, Andrew Deering, Esther Hodge, Carol Turner, Marjory Collins, Miriam Keiffer, Joanne Steele, Lolly Hirsch, Marion Masone, Colette Price, Howard Parsons, Joanne Evans Gardner, Barbara Sang, Ellen Bissert, Pat Howe, Michelle Vian, Florence Rush, Joan Joesting, my son Randall, and many members of the Association for Women in Psychology, The Women's Liberation Workshop of London, the New York Radical Feminists, and the National Organization for Women (NOW).

I also thank the hundreds of patients and former patients who responded to questionnaires, allowed themselves to be interviewed, spoke to me informally about their psychotherapy experiences, gave me written accounts, and repeatedly asked, When is the book coming out? They would not let me forget the importance of the topic, which served to keep my own interest and motivation alive.

I was also encouraged by the school psychologists who confided that they would prefer to adopt a behavioral, rather than a psychodynamic approach, if "politics" permitted, and by many of my students, particularly those who were parents or teachers, who told of damage done to children by the diagnoses and accusations of mental health professionals.

A very special kind of gratitude is reserved for those who read and commented on various portions of the manuscript. Most important on this list is Helen Payne who read, or allowed me to read to her, large portions of the first draft, and who gave the kind of support at that difficult stage without which I might have floundered endlessly in revisions. Helen also helped me attack the unexpectedly arduous task of putting the notes together. I do not like to think of how things might have gone without her guidance and skill.

Others who read portions of the manuscript and gave comment, sometimes invaluable suggestions, and always support and encouragement, were Helene Silverstein, who also helped with interviews, Evan Morley, Virginia Blaisdell, Naomi Weisstein, Jennifer Abod, Mathew Vittucci, Joanne Steele, Jean Ferson, Ruth Grant, Frances Foster, Debra Kirby, Mary Orovan, and Wilma Scott Heide, and my editor, Linda Schjeldahl.

And for the invaluable help that came from just letting me talk over some point, or from the contribution of an important insight of their own, or both, there was Lolly Hirsch, Evelyn Harris, Florence Rush, Helene Silverstein, Mary Coddington, Selma Bunks, and many, many others.

I also want to thank my colleagues at scientific conventions and meetings who expressed interest and gave their encouragement toward this undertaking. These include several members of the Society for Psychotherapy Research.

Claudia Stephens deserves my gratitude for the accuracy and astuteness with which she assisted in organizing notes, taking care of correspondence, and retyping. Others who helped with sundry details were Ruth Grant and Mathew Vittucci, who helped with references, William Kornsey, who helped with library research, my son, Daniel, who worked on the bibliography, and Mary Orovan, Nora Budzilek, and my mother, Lois Miller, who contributed assistance to various aspects of manuscript preparation.

My deep gratitude and awe at their being able to manage the horrendous task of typing from handwriting goes to Claudia Stephens, Elaine Greytak, Norma MacDaniel, and Elinor Carlson.

I am grateful to my son Russell who shared the house with me during the months of writing and, in countless ways, demonstrated his respect for me and my work.

Finally, I want to thank Dr. Melitta Schmideberg who agreed to let me quote at length from her articles even when she was not sure she was entirely happy with my approach, and Simone de Beauvoir, first person to read the entire manuscript, and whose comments about it were in themselves sufficient to justify the whole enterprise.

I wish to thank the following authors and publishers for permission to reprint portions of their work:

Arbor House Publishing Company, Inc., for permission to reprint from *The Making of a Psychiatrist* by David S. Viscott, copyright © 1974 by David S. Viscott

Grove Press for permission to reprint from *Joy* by William C. Schutz, copyright © 1967 by William C. Schutz

Saul I. Harrison, Donald J. Carek, and Little, Brown and Company, for permission to reprint from *A Guide to Psychotherapy* by Saul I. Harrison, M.D., and Donald J. Carek, M.D., copyright © 1966 by Saul I. Harrison and Donald J. Carek

Lewis B. Hill and the University of Chicago Press, for permission to reprint from *Psychotherapeutic Intervention in Schizophrenia*, by Lewis B. Hill, M.D., copyright © 1955 by the University of Chicago

John Murray (Publishers) Ltd., for permission to reprint from *This Stranger, My Son* by Louise Wilson, copyright © 1968 by Louise Wilson

Holt, Rinehart and Winston, for permission to reprint from *The Modes and Morals of Psychotherapy* by Perry London, copyright © 1970 by Holt, Rinehart and Winston, and from *Fundamentals of Experimental Psychology* by Charles L. Sheridan, copyright © 1971 by Holt, Rinehart and Winston

Princeton University Press, for permission to reprint from *The Freud/Jung Letters,* ed. by William McGuire, trans. by Ralph Manheim and R. F. C. Hull, Bollingen series XCIV (copyright © 1974 by Sigmund Freud Copyrights Ltd. and Erbengemeinschaft Prof. Dr. C. G. Jung)

Psychology Today, for permission to reprint from "The Long Weekend" by Frederick H. Stoller, reprinted from *Psychology Today* magazine, December, 1967, copyright © 1974 Ziff-Davis Publishing Company

John Wiley and Sons, Inc., for permission to reprint from *Handbook of Psychotherapy and Behavior Change* by Allen E. Bergin and Sol L. Garfield, copyright © 1971 by John Wiley and Sons, Inc.

F. E. Peacock Publishers, Inc., Itasca, Illinois, for permission to reprint from *Current Psychotherapies* by Raymond Corsini, editor

PSYCHOTHERAPY: THE HAZARDOUS CURE

1
The Psychodynamic Psychotherapy Experience

PSYCHOTHERAPY

Insight, or psychodynamic, psychotherapists assume causation to lie within the patient; they utilize emotional response of the patient to the therapy relationship; and they expect that improvement will result from a developing comprehension of the underlying dynamics of her personality. This process comes about through more or less "nondirective" interviews in the therapist's office in which the therapist offers little or no direct advice and it is usually up to the patient to bring forth "material" for examination. The therapist's job is to understand the patient better than she understands herself, and then to guide her to self-knowledge, usually by developing interpretations and eventually communicating them to her. Acceptance and recognition of her own previously unconscious processes is, if not a cure in itself, a major step on the way to "recovery."

Traditional insight therapy conforms to a disease or medical model, and the quasi-medical terminology with which psychotherapists talk to one another and their clients will be used in much of this book in order to reflect its use in the psychiatric literature. In psychotherapy, the *patient* is *sick*. The *pathology* is of *internal origin*. *Symptoms* are useful in indicating that a hidden illness is present. *Remission of symptoms* is not only not a *cure,* but could actually postpone *recovery*. Direct removal or alleviation of symptomatic distress is usually not desirable because (1) the symptom is not the illness, and therefore treatment of symptoms alone could lead to the development of new, perhaps more serious, symptoms if the underlying cause is not eradicated, and (2) the anxiety produced by symptoms provides motivation for continuing treatment. A *doctor* directs the therapy, usually makes a *diagnosis,* and often identifies the patient's *syndrome* with a technical term. Note that while the terms are medical, *the sickness is not organic.* The psychodynamic psychotherapist does not expect that discernible lesions in the brain or other parts of the nervous system, or any part of the body will ever be found to be the cause of the "disease" he treats. The illness is purely "psychological"; it is the way the organism functions, not the physiological structures, that are at fault. The patient's symptoms stem from psychic complexes based in childhood trauma, or on maladaptive and illogical unconscious forces which determine behavior. The basic principle can be defined as "it's all in your head" where "head" does not refer to a physical structure. In traditional insight therapy, no drugs, no change in diet, no surgery, no physical regimen is ever indicated. The treatment is talk. Psychoanalysts, who in this country are almost all M.D.'s, do not conduct physical examinations of their patients. Other psychiatrists, generally still very much under the influence of psychoanalysts and psychoanalysis, rarely conduct physical examinations, although they do prescribe physical treatments, particularly when they deal with patients who are not psychotherapy patients, such as those confined in mental hospitals.

The underlying concept is that action results from motives, that disordered behavior is the result of peculiarities inside the individual, and that therapy aims to loosen the bond between the inner states and the disordered behavior they produce.[1] Under the gentle Socratic guidance of the psychotherapist, the patient engages in dialogue with herself in keeping with the ancient ideal (Know Thyself), and in expectation that the truths discovered thereby will free her of her problems. To the orthodox Freudian, the analyst was both anonymous and "objective." Lately, the emphasis has turned to the patient-therapist *relationship*.[2]

The first private practitioners of traditional insight psychotherapy were psychiatrists. Within recent decades, clinical psychologists have tended to forego their previous limited role as personality assessors and diagnosticians and open offices of their own, as have social workers. In *The Fifth Profession*, Henry, Sims, and Spray note an overall similarity of both techniques and clientele despite theoretical differences and differences in professional training among psychoanalysts, psychologists, social workers, and psychiatrists. But in the public mind, of course, the medical doctor is supreme. The columnist Ann Landers recently stated emphatically that the professional of choice as psychotherapist was the psychiatrist *because of his medical background*.

FREUD

It is often claimed that Sigmund Freud is rightfully ranked with Copernicus and Darwin in forcing drastically changed conceptions of the place of human beings in the universe. According to this view, Freud forced humanity to recognize that our rational superiority over other animals was but an other example of our delusions. We might do well, however, to reexamine this kind of thinking. Freud was not, after all, the first to postulate unconscious processes. Pierre Janet and others had done so before him.[3] Furthermore, there is some question as to the value, validity, and, indeed, the logical tenability of the idea of the unconscious. An alternative view finds it more helpful to *unpostulate* unseeable inner events as J. B. Watson did when he founded behaviorism.

Freud has been called a determinist because he saw meaning in human actions. Common slips of the tongue and other "errors" were *motivated*, not capricious or accidental. Thus, he assumed causation—behavior was determined. Like Sherlock Holmes, Freud sought clues to the unknown (in his case, unconscious dynamics) among the banalities of everyday life. Unlike Holmes, Freud linked observable "clues" to internal events for which he felt no need for scientific validation. This is his Achilles' heel. The very essence of the talking therapies is here. All of them, as we will see repeatedly, permit one person to stand over another and presume to see within. The therapist is given free rein to know the patient better than she knows herself, and there are no objective handles for her to grasp. No wonder psychotherapy has so often been referred to as the modern religion. As the penitent speaks to the priest who speaks to the unseen God, the patient speaks to the therapist who speaks to the unseen Unconscious.

Freud is widely hailed as one of the creative geniuses of recent times. He is the most influential of all psychotherapists. In a recent survey in which one thousand psychologists were asked to name the five persons who most directly influenced twentieth-century psychology, Freud ranked first more than three times as often as Pavlov, his nearest competitor.[4] Furthermore, although *pure* psychoanalysis—strictly defined in terms of five times a week, on the couch, using free association and dream analysis, a predominantly silent, bearded, European analyst, etc.—is now relatively rare, most individual therapy by private practitioners is based on psychoanalysis and resembles it in important ways. It is beginning to appear that the "creative giant" took us, not a step forward, perhaps not a full step back, but a step sideways that inhibited progress in certain areas of psychology and psychiatry for half a century. It may be argued that he gave us sex, but in fact the acceptance of his theories might be explained by the presence, especially in the United States, of a culture ripe for just that change.

Freud's "shocking" ideas arrived on the American scene at a time when psychiatry had spent decades in a search for organic explanations of mental conditions, a search initiated by the discovery that the psychosis "general paralysis," or "general paresis," was the end result of syphilitic infection. Freud presented his cases and his cures using the "mystery solved" manner, in which the symptoms were baffling at first but were ultimately all tied together in a rational explanation of cause and effect, a technique common among neurologists of that day. The response was electrifying. For the frustrated psychiatrist or neurologist—at least, for some of them—the linking of "conversion hysterical" paralysis or blindness to childhood trauma, and the dramatic recoveries described, were truly impressive.*

The patient's symptom, Freud explained, served symbolically to protect her from reliving the events that were the sources of real distress. Maybe the unconscious forces were insistent, impolite, and even uncivilized, but illogical they were not. Part of Freud's initial appeal, especially to those in the arts, lay in the fact that his psychology was exciting, dramatic, and *literary*. (The appeal continues. On college campuses today, one finds Freud read rarely for psychology courses, more often for courses in literature.) The prospect of being analyzed promised a fascinating exposure of hidden thoughts and impulses. That some of those might be sexual titillated a culture wresting itself from the grip of Victorian rigidity.

Furthermore, psychoanalysis was the perfect blend of the impressive vocabulary and authority of science and the inherent incomprehensibility of religion. Psychotherapists developed a new ethic of "optimum functioning," "self-actualization," and "happiness." Ultimately, "being analyzed" was regarded as the hallmark of a progressive and liberal attitude (without the stress and possible dangers inherent in

* They were probably due to what psychiatrist Arthur K. Shapiro calls the "placebo effect." Shapiro defines a placebo as "any therapy . . . that is deliberately used for its nonspecific psychologic or psychophysiologic effect, or that is used for its presumed specific effect on a patient, symptom, or illness, but which, unknown to patient and therapist, is without specific activity for the condition being treated" (A. K. Shapiro, "The Curative Waters and Warm Poultices of Psychotherapy," p. 22). It is said that virtually any form of treatment works during the period of optimism that follows its introduction. More commonly, placebo is thought of as the "sugar pill" with which the physician intends a psychological effect.

being involved in social or racial issues)."*⁵ Not surprisingly, then, the artistic subculture was among the first to express enthusiasm for the new psychology. Mysterious, glamorous, and inherently human, it exposed drama beneath the mundane exterior of ordinary life. Even the most dull and pedestrian existence was but the superstructure over dynamic, even brilliant, unconscious complexes and maneuvers. Analysis was the pathway to the most fascinating secrets of all—those of the human mind.

Physicians' acceptance of psychoanalysis was sometimes immediate, sometimes resisted, generally touch and go, and never really complete. The low status of psychiatry in the medical hierarchy today attests to the conflict. Yet, by the 1950s, most psychiatric departments in medical schools were headed by psychoanalysts. Furthermore, other physicians often, in fact *too* often, adopted the "it's all in your head" approach when symptoms were vague and not due to identifiable physiological pathology.

Following its flowering during the lifetime of Freud, psychoanalysis itself began to lose the vigor of those early days. In 1965, medical psychologist Joseph D. Matarazzo characterized psychoanalysis as "parochial teaching based on six decades' old clinical observation of one sensitive and brilliant man"⁶ which cannot compete with newer trends and theories from the universities and medical schools. Although the prestige and influence of psychoanalysis was such that analysts were appointed to leadership positions in psychiatric departments in medical schools and hospitals, training in psychoanalysis requires extensive further training, not in medical schools, but in special psychoanalytic institutes. Today, more psychoanalysts are leaving the field than are entering it. Despite actual *increases* in psychoanalytically derived therapies, only one psychiatrist out of every twenty sought postgraduate analytic training in 1968 as compared with one out of seven in 1945, and less than 2 percent of those receiving

---

* Psychotherapy's decline in popularity on the political left coincided with an upsurge of optimism. Now, when activism is again unpopular, psychotherapy has entered "supernova" phase. The current involvement of the 1960s social activists in psychotherapy offshoots suggests a relationship between the two.

psychiatric treatment are getting "orthodox" psychoanalysis. This makes it the least used of over forty forms of psychiatric therapy.[7]

Many attribute this trend to the lack of development of analytic practice and theory. Although concern is often expressed within analytic circles, it is like talking about the weather. No one seems able to make a contribution that is incorporated into the mainstream. It has been like this almost since the beginning, when Adler and then Jung left the ranks; any deviation from the words of the master are viewed as dissension rather than as progress and each potential innovator has learned to keep quiet or go out and found his own "school." To some degree, the stagnation was more apparent than real. During Freud's lifetime there was considerable development, and because his writings contain contradictions as the theory changed, innovators were often able to present their concepts as not really departing from the essential conceptions of the great originator.

THE IMAGE OF THE THERAPIST

When psychotherapists write overall descriptions of the process of psychotherapy, the image of the therapist tends to be flattering: "He is invariably assumed to be tolerant, understanding and caring."[8] Leonard Krasner, a behavior therapy advocate, noted that the ideal psychotherapist has been described by various writers as

mature, well-adjusted, sympathetic, tolerant, patient, kindly, tactful, non-judgmental, accepting, permissive, non-critical, warm, likeable, interested in human beings, respectful, cherishing and working for a democratic kind of interpersonal relationship with all people, free of racial and religious bigotry, having a worthwhile goal in life, friendly, encouraging, optimistic, strong, intelligent, wise, curious, creative, artistic, scientifically oriented, competent, trustworthy, self-aware, insightful of his own problems, spontaneous, having a sense of humor, feeling personally secure, mature about sex, growing and maturing with life's experiences, having a high frustration tolerance, self-confident, relaxed, objective, self-analytic, aware of his prejudices, non-obsequious, humble, skeptical but not pessimistic or self-deprecatory, trustworthy, dependable, consistent, open, honest, frank, technically sophisticated, professionally dedicated, and charming.[9]

The practice of intensive individual psychotherapy "provides rich nourishment for one's omnipotence and omniscience strivings."[10] Psychotherapists whose personal lives are not at all tranquil and controlled "find in the practice of therapy a kind of splendid calm [in] which they and their patients conspire together to believe the benign influence of the therapists' perspective."[11] The therapist is "likely to enjoy the autonomy, status, glamour, economic reward, and perhaps most important, the feeling that he is productively engaged in the purposeful act of helping relieve another individual's suffering."[12] Psychoanalyst Lawrence Kubie asserts that

the highly charged psychotherapeutic relationship is one of the most important relationships in the world but also one of the most subtle and difficult. It puts demands on us as psychotherapists for which the race is hardly ready. We have not reached a degree of maturity or a quality of wisdom and generosity that justifies our attempting to play this role at all. Yet the pressing needs of sick patients force us to attempt it.[13]

In fact, psychotherapists writing about themselves and their task cover a range from the highly immodest characterizations given above to genuine concern and doubt about the effectiveness of their enterprise. Psychotherapy researchers Allen E. Bergin and Hans S. Strupp comment that "the theme that the therapist is often 'lost' . . . constitutes a remarkable contrast to the many treatises on psychotherapy from which the novice derives the expectation that the therapist is never, or only rarely, at loose ends."[14] Kenneth Mark Colby, a former psychotherapy practitioner, and one of Bergin and Strupp's consultants, said that while he was often able to provide beautiful explanations, the truth was that he "really didn't know what he was doing." He said, "getting money for doing something like this, you begin

to feel like a quack." He had in fact stopped being a therapist after having questioned the activity.[15]

More often, however, therapists come "to believe in their
own omnipotence" and to view therapy as something more
than "an arrangement in which a patient pays a doctor some
money which obligates the doctor to listen and keeps him
from going away no matter how badly he is treated or what
the patient says to him."*[16]

AIMS OF PSYCHOTHERAPY

Although patients come to psychotherapy with specific
hopes and wishes, therapists have goals based in part on the
exigencies of practice and in part on the theoretical formulations which underlie treatment procedures. A pivotal assumption is that the patient is driven by unconscious forces lying
deeply imbedded in her mental apparatus. How she feels is
the product of intrapsychic mechanisms, and therapy is
largely a passive examination of the patient's verbal utterances.

Freud considered the aim of analysis to be the replacement of a symptom "by an act of conscious choice," an objective reflected in psychologist Ernest Kramer's statement
that, as a therapist, he hopes to produce "a change in the patient's perceived world; a change which brings about a
diminution of the suffering which brought [her] into therapy
and which gives [her] the experience of choosing among a
wider range of possibilities in living than [she] seemed to
have before."[17] This is an unusually explicit statement. Therapist goals are typically more vague.

A complaint frequently enunciated behind the closed

* Psychotherapist Jay Haley recasts the situation to describe the
psychoanalysis transactionally as a "dynamic psychological process
involving two people, a patient and a psychoanalyst, during which
the patient insists that the analyst be one-up while desperately
trying to place [her] one-down, and the analyst insists that the
patient remain one-down in order to help [him] learn to become
one-up. The goal . . . is the amicable separation of analyst and
patient" (Haley, *Strategies of Psychotherapy*, p. 193).

doors of professional meetings is that the goals of psychotherapy are not only too inexactly perceived, but often totally
unknown or inexplicable to the patient. Sometimes they are
in direct contradiction to those she holds for herself. Among
different goals that have been articulated by various psychotherapists are removal of symptoms, reorganization (or "reconstruction") of the personality, adjustment to society, self-
fulfillment (or "actualization"), and curing pathology. These
goals not only differ, they are often incompatible with one
another. How therapists manage to attract and retain patients despite the confusion within their discipline is a matter
of psychotherapy's public image and of certain strategies employed by practitioners which we will discuss next.

WHAT BRINGS PATIENTS TO
PSYCHOTHERAPY?

Psychiatrist, psychologist, writer, and practicing psychotherapist Jerome D. Frank has wondered whether mental
health education's main effect has been to "teach people to
regard certain kinds of distress or behavioral oddities as
illnesses rather than as normal reactions to life's stresses,
harmless eccentricities, or moral weaknesses."[18] Viewing normal behavior as diseased, he observed, causes alarm and increases the demand for psychotherapy.[19] Psychiatrist and
former analyst Melitta Schmideberg reports that, beginning
in the 1920s and 1930s the public, especially the American
public, "attached much glamour to analysis, analysts, and
even to being analyzed. . . . The mass media helped to
make psychoanalysis popular; women's magazines in particular wrote steadily on mental health problems from an analytic point of view. The New Yorker had at least one joke on
analysis in every issue. A well-known analyst had his own
public relations man; . . ."[20]

Perhaps the segment of the public that responded to psychoanalysis consisted, at least in part, of persons with an un-
fulfilled wish for intimacy, an urge to express oneself and be
praised for it, or absolved, as William Schofield, author of
Psychotherapy, The Purchase of Friendship, suggested. But

the reasons most often given by patients are depression, anxiety, feelings of inferiority, and interpersonal problems. More women name depression as the reason for entering psychotherapy than any other reason, although marital difficulties and anxiety are mentioned very often.[21]

Anxiety in the psychiatric patient is an advantage.[22] Frank says that intellectuals or people from the upper classes who look to psychotherapy to help them overcome vague self-dissatisfactions or to find more meaning in their life and so-called sociopathic personalities who are forced by others to obtain treatment are among the most difficult to treat because the psychotherapist's "usefulness to these types of persons depends in part on his *creating* or unearthing some source of distress or otherwise *convincing* them that they are ill [my italics]."[23]

Psychoanalyst Anthony Storr has observed that today's patients rarely fall into standard diagnostic categories:

> Most patients . . . seek analysis because their lives are unhappy and their personal relationships disturbed and unrewarding. Thus, a representative analytical practice might perhaps contain a minister of religion with doubts about his faith, a woman whose husband has left her for another, a male homosexual complaining of depression and isolation, a psychiatric social worker with emotional difficulties in dealing with her clients, a businessman with a duodenal ulcer, a composer whose inspiration has deserted him, and a mother whose chief complaint is of an inability to handle the upbringing of her children.[24]

In *Social Class and Mental Illness*, published in 1958, Hollingshead and Redlich point out that the incidence of serious mental illness is greatest among the lowest socioeconomic classes. The highest class, which contains 3 percent of the general population, accounts for only 1 percent of the psychiatric population. In contrast, the lowest class, 18.4 percent of the general population, accounts for 38.4 percent of the psychiatric population. Furthermore, the types of disorders differ, with feelings of anxiety about interpersonal relationships, inadequacy, and guilt characterizing the major complaints of the middle and upper classes, and psychosis (especially schizophrenia) and sociopathic disturbances (troublemaking, delinquency) characterizing the psychiatric problems of the lower classes.[25] Explanations for the differences in type of disorder are most often given in terms of the early training that individuals in different socioeconomic classes receive, although the data from such studies only tell us about correlations; whether deprived conditions lead to schizophrenia or schizophrenics tend to end up in the lower classes because of their illness cannot be determined from such studies.

Sociologist Thomas J. Scheff reported the results of an investigation of users and nonusers of a student psychiatric facility in an article published in the *Journal of Health and Human Behavior* in 1966. Scheff concluded that there exists a "psychiatric public" whose members have fewer symptoms but present themselves more frequently for treatment.[26] In another study examining attitudes toward seeking professional help, four important dimensions were found: recognition of the need for professional help, interpersonal openness, lack of fear of stigma, and confidence in the mental health profession. With the exception of interpersonal openness, the list suggests that the tendency to seek out psychiatric care is more closely related to education than to intensity of distress.[27]

Probably one of the most effective propaganda media for the encouragement of the use of mental health facilities and personnel, the recognition of symptoms, and the reduction of the stigma most people associate with mental illness is the undergraduate psychology curriculum. The courses in personality, "abnormal" psychology, and other clinical psychology subjects are often taught by a clinical psychologist with a part-time psychotherapy practice, or by a private practitioner who teaches a course or two on the side. Such instructors are rewarded economically by letting their students know that their services are available, and by presenting themselves in a favorable way before the public—both the public in general and the public in the classroom. Even when the instructor is not a psychotherapist, she or he is likely to speak well for psychotherapy. So do the Introductory Psychology textbooks. Although the majority of citizens have not responded favorably to efforts by mental health organizations to consider mental disturbance "an illness just like any other illness," psychology students are a subgroup that receive a particularly large dose of "the message" and frequently "get it."

The educated reading public is also the object of direct communication from members of the psychotherapy professions. Books about psychotherapy constitute an important nonfiction category. One publisher's representative, in turning down the proposal for this book, was very frank about it if not entirely logical. The editor said, "We couldn't possibly publish a book that criticizes psychotherapy. We have made a great deal of money from the works of leading psychoanalysts and other psychotherapists and it wouldn't be fair to publish a book that is not respectful of them."

Nora Budzilek, psychology graduate student at the University of Bridgeport, recently attempted to learn who patients were and whether they associated with one another. She interviewed twenty suburban women and asked them first to supply some information about three close friends of their choosing, including whether the friend had been or was a psychiatric patient. After talking of her three anonymous friends, the woman was asked if she would object to answering the same questions about herself. Every woman cooperated. Budzilek's results indicate that a woman who had been a psychiatric patient was much more likely to have patients among her closest friends, while a woman who had never been in therapy did not have friends in therapy or said that she did not know whether her friends had psychiatric histories.[28] These findings suggest that members of the psychiatric public talk to one another about therapy, and, possibly, that they are more likely to become the close friend of someone who, like themselves, has been in psychotherapy.

Charles Kadushin, Professor of Sociology and Education at Teachers College, Columbia University, summarizes the characteristics of those he calls the Friends and Supporters of Psychotherapy. They are "culturally sophisticated"—they go to concerts, plays, art exhibitions, and cocktail parties. They are very likely to have occupations in psychological and artistic fields, be under forty-five years old, and not be religious. Furthermore, since not all Friends have these characteristics, "those persons who are not naturally exposed to the Friends must be more directly recruited to membership through mass media favorable to psychiatry and through previous experience with psychotherapy."[29]

Kadushin notes that Friends who become patients differ from non-Friends in each step of the process of deciding to enter therapy. Their problems are more likely to be interpersonal, or dissatisfaction with themselves, and they are more likely to know of psychotherapists through their associates. Most Friends and Supporters of Psychotherapy are people who are or have been patients, and likely will be patients in the future. Becoming a patient again and again is extremely common:

> Only 12 percent of analytic and 5 percent of hospital-clinic applicants are beginners. The rest have previously been to at least one professional for consultation about problems related to the very ones now brought to a psychiatric clinic . . . the fact is that the major role of psychiatric clinics is to take in other professionals' wash. . . . Seventy percent had been to three or more different professionals before applying to a hospital psychiatric clinic.[30]

Kadushin concludes that analytic clinics and private psychotherapists are treating, not those most in need of psychiatric care, but the Friends and Supporters of Psychiatry.

Throughout this book, I will use the term "Friends" to refer to all those who espouse a psychodynamic ideology regardless of the form in which it is expressed. Thus not only patients, former patients, and mental health workers, but literary critics, novelists, film makers, and historians who may never have been patients themselves may be included as Friends. Like sociologist Charles Kadushin, I use the terms "psychiatry" and "psychotherapy" interchangeably when referring to Friends. Other terms which have been used are "psychiatry public" and "patient types." The last term is clearly derogatory.

Sociologist Pauline Bart suggests that "regardless of the

distribution of psychosomatic illness, it is only in psychologically sophisticated circles that the psychogenic contribution to the discomfort is recognized."[31] The women in Bart's study who sought psychiatric rather than neurological treatment were of higher socioeconomic and educational status, more likely to be employed, have an urban background, be married to professionals, and be Jewish. Women who lacked "psychiatric vocabularies" themselves rejected doctors who "interpreted their symptoms in psychiatric terms."[32] Another characteristic of the Friends of Psychiatry among patients is that in many ways they resemble the psychotherapists themselves; both tend to be urban, upwardly mobile, and Jewish or Protestant rather than Catholic. But more Friends are female; the vast majority of therapists are male.

Much has been written about the type of patient preferred by the therapist. In fact, therapists are amazingly unabashed in their descriptions of favored patients. Favored patients are never the "sickest." In an article published in the 1962 *Annual Review of Psychology*, Strupp observed:

> It is becoming increasingly clear that therapists have fairly specific (and valid) notions about the kinds of attributes a "good" patient should possess as well as about those attributes which make a patient unsuitable for the more usual forms of investigative, insight-producing psychotherapy. Patients considered good prognostic risks are described as young, attractive, well-educated, members of the upper middle class, possessing a high degree of ego strength, some anxiety which impels them to seek help, no seriously disabling neurotic symptoms, relative absence of deep characterological distortions and strong secondary gains, a willingness to talk about their difficulties, an ability to communicate well, some skill in the social-vocational area, and a value system relatively congruent with that of the therapists. Such patients tend to remain in therapy, profit from it, and *evoke the therapist's best efforts* [my italics].[33]

According to this, the therapist's ideal is everybody's ideal. Two years after Strupp's article, Schofield published his book *Psychotherapy: The Purchase of Friendship* in which he introduced the term "YAVIS Syndrome," YAVIS being an acronym for the attributes of a desirable patient: youthful, attractive, verbal, intelligent, and successful.

Ironically, the qualities that make a good patient are also associated with improvement without treatment.[34] Furthermore, the healthier the patient is to start with, the more satisfied the therapist with the result of his treatment, even when actual change is very slight.[35] Psychotherapists tend to shy away from patients with poor prognoses. Arthur Shapiro noted that "patients are now the least ill of any group, and have comparatively favorable prognoses even without therapy. The criteria for selection may have evolved during the past sixty years into an empirical recognition of those patients most likely to respond to psychoanalytic treatment and perhaps to any appropriate treatment. . . ."[36] Furthermore, "the patient's ability to pay a large fee for a long time is a prerequisite for treatment and the therapist's interest."[37]

According to the therapists themselves, then, psychoanalytic treatment and most of its derivatives depend on patients who are bright and cooperative, who realize their need for treatment and come regularly, who verbalize freely, tell the truth, and are able and willing to pay. Obviously, such a combination of conditions occurs rarely.

Yet it is this small proportion of persons who support the therapy enterprise—they, the federal government, and certain private foundations. In many cases, companies hold insurance policies which cover private psychiatric care for their higher level personnel and their families. The current campaign to include psychotherapy by psychologists in autonomous practice (not under the supervision of medical doctors) in Blue Cross-Blue Shield policies actually would not spread the availability of psychotherapy to disadvantaged or working class groups. Most of them are not covered by such policies and, unlike Friends, they would be reluctant to utilize psychotherapeutic facilities even if they were available. The rise of psychotherapy in the United States and in Europe may be due to a deficiency in human relations in Western society, as is so often said. But it is most popular where it has been promoted by the media, where people can afford it and where it has public support.

SYMPTOMS

Although symptoms are usually what brings a patient into
therapy, psychoanalytic therapists have tended to give them
short shrift. Symptoms are useful in "motivating" a patient to
continue treatment, but they are not illnesses in themselves;
they are merely indications of an underlying problem, and it
is that inner problem which should be the aim of therapeutic
intervention. By this reasoning, a patient who enters treatment because of a snake phobia and leaves three years later
with her snake phobia intact, may be judged "greatly improved" because "personality reconstruction" had taken
place. Conversely, a patient with severe depression who after
a few months with or without treatment is no longer depressed, has not been cured, since there was no personality
reconstruction. With personality reconstruction something
that can be seen only through the tinted glasses of the psychotherapist researchers, relief of symptoms or patient claims
of improved functioning can easily be discounted. According
to Strupp and his colleagues, it is a "well-known clinical observation that while patients often enter therapy with a few
specific symptoms for which they wish relief, as therapy
progresses, they begin to perceive a wider variety of situations which are contradictory, incompatible with adult purposes, and the like."[38] With "deeper probing, they gain insight" and may leave "feeling benefitted" but with no
"symptom relief."

A person with no change in her phobic reactions but
greater self-awareness may or may not be judged "improved," depending on who does the judging. According to
Schmideberg, writing in 1960:

> A rather paradoxical situation has arisen in psychiatry. It is
> often feared that it may be dangerous to suppress symp-
> toms, while on the other hand, obviously the aim of all
> therapy must be to cure them. But how are we to decide
> whether a symptom has been suppressed or cured? This

therapeutic uneasiness is often transmitted to the patient, and interferes with [her] progress. . . . Whereas in medicine we speak about an "alleviation of symptoms" or the "relief of suffering," in psychiatry we hear of "losing symptoms" as though something valuable had been lost, and "suppressing symptoms" or "increasing repression" are expressions reminiscent of oppression.[39]

Schmideberg calls for an evaluation of symptoms in terms of their consequences in the patient's life.

Anthony Storr, a practicing psychoanalyst, finds the issues of symptoms and symptom relief less relevant "once the analysis is under way . . . It is not uncommon to hear analysts say with relief about a patient that [she] has passed the stage of bothering with symptoms at all, irrespective of whether they have disappeared or not, and this lack of concern is reckoned as a sign of progress in analysis. . . ."[40] Storr also notes that most patients who "present themselves for analysis" these days "do not have any clear-cut symptoms in any case."[41]

From the psychodynamic view, the symptom is not the basic issue. The removal of the symptom will not only not affect the root cause, but will adversely affect the delicate protective organization that allows the patient to function, however neurotically. Here is the rationale for the view that patients are frail and easily hurt and therefore should not be "tampered with" except by persons of the highest professional training and competence. To remove a symptom is to open a Pandora's box, to leave the patient weak and defenseless, and, without question, to expose her to the development of more serious pathology in which other, more virulent and disabling symptoms will substitute for the "lost" one.

There has been a steady accumulation of evidence that symptom substitution rarely occurs and that when it does, or appears to, it is readily amenable to treatment.[42] Later, when we examine behavioral orientations, we will discover a therapy based on the entirely opposite idea—that symptoms are harmful, and that their removal tends to initiate positive chains of events that have many beneficial ramifications.[43]

THE IMAGE OF PSYCHOTHERAPY

To the general public and to some degree, to the professionals themselves, psychotherapy is surrounded by a certain mystique for which there are three separable sources.

The popularity of psychotherapy today is in part because it is imbued with a sense of the alien and the secret.[44] Like medicine itself psychotherapy's historical roots lie in magic, superstition, and religion. The mysticism, faith healing, and hypnotism with which many people still associate psychotherapy were in fact the immediate precursors of psychoanalysis. By Jerome D. Frank's broad definition of psychotherapy as a set of contacts between a socially sanctioned healer and his client, where treatment consists primarily of gestures, words, and other communicative acts or utterances, psychotherapy began in prehistory. Current psychoanalytically derived therapies are merely modifications of superstitious methods of healing.

A second contribution to the aura of mystery and power associated with psychotherapy is its professional relationship with modern medicine. Psychiatry, and therefore to some degree all forms of psychotherapy, benefit from the propaganda machinery by which the vested interests of medicine promote the physician's image.[45]

Finally, there are the specific stratagems employed by the therapist himself through his attire, his language, and all aspects of his public behavior. Shapiro speaks of the magic and mystery, which he notes is called one-upmanship by Haley, engendered by "an unapproachable and prestigious physician, who [is] a master of esoteric dynamic theory not easily understood by the uninitiated."[46] Technical jargon is in fact a kind of inner-sanctum code system, meant, quite deliberately, to keep others out and to impress. British anthropologist Geoffrey Gorer speaks of "words of power." He notes that "many people appear to feel that when they have applied a psychoanalytic or quasi-psychoanalytic term to a person or a situation they have somehow gained control over the person or the situation, rendered it or him understandable, safe, in-

nocuous."[47] It is also helpful that the theories and practice
are "elaborate, detailed, time-consuming, expensive, fashionable, [and] esoteric."[48] Specific therapist behaviors that
serve to promote the desired image in the patient are described in Shepard and Lee's book *Games Analysts Play*.
They include ploys to hide the therapist's inexpertise, ignorance, or feelings of inferiority.[49]

Some clinical psychology graduate students recently reported their observations of the effect that administering
therapy has on the social behavior of the therapists. Other
students and more experienced psychotherapists in a department of psychology at a state psychiatric hospital "concurred
that the psychotherapist is an artificial human being; he is a
nonreal entity who relates in a nonreal way with the people
who seek his services."[50] This comes about in part through
"desensitization" due to repeated association with pathological persons who are threatening to most people. His behavior is also affected by that of people he meets in social situations: "people tend to go to extremes when they meet a
psychologist or psychiatrist in terms of revealing their pathology to him; that is, they may be hostile to him because he is
a reminder to them of their inadequacies or they may wish to
talk to him about a problem they have, a friend has, etc."[51]
Eventually, the therapist tends to withdraw from social activities and devote himself to reading, research, and his practice. He "lives" through his patients: "The influence and
control he is capable of utilizing with people in no small way
has a grandiose and ego inflating flavor to it."[52]

THE INITIAL INTERVIEW

Textbooks on the practice of psychotherapy often devote a
chapter, sometimes several, to the first interview between patient and therapist. Since private practitioners of intensive
psychotherapy see relatively few patients, most do not have
secretaries. Appointments are usually arranged on the telephone directly with the doctor who received the message left
with his answering service. The patient, therefore, has already spoken to him. He may also have received materials

from a referring physician or agency. In the patient's mind, there is likely to be fear and some suspicion; therefore, one of the therapist's tasks is to encourage the patient to return. Whatever degree of awe and confidence the patient had before she walked through the door may be lost in the reality of an actual office with furniture, draperies, and ash trays, the desk with its high-backed chair behind it, and a therapist who walks, talks, and wears particular clothing. Sometimes, all of these things may enhance the mystique.

Drs. Harrison and Carek, who devote three whole chapters to the initial interview in their book *A Guide to Psychotherapy*, say that one of the first goals of the therapist is development of rapport, or the construction of an emotional bridge between the therapist and the patient. They note that the patient may continue to "envelop the therapist with an aura of magic whereby [she] magnifies the therapist's actual power."[53] This unrealistic attitude of the patient "may facilitate amazingly powerful effects. Such attitudes can enable a therapist's words of encouragement to relieve a patient of symptoms, or a practitioner's imprudent words to precipitate iatrogenic [treatment produced] illness."[54]

The patient is still "nervous" about coming for psychiatric treatment; the strange situation is itself still frightening. There is the image of being a "psychiatric patient" to get used to, and there is some awareness of the probable cost in time and money. Although Harrison and Carek list "being helpful to the patient" as one of the main goals of the initial interview, they caution therapists against too much relief of anxiety lest the patient not return. Indeed, where anxiety does not exist already (for instance, in patients who come at the insistence of another—parents, husbands, court) the therapist "may well have to accept the challenge of somehow provoking the anxiety that will make the patient want to change."[55]

Although much is written about preferred types of patients and "unsuitability for psychotherapy" or for particular types of therapy, those who initiate private therapy tend to meet the economic criterion. Often a therapist warns the patient at her first visit that he cannot tell immediately whether psychotherapy might be helpful, and that it may take two or three initial judgments to collect background information. After that, the first couple of months can be viewed as a trial period in which readiness and willingness for extensive psychotherapy can be judged. Despite the seeming reasonableness of these tactics, they can also serve as ploys, in Shepard and Lee's terms. By holding out the possibility that therapy (with its expense and possible embarrassments from various sources) may not be needed at all, he encourages her to come at least for the initial series; and probably for the trial period. This provides more opportunity for the development of the "rapport" on which long-term therapy may be based. It is interesting that despite these standard efforts to "sell" therapy to the patient during the first few sessions, it has been estimated that more than half of those who begin therapy do not continue for more than four to six sessions altogether.[56]

Some therapists have learned to detect signs that a patient will discontinue early, in which case he can try to keep the door open for future contacts by preventing her from viewing her termination as a total rejection of therapy. It is "better business" to create such a feeling, if possible. While the therapist may be geared to long-term therapy, he is willing to concede that there may be those for whom a few sessions may, in fact, have beneficial effects, possibly due to placebo (or nonspecific) factors in which patient expectation plays a larger role than therapist techniques.[57]

Psychoanalysts, most fully committed to long-term therapy, consider premature termination of therapy to be a dynamic symptom in itself, even in cases where the reason for stopping experienced by the patient is alleviation of the symptom or problems that brought her to therapy in the first place. This, say the analysts, is a pathological reaction. They have dubbed it a "flight into health," which occurs in patients whose need to maintain neurotic symptoms is so strong that they prefer to mobilize the appearance of having no pathology rather than subject themselves to the possibility of uncovering "repressed material." From this viewpoint, the therapist feels quite justified in warning the patient about what is happening and what can be expected. Many patients have reported that they were induced to remain in treatment because of what can only be called outright threats:

> Your problems are deep-seated, but very severe. Psychotherapy is absolutely necessary if you are to continue to function.

> I can predict a worsening of your condition without treatment—and a more severe relapse next time.

> Unless the underlying causes are located and treated, there is every reason to believe that the pathology beneath the surface will grow. I would not answer for the eventual consequences.[58]

Such statements can be terrifying and very effective for the patient who holds respect, even awe, for the therapist.

Many patients were influenced by psychoanalytic public relations material, as well as subtle and not so subtle behavior of the therapist, to believe that psychoanalysis was the very best and most desired treatment and that should they be found to be "unsuitable" for analysis it would be a sign of personal inadequacy. This can come as an emotional shock. Schmideberg has pointed out that the high expectations patients have about analysis contribute to the sometimes severe problems they have when the treatment fails.[59]

GROUND RULES

Very early in treatment, preferably but not necessarily at the first interview, the guidelines for the therapeutic situation are discussed. In classical psychoanalysis, severe restrictions were imposed. The patient agreed to make no major alterations in her life such as changing jobs, marrying, or getting a divorce, not to discuss either her problems or the analytic sessions with anyone, and not to read about psychoanalysis or psychotherapy. In any type of psychotherapy, the matter of fees and appointment times must be settled. Freud himself initiated the practice of patients in long-term therapy "leasing" time from the therapist. This means that the therapist is always available to the patient at the designated hours, and that the patient must pay for that time even if something un-foreseen or unavoidable prevents her from keeping the ap-pointment. Some therapists use a semireleased time system in which the patient does not have to pay if she provides sufficient advance notice.

The patient is also informed that success will depend pri-marily on her cooperation and on how much she "wants to improve." If procedures such as free association and dream analysis are to be used they are discussed. She is also told not to expect immediate relief, that therapy may in fact lead her to feel worse at times, but that this is common during psychotherapeutic treatment and should not be construed as a sign of failure.

Perry London has described the actual conduct of a psy-chotherapy session as follows:

> The patient and doctor greet each other and take positions in the doctor's office. If the patient lies down on the couch (classical psychoanalysis), the doctor generally sits behind [her] head towards the side, in order to see [her] without being seen. If the patient sits (client-centered, Sullivanian, and so on), the doctor usually sits facing [her]. In either case, the positions tend to be fixed and constant for all ses-sions; neither party will ordinarily get up or move around the room during the session, nor will there ordinarily be any physical contact between them. Talk is the legal ten-der of expression and communication here, talk and not motion; there are therapists who say one must never take notes, but listen in rapt attention, motionless. For some, even talk means only speech and no other kind of words, as with therapists who discourage or forbid patients to make agendas or other notes about themselves or read them during the session; notes are words, but not talk.[60]

TRANSFERENCE

At the outset, the patient is warned that therapy is emo-tionally involving and that she can expect to experience in-tense reactions, some of which will be directed toward the therapist himself. "It is part of the treatment," she is told. "There will be times when you hate me and want to leave.

At other times, your feelings toward me will be more positive."

Indeed, in most long-term intensive psychotherapy, the patient develops emotional feelings about the therapist. Often, not always, these are strong feelings of attraction with erotic components. Freud maintained that these reactions were not really reactions to the therapist himself who, in classical psychoanalysis, preserves anonymity and "objectivity" and therefore does not exhibit enough of himself to provide a basis for either anger or attachment. These strong emotional reactions are, according to Freudian theory, feelings that the patient has held toward significant persons in early life; they are being "transferred" to the therapist, and this is not only desirable but a central aspect of the treatment process. One reason Freud declined to treat psychotic patients was because he believed that they tended not to experience transference reactions.

Several types of transference have been delineated. There is always some tendency under normal circumstances to react to persons with basic trust, more trust or less depending on one's previous experiences. Psychoanalysts call this "basic primal transference," and believe that this individual initial approach to people is formed in early childhood. A second type, "spontaneous transference," is based on superficial aspects of the situation: when a person's name produces good or ill feelings because of prior experiences, for example, or when one has had unpleasant experiences with other physicians and so initially responds negatively to a new doctor. "Transference reactions," the third type, are derived from "repressed infantile feelings which make their appearance as emotional needs that involve the person currently present."[61] Over a long time period these transference reactions will "crystallize" into a full-blown "transference neurosis" if regression is appropriately "controlled" through psychoanalytic techniques.[62]

Transference, including the transference neurosis, was hailed by psychoanalysts because it brought real feelings into the analytic chamber where they could be dealt with directly and immediately. Transference is at the very core of psychoanalytic treatment. The feelings that constitute it are repetitions or displacements of reactions to persons in childhood. Instead of just recalling them, the patient repeats them as reactions to the analyst. This reenaction of the past in analytic sessions supposedly permits early conflicts to be understood and handled. Thus, according to some writers, psychoanalysis *is* transference analysis.[63]

Freud believed that transference developed more readily in neurotic individuals, but it has since become clear that the therapist's behavior, or lack of it, plays a crucial role. Sympathetic listening combined with deliberate anonymity, lying supine on the analyst's couch in a defenseless posture,* free association, the description and analysis of dream and fantasy "material," and frequent sessions contribute to the likelihood that a transference neurosis will develop. London notes that the "therapist's personal anonymity helps promote the transference reaction by withholding information which would give the patient a realistic basis for evaluating and responding to him."[64]

There is no evidence that ability to develop a transference reaction is a measure of degree of disturbance. As Freud himself was aware, psychotics, generally assumed to be the most disturbed of patients, often fail to develop these reactions.

Transference is in fact puzzling. That strong emotional reactions to the psychotherapist typically occur is undeniable, but why they develop and what should be done about them is far less clear. For one thing, the experience can be painful for the patient. She may wish to leave therapy, and sometimes does. There may be "symptomatic shifts" in which, according to the analysts, the patient feels some degree of symptom relief which helps convince her that therapy is no longer needed. In extreme cases, the patient might take a new job or even marry to escape the feelings of transference.[65] Techniques for preventing such behaviors include

---

* And an erotic one. Patients report that it is the sexual suggestibility of the position that causes couch resistance. I have not located research reports which compare the reactions of women with men to the analytic couch.

early warning that such feelings are to be expected, reducing the number of sessions per week, letting up on the anonymity somewhat, or giving interpretation of the transference immediately.[66] In psychoanalysis, a "full-blown, regressive transference" is considered to be part of treatment, under the assumption that by activating representations of infantile conflicts the underlying illness based on these conflicts will be cured. In this way, psychoanalysis can be a very unpleasant experience, and, by the admission of the psychoanalysts themselves, damaging rather than beneficial.

Many psychotherapists today indicate that they try deliberately to discourage extreme transference, although how successfully is unknown. In *The Psychiatrists,* Rogow notes that patients often return to therapy, that, in a sense, it is "never really over."[67] Although "resolution" of transference is a standard aspect of psychoanalytic psychotherapy, it has been found that patients' appraisals of their therapists were higher immediately after therapy than they were several years later, which suggests that "transference feelings" were far from resolved at termination.[68] Psychiatrist Richard D. Chessick says:

> The glue that holds patient and therapist together through thick and thin of psychotherapy over the years of time is the mutual gratification in the transference-countertransference [the therapist's reactions] structure. . . . From the patient's (unconscious) point of view it is gratification in the transference that keeps [her] coming.[69]

Chessick warns that the therapist must carefully adjust the amount of "gratification" obtained by the patient: should she receive too little gratification, she might "fall apart"; with too much, there would be no "growth."[70]

From my own interviews with patients and former patients, I have received the impression that there is little that is unconscious about the transference feelings. They may be strongly experienced. Patients talk about having romantic feelings about their therapists, about keeping embarrassing secrets, particularly admission of their attraction for him, and of having therapy, the regular face-to-face meetings with a man to whom they are attracted, lift the boredom and introduce a measure of excitement into a drab existence. Years after the last therapy session, an accidental meeting with the therapist may produce the tingling excitement that would accompany an unexpected meeting with a former lover. Harrison and Carek recommend complete termination rather than tapering off "lest one keep open the 'wounds of therapy.'"[71] Such advice is also given to a person trying to overcome the pain of an unrequited love.

Transference reactions have been observed to run a relatively predictable course. Generally positive feelings toward the therapist continue to rise throughout the entire course of treatment while negative feelings reach a peak about midway and thereafter drop to a very low level, even lower than at the beginning of therapy. Thus, feelings fluctuate between positive and negative during the first half of therapy. But it depends on the patient. "Good" patients show the pattern just described, "poor" patients fluctuate at a lower level and never develop intense positive feelings.[72]

The issue of transference is serious. In intense positive transference, the patient feels that she is falling in love. She fantasies scenes in which the therapist dances with her, embraces her, asks her to go away with him, wants her to be the mother of his children, tells her she is his favorite patient, the most exciting person he has ever known, or that *he* is the one who needs help and she is the only one who can give it to him. Her feelings are romantic and erotic, and her dependency on him increases. She is in love, and has now to face the problem of getting over it. How the therapist handles the situation makes a great deal of difference in how much she suffers. Some psychotherapists have expressed recognition of the problem. Recommendations on how to reduce transference intensity have more and more found their way into therapy manuals.

Although there may be problems concerning transference, it also has relevance to the therapist's economic security. Ironically, the therapist promotes this reaction by giving *less* of himself to the therapy relationship, by saying and doing relatively little. The temptation to sit back and rake it in must be strong. There are even those who doubt, not that the feelings exist, but the validity of the theory that underlies seeing them as transference. Professor John M. Shlien of the Graduate School of Education of Harvard University calls transference an obfuscation:

> . . . a fiction invented and maintained to protect the therapist from the consequences of his own behavior. . . . Often there is no original experience to transfer. Warmth, for example, may feel good because it's "wired-in" and not because the person experienced it this way in childhood.[73]

COUNTERTRANSFERENCE

The term "countertransference" is widely used to refer to the therapist's feelings, positive and negative, about the patient. Since the ideal analyst in Freudian therapy is neutral and objective, countertransference is generally considered to be counterproductive, an unfortunate accident to be speedily corrected. In some cities, countertransference groups, a kind of group therapy for psychotherapists, meet regularly to deal with the emotional reactions of its therapist-members to their patients. The term countertransference implies that the feelings are reactions to the "transferred" emotional reactions of their patients, but, in practice, *any* feelings of the therapist toward the patient are commonly referred to as "countertransference phenomena."[74] This seems somewhat illogical because while the therapist is a relatively unknown individual to the patient, the reverse is not the case. The patient is in fact very exposed. If the therapist develops feelings about her, it seems reasonable to assume that those feelings are reality-based, evoked by the patient herself, and not merely reactions to her projections or carry-overs from other patients or members of the therapist's family.

Countertransference feelings are sometimes hostile and rejecting. Arthur K. Shapiro notes that such factors as the patient's motivation for treatment, the therapist's expectations concerning prognosis, the nature of the diagnosis, the patient's age and specific problem, and even the fee paid may affect the psychotherapist's feelings for his patients.[75] It has also been noted that therapists tend to be less attracted to patients of lower socioeconomic status.[76]

Chessick, borrowing from Karl Menninger, lists some of the signals by which a therapist can recognize his countertransference: incomprehension of the material the patient produces when it resembles the therapist's personal problems, depression or uneasiness after the session, lateness, running overtime, forgetting an appointment, drowsiness, erotic or affectionate reactions to the patient, talking excessively about the patient to colleagues, fearing that the patient will discontinue therapy, sudden losses or increases of interest in her "case," angry arguing, becoming disturbed by her behavior, or thinking about her afterward during leisure time.[77]

What to do about countertransference is not generally agreed on. Harrison and Carek, like most psychoanalysts, emphasize the importance of being sensitive to one's countertransference. They cite trying to impress by name-dropping or feeling a sudden surge of concern for a particular patient's welfare as additional signs of countertransference, and suggest that at certain times with selected patients it may be helpful to reveal countertransference feelings to the patient so as not to confuse her. But only negative feelings. Positive feelings are best not revealed to the patient because to want to admit them is likely to represent an "acting out" of the countertransference feelings themselves. Harrison and Carek admit that, in fact, the same can be said of negative feelings, that the psychiatrist's wish to reveal them may be "unconsciously" motivated to harm the object of his dislike.[78] Altogether, therapists are reluctant to discuss their genuine feelings about the patient. Chessick feels it is unwise to discuss countertransference with patients, although it is advisable to let them know about those reactions of the therapist "based on real provocation." How the therapist is able to differentiate between the two may be a problem.[79]

In fact, the whole issue of countertransference is a sticky one. It undermines the therapist's sense of control over himself and, hence, over the therapy process. Yet it has been pointed out that the concepts of transference and countertransference protect both patient and therapist against recognition of, and consequent anxiety about, what is actually going on between the two persons.[80] The evidence from patients strongly suggests that the transference neurosis often feels like, looks like, and acts like being in love. It leads the patient (or therapist in the case of countertransference) to be concerned with the impression made on the object of erotic and/or romantic desire, to enjoy simply being in the presence of that person, whatever transpires, to be sensitive to signs of rejection, and to be virtually paranoid when it comes to finding subtle indications of reciprocated feelings.

Apparently the frequency with which the phenomenon occurs in psychotherapy is greater the closer the procedures resemble classical analysis, but it is not unheard of in other recognized therapies. Evidently it would be intolerable if it were not conceived of as part of treatment. Yet some persons get "treated" without it, and it appears increasingly in the literature as a somewhat controversial, if not actually shady, topic. Phyllis Chesler has publicized cases of women in which sexual relations between patients and therapist actually occurred.[81] Questionnaire data suggests that seduction in therapy may occur as frequently as one in a hundred cases, and, as an internationally distinguished former analyst and journal editor said, "Two people alone together in a dimly lit room discussing intimate personal details of life—what else can one expect?"

When countertransference feelings become so strong that the patient becomes more important than anything else in his life, the therapist is said to have developed a "countertransference neurosis." Unlike the patient's transference neurosis, conceived by analysts as a positive step provided it can be treated and resolved, the therapist's countertransference neurosis is always pathological.[82] Recently a New York State psychotherapist noted that therapists have been found to hold initial biases favoring some patients and disfavoring others. Among those viewed more favorably are those with similar racial and religious background to that of the therapist. Also favored are patients whose clinical diagnosis suggests good prognosis, and patients exhibiting "high motivations" for psychotherapy.[83] Such initial biases can be the stuff from which countertransference neurosis is made.

INTERPRETATION

The art of interpretation includes at its center the art of translating unconscious symbolism. The dream imagery, for example, is treated as symbolically referential to the "real" unconscious compulsive mechanisms motivating conscious life. It is the rationalization of these techniques rooted in the art of symbol translation that Fromm together with the other reformists must furnish. For without the esoteric technique, analysis would collapse into common ordinary counseling.

HARRY K. WELLS, *The Failure of Psychoanalysis*[84]

Perhaps Freud's major contribution was the license he gave to interpretation through "psychic determinism" and the "objective analyst." Having structured a real but invisible underlying dynamic in the Id, Ego, and Superego triumvirate from which causation emanated after the first years of life, he gave practitioners the magic they needed to elevate themselves to the rank of seer. Nothing is more intrinsic to psychoanalysis and all its offshoots—even down to the encounter groups of Esalen—than that the individual give over her knowledge of herself and her motives to the therapist (leader, group member) who makes that knowledge "whole." As the mystic *sees* God, the therapist sees the patient's inner self. What he does with his "knowledge" depends partly on his theoretical and technical orientation, partly on his idiosyncratic inclination, or on his own personal situation. The following examples are typical:

The reason why you were late to the session today is that you are feeling hostile toward me.

When you burn the potatoes or oversalt the gravy, you are really showing a form of protest. These domestic "mistakes" are bids for your husband's attention.

The loss of the ring was not really an accident, but an attempt to dissociate yourself from its giver.

Your extreme fondness for your son masks an inner hostility that may erupt at any time. Excessive fears for his safety are really disguised wishes that he will be harmed. This is all, of course, deeply unconscious.

We human beings love interpretations and we seek them in many contexts. Current events are interpreted as part of a divine plan for humanity. The continued popularity of the Bible, the Koran, and other great religious sources undoubtedly lies partly in their vast potential for interpretation. To interpret is to suggest or to pronounce a cause, an explanation. Human beings hunger for an explanation for suffering, to create order out of what seems chaos. Interpretation provides some relief from fear.[85]

But interpretations can be dangerous. In the past, for example, women were often accused of witchcraft by conscious or unconscious lies based on an accumulation of interpretations. The woman falls to the ground on the way to the market place; this shows that she has tried to fight off the devil, but failed. The witch smiles and tries to be kind to people; the devil has made her his emissary and part of her job is to entice more people into the evil web. The witch shows fear as her accusers multiply; this is because she knows of her guilt. The witch shows no fear; her sorcery protects her. Once the accusation was made, it was very difficult to escape. So long as the devil was unseeable, except indirectly, and proof of witchcraft lay in the interpretation of events not harmful in themselves, a woman's being accused was a chance occurrence or a political one.

Hale, in Volume I of *Freud and the Americans* notes that among reasons for the acceptance of psychoanalysis by physicians was its provision of a "conceptual model of the neuroses that could also be applied to the psychoses. This included that elastic term, the 'complex' . . . an organized constellation of ideas and affects. . . ."[86] Some writers have included among Freud's most important contributions his suggestion that neurosis and psychosis are poles of a continuum, but that is lately being questioned as evidence of specific organic impairments or deficiencies are found to be responsible for particular syndromes at various points on the continuum.

The crucial concept, with which psychotherapeutic interpretation is rationalized, is repression, a "mechanism of ego defense" in which the conflicting or the unpleasant is blocked out or pushed aside unconsciously so that the patient is not only unaware of her "repressed material" but also unaware that repression has occurred. There is, therefore, no way that she can interpret herself. The therapist's interpretations, on the other hand, are assumed to be an objective account based on actual data.

During the development of psychoanalysis, therapeutic strategies were gradually altered. At first, interpretations were withheld so that the processes of free association and dream reporting could eventually bring the patient to self-awareness of unconscious processes. Later, the concept of analytic "tact" was developed, according to which interpretations were gently offered when the timing was right.

Another set of instructions on the making of interpretations is given by David Viscott in *The Making of a Psychiatrist:*

> Always interpret the style of the patient's behavior before you interpret what they tell you. If someone is very hostile and angry and telling you about a flower show they went to, point out that they are angry. Don't get tricked into talking about the flower show. When a patient tells you something painful and does it in a way that doesn't show [she] is feeling pain, point out the discrepancy to [her] and ask if [she] understands it.[87]

Viscott goes on to emphasize the necessity of allowing patients to move "at their own pace," rather than being pushed or pulled by the therapist. On the other hand, he continues,

> if only one person sitting in the room with the therapist has insight into the patient's problems, it should be the therapist. . . . If it's the patient who has the insight and you (the therapist) don't, *you've* got a problem.[88]

This underscores the role that interpretation plays in the maintenance of the therapist-patient hierarchy.

Chessick has noted that a "good" interpretation "increases

the faith of the patient in the therapist, and thereby reduces anxiety and heightens a sense of security. Simultaneously it reassures the therapist as to his own competence. . . ."[89] Nor are these desirable effects dependent on whether the interpretation is "exact" (correct) or "inexact" (incorrect or not entirely correct). It has been asserted by several psychotherapists that an interpretation need not be true in order to have a beneficial effect on the patient, that if the therapist believes that a given interpretation is therapeutic, it becomes so.[90]

It is traditional that the patient's acceptance of these "insights" is at the heart of psychodynamic therapy. Former president of the American Psychoanalytic Association Franz Alexander viewed the essential moments of change in therapy as those times in which a disturbing or traumatic past experience is reexamined in a new context. Personality theorist George Kelly saw progress when the individual recognized that her life is collapsing around her, and began to rebuild her "personal constructs." Alfred Adler used therapist interpretations in order to correct "erroneous conceptions," a principle expanded by Albert Ellis whose "Rational Therapy" allows the therapist directly to supply a more correct "philosophy." In trying to increase their effectiveness, some therapists imbue their interpretations with mystique by "delivering" them in a "special tone of voice."[91] In an article comparing psychotherapy to brain washing, Robert H. Dolliver notes the tendency among some therapists to repeat an interpretation "many times, until the client finally accepts it."[92] It is possible to jam an interpretation down a patient's throat or to use more subtle means such as rewarding "good patient" behavior.[93]

Interpretation is generally viewed by psychotherapists who use it to be evidence of their professional mastery. Viscott recounts an interpretation he made about a young male patient:

'The hour isn't over,' I said. 'You just now got up to leave the same way you ran out of the bedroom and went to class the day you found your father dead. The feelings are the same.'[94]

He notes that in making this statement he had tied an event in the therapy situation to an event in the past, the essence of a "total" interpretation.

> When it works [it] can be breathtakingly effective. The patient has a concrete example of how he really feels and his therapist gets an enormous sense of power. It can be very heady.[95]

Significantly, in discussion of their therapy, patients seldom mention insights given to them by therapists. Instead they stress being able to talk with someone about their problems "in an atmosphere of interest, warmth, and tolerance. . . . The leitmotiv that sounds again and again in the patients' replies is the importance of sharing uncertainties and urgencies with an individual who will listen with respect and treat with dignity their person."[96]

Interpretations can harm. Donald W. Light, Jr., of Princeton University warns that if the psychiatrist "overinterprets" a subtle suicide sign he may actually suggest the idea to the patient.[97] Clinical psychologist Rose Zeligs feels that even in less acute situations, the therapist should be wary: "To try to interpret another person's feelings and fantasies and what exists in [her] unconscious is a difficult and almost impossible task. To jump to conclusions about it without having the confirmation of the other person is wrong and may also be harmful."[98] Melitta Schmideberg, who writes of her experiences with patients who were previously in treatment with psychoanalysts and for whom therapy had been a failure, makes the following comments:

> The patient resents the humiliating and frustrating aspects of the analytic situation, its inequality, the *hurting interpretations*, the highlighting of [her] pathology and shortcomings, the fact that [she] does not get better. . . . If the patient gets worse, the analyst resents this, but, since according to analytic tradition he has no right to show resentment, he expresses it by *further hurtful interpretations* . . . [my italics].[99]

Unfortunately, the therapist's interpretations cannot be verified by objective confirmation. The sessions are private, only therapist and patient are witnesses, and, even when it is "supervised," standard practice usually forces the supervisor to rely on reports supplied by the therapist rather than on direct observation. The same patient behavior might give rise to various interpretations. A silent patient, for example, might be viewed as *resistant* by Freud, *anal erotic* by Ferenczi, *showing defensive ego operation* by Anna Freud, and *reacting to the analyst's countertransference* by Zeligs.

Florence Rush, formerly a psychoanalytically oriented social worker, describes the horror with which she reacted to the diagnosis and interpretations made of her clients by the psychiatrist at staff conferences. After a while, she began to develop anxiety symptoms of incessant trembling for which she herself sought psychiatric help. After several months, her therapist wrote the following:

> Patient never freed herself from the oedipal triangle. She loved her father and competed with her mother for her father's affection. The father love was transferred to her therapist. Since the original conflict remained unsolved, she displaced the infantile father image onto Dr. Farley, also a psychiatrist. Because Dr. Farley admired her work, his attentions resulted in the unconscious fulfillment of the forbidden infantile wish. This situation was complicated by Helen, the supervisor who represented "mother" and "competitor" and who might punish the patient for her fantasized success at taking her mother away from her father. Overwhelming guilt, fear, and anxiety resulted in the attacks of trembling and shaking.[100]

Rush reports that after viewing "the dynamics," Dr. Green "said with feeling, 'The reality is that once and for all you must give up your father. You can't have him.'" She accepted the interpretation:

> Although I never felt any conscious desire to have my father, I felt ashamed of my repressed unconscious wishes. . . .[101]

That a person should be ashamed of unconscious wishes is illogical. That such shame exists, even among sophisticated patients, contributes to what Haley calls being one-down. It might also be conjectured that therapists encourage the feeling because of the desirable effect it might have on the patient's anxiety and motivation to continue in treatment. Rush goes on to say that she "did admire Dr. Green's ability to so skillfully put his finger on the problem."[102] However, her symptoms grew worse, she left her job, and for a year found relief only through the use of tranquilizers. Although she did not return to the psychotherapist after beginning the use of the medication, eventually she fully recovered. Years later, she felt that her problems were in fact *caused* by the interpretations, first of her clients, then of herself, by psychiatrists.

To be in a situation where only someone else, not oneself, can know one's mind is in itself unsettling. Haley recognizes that "the uncertainty of a patient can become profound when she is encouraged to believe that [she] is driven by forces beyond [her] control which the psychoanalyst can understand and interpret but [she] cannot."[103] The totally untenable position of a patient who tries to argue with an interpretation is a direct consequence of psychoanalytic theory which holds that repressed "material" will fight to stay repressed. Thus therapists often feel that a particularly vehement argument against an interpretation suggests its validity.

Interpretation is not an activity confined to the psychotherapist; it has become part of the lifestyle of the culture. In the late forties and early fifties, I can recall the scene in the college cafeteria in which dreams were "analyzed" regularly over lunch, usually with a male upperclassman or graduate student playing therapist and pretty female students the recipients of his voluntary services. In those days, every elongated object from a pencil to a skyscraper was a phallic symbol, every rounded object representative of female genitalia, and the Oedipal game was new and exciting. Edwin Holt tells the following anecdote:

[There was] a party at which a man with a penchant for stretching the truth . . . innocently began to describe his dreams. Another guest interrupted: "I beg your pardon, Sir, but since you are not a Freudian, you are unwittingly making the most intimate revelations. I do not wish to be an eavesdropper, even in such a way."[104]

Today Friends of Psychotherapy often interpret each other's behavior, sometimes even making diagnoses, and often referring one another for therapy.

Being interpreted puts one in a bind. It is not possible to argue against an interpretation because if the process is that of repression it had all happened unconsciously and one is not expected to be, in fact could not be, aware of it. Even among friends, to protest that an interpretation is inaccurate is to prove its validity.

Unfortunately, just as in the case of transference, interpretation is not likely to be given up easily in psychotherapy practice because of the rewards it brings to the patient, and to the therapist. Chessick, in rebutting the assertion that therapy resembles brain washing or indoctrination, says:

> the therapist stays conscientiously with the patient's material and emphatically resonates with the patient's unconscious. He is then able to interpret the patient's unconscious accurately and is not presenting his own preconceptions *de novo* to the patient.[105]

But where does it all end? In an earlier chapter, Chessick said of one of his patients:

> [he finally] developed an affair with a female artist, which represented an acting out of his transference longing toward me, enabling him to avoid the direct pain and the homosexual aspects of such longings, which were extremely intense and most primitive. . . .[106]

Here is an analyst interpreting a transference. But, how can we be sure? Perhaps Chessick's interpretation is in fact the result of *his* "countertransference" and the projection of *his* own homosexual longings onto the patient, a reaction to *his* hurt and jealousy over the patient's heterosexual affair. What assurance does a patient have that she, or he, will not become the victim of the psychotherapist's unconscious needs and complexes?—The therapist's credentials? His years of experience? His personal analysis? The prestige of the institution at which he was trained? His own publications? None of these provides any assurance of the psychotherapist's freedom from such biases.

THE INTERPRETATION OF RESISTANCE

When we undertake to cure a patient of [her] symptoms [she] opposes against us a vigorous and tenacious *resistance* throughout the entire course of the treatment. This is such an extraordinary thing that we cannot expect much belief in it. It is best to say nothing about it to the patient's relations, for they invariably regard it as a pretext set up by us to excuse the length or the failure of the treatment.

SIGMUND FREUD, *A General Introduction to Psychoanalysis*[107]

The supposition that the patient's illness serves as a protective response to threat and that treatment involves uncovering painful hidden material means that it will be necessary for the therapeutic process to struggle with active "resistance." This is defined as "opposition to therapeutic efforts, especially a defensive reluctance to explore repressed material."[108] Psychoanalytic technique is largely the technique of exploring resistances. The analyst focuses mainly on the resistances the patient brings up which contravene the treatment process.[109]

Among the myriad forms that resistance can take is the "flight into health" in which the patient's problems disappear too early in treatment. Another is refusal to accept the interpretations of the therapist. "But I really love my mother (children, husband)" becomes evidence not that the therapist's interpretation may have been in error but that the patient is resisting.

In the view of the therapist, a most disconcerting form of resistance is when therapy is broken off altogether. Such extreme behavior removes the patient from the therapeutic influence. Although, as we have seen, most interpretations are not immediately voiced, interpretation of resistance may be given quite early in treatment, frequently accompanied by admonitions indicating the importance to the patient of continuing. The patients and former patients I have interviewed have reported therapists saying such things as:

You are a very sick woman.

You would not last two months without therapy.

You can only expect to get worse.

If you quit therapy now, I will not be responsible for the results.

They also reported that resistance was brought up early in their therapy. Explaining resistance at the outset helps keep the patient from obeying her early impulses to flee. The therapists said such things as:

You will often feel that we are not getting anywhere, but that very feeling can be a sign of progress.

You may come to feel fondness for me, or to hate me intensely. Such feelings are expected. They are a part of therapy.

Although the concept of resistance was born within the Freudian framework, many psychologists believe that "regardless of one's theoretical allegiance, the significance of the resistance phenomenon in therapy is hard to overestimate."[110] Yet the concept has been taken to such an extreme that a countertendency has developed away from emphasis on the flagrant interpretation of resistance. When a therapist can willy-nilly and without any basis except his clinical judgment define any patient behavior as motivated by the therapy situation the authoritarianism that arises leads to intolerable abuses. Many of the resistance interpretations have begun to appear simplistic. It has been officially admitted that a flat tire or last-minute phone call *could* cause lateness, that a patient's silence might indicate thoughtfulness and doubt, or hostility induced by the therapist's behavior, or even that a decision to discontinue therapy might be because the patient's financial circumstances were strained, or because therapy showed no signs of helping her.[111]

It is terrible to contemplate the therapist in his private practice who daily sees no signs of improvement. In a corner

of his mind, he begins to question the validity of what he is
doing, but his professional commitment and his indoctrination through the long years of training do not allow him
to entertain doubts at this stage. He has, after all, undergone
personal therapy in which he submitted himself to the authority of another and spent many sessions in analysis of *his*
resistances to therapy as indicated by *his* feelings of misgiv-
ings, "blocked" associations, lateness, and other "clear" signs.
Schmideberg said that many analysts came to accept

> the tenets of analysis as "truth" in a pseudoreligious way
> by trying to fit their patients to the preconceived theory
> and by taking for granted, without substantiating it, that
> this "truth" is necessarily healing. . . . As a rule, [they
> have] not learnt to handle deterioration by means other
> than interpretation, and when the situation gets out of
> hand they often resort to panic measures . . . [The thera-
> pist] resents patients who do not respond to his efforts and
> who challenge his faith in analysis, and sometimes he even
> becomes afraid of the patient.[112]

A patient who senses the therapist's turmoil might be accused of resisting. In coming for treatment she has indicated
her acceptance of the role of patient in need of help and has
also accepted his role as therapist, capable of helping. From
the beginning, she is also likely to accept his interpretations.
Later, when she has revealed much of herself, told many "secrets," admitted to many faults, spent so much time and so
much money, she has developed a deeper commitment and a
more tenacious faith in treatment and in the particular therapist, even if she has not developed a romantic or erotic
"transference" of emotionality. When he suggests, however
gentle or tentative his tone, a meaning behind her behavior,
these forces may compel her to adopt his view. Patients come
to therapists in a weakened condition, usually depressed and
anxious. They want the therapist to be an authority, to take
care of them, to help. For this, they are willing to give up
privacy and integrity. "Take me apart if you must, but put
me back together better, please," they plead.

Those who are forced to participate in psychotherapy sessions against their will are very different. A fifteen-year-old

girl with whom I consulted had retained her integrity by never seeing the therapist as an authority and by never really revealing herself to him. It is among the young people whose parents, school authorities, or courts insisted that they "receive treatment" that the term "shrink" seems most popular. Believers among adults prefer "analyst," even if he is not a psychoanalyst, or "psychotherapist," or "doctor."

For the voluntary, usually female, adult patient in private therapy, upon whom this book is focused, the therapist is an authority, if not a God. She strains her very perception of reality in order to believe what he says and accept his judgment. Evidence of the psychotherapist's fallibility may be more threatening to her even than her own vision of herself as torn apart by inner conflicts. The passivity of the psychoanalytically oriented psychotherapist undoubtedly had much to do with the continued popularity of psychotherapy for almost seventy years, because the less he said, the greater her ability to retain her belief in him.

Viscott, in *The Making of a Psychiatrist*, gives two accounts of elaborate patient behavior stimulated by an absence of therapist behavior. In a psychiatric residents' therapy group, when the leader had a flat tire and did not arrive on time for the session, the group used the time to spin involved explanations and interpretations, and displayed emotional reactions ranging from affection and concern to outright hostility. The group members tended to assume that the lateness of the therapist was deliberate or had interpersonal meaning.

The second example was of a young male patient (also a psychiatric resident) whose therapist fell asleep one day during their 6:30 A.M. session. The patient began the session by announcing that he felt something the analyst had said at the previous session was incorrect.

> Usually I can tell how he reacts to something, but this morning I couldn't tell because he was silent. I mean, he's often silent, which means "keep talking." Right?[113]

The patient went on talking. From the continued silence, he judged that he was "on the right track," and began to free associate.

[This] opened up a whole new area. Still no comment. I said, "I understand you're trying to see how much stress I can take!" Still no comment.[114]

The patient becomes angry at first, then anxious, afraid "something has happened" to the therapist. He reports his various feelings, but still gets no reply:

Then I get this brilliant insight and I say, "It's this way with all authorities and me. I get afraid of my own anger at them and knuckle under. I'm afraid of my own anger. How about that?" I'm saying to myself this guy is really a brilliant analyst! What brilliant technique, superb self-control, being quiet like that and not saying a word, letting me go through all this anxiety knowing just how much I can take, knowing I'm safe because he won't let me go too far. I told him how much I appreciated his ability to stay silent. I really did, and for the first time I understood what they meant when they say the analyst's love *is* his silence. . . .[115]

Silence by the therapist promotes both ambiguity and anxiety, and these, in turn, increase the therapist's influence and the patient's motivation to remain in treatment.[116] It has been suggested that the silence of the analyst produces a state of hypersuggestibility comparable to that of hypnosis.[117] It is therefore "one of the most potent tools" in the therapist's repertoire. It is also the background against which any verbalizations or other reactions of the therapist are very sensitively and seriously attended to by the patient.

On the other hand, silence is often bitterly resented by patients, particularly when they give retrospective accounts of their therapy.[118] There is a difference between silence and sympathetic listening. Some therapists are very directive; they shout interpretations at their patients. Other therapists are very explicit about revealing their own emotional reactions to the patient's behavior. But the major difference between such techniques and those of the passive psychoanalysts may be in how much sensitivity in reading therapist messages the patient is required to develop. Most of the new psychotherapies that have achieved popularity still depend on a basic assumption of inner causation with an emphasis on thoughts, feelings, and interpersonal relationships, and on the assumption that a person may be better understood by another than by herself, thereby making it reasonable for her words and actions to be interpreted. Therapy is perceived as a kind of battle in which the patient's resistance must be overcome if cure is to take place.

THE RESPONSIBILITY BELONGS
TO THE PATIENT

A major difference between the treatments of medicine and those of psychotherapy warrants discussion. Both goals and procedures of psychotherapy tend toward vagueness and nonobjectivity, whereas medicine is almost always explicit and objective at least about one if not both. The responsibility of the physician is defined with relative clarity. He diagnoses and prescribes. With the patient's willingness and cooperation, the indicated treatment is carried out. Too often, the explanation given the patient is incomplete, so that the consent to treatment given may fall short of the criteria of "informed." But the physician's responsibility is primarily that of recommending treatment. He is not responsible for seeing that the patient carries it out. A physician who failed to recommend a standard treatment for a clearly diagnosed condition might risk a malpractice suit, but having made the recommendation, he will not be liable for any results of the patient's refusal to have it administered.

Analytic psychotherapy, born among medical men and envious of the status of medical treatment, has carried over this concept of responsibility without taking into consideration that the treatment and the personal influence of the therapist cannot be separated. Treatment is not something recommended and then objectively administered. It emanates from the intricacies of a personal relationship in which the vision of both patient and therapist may at times be blurred. This makes the therapist quite unlike the surgeon cutting off a specific piece of tissue, or the general practitioner prescribing a specific dosage of a known chemical. It therefore would appear to be nonsensical to speak of patient "responsibility" in psychotherapy comparable to the medical sense of carrying out or permitting to be carried out a prescribed therapy. Yet this is what has been done. Over and over in the statements of psychotherapists runs the theme of patient blame, sometimes carried to amazing extremes.

Patients have told about being rejected by therapists who said that they had "refused to cooperate" and did not "really" want to get well. The "dynamics" of mental illness are described in textbooks as the consequences of the victim's seemingly voluntary actions. For example, this passage describes the "active-dependent" or "gregarious personality":

> The tendency . . . to seal off, to repress and make inaccessible portions of [her] meager inner life, further aggravates [her] dependence on others. By insulating [her] own emotions and cognitions from the stream of everyday life, [she] effectively denies [herself] the opportunity to learn new alternatives for behavior, to modify [her] self-image or to become a more genuinely skillful and knowledgeable person. As long as [she] blocks the fusion which should occur between the new experiences and self, [she] remains stagnant, unaltered and impoverished. Deprived of opportunities to learn and to grow, [she] perpetuates the vicious circle of [her] dependency on others. . . .[119]

Neurosis is something the patient does to herself. Treatment depends on her willingness, commitment, responsibility, and courage.

Patients are often blamed for their failure to trust the therapist, for their "manipulativeness," for their failure to obey the rules of therapy, for their "seductiveness," and for their irresponsibility. Even suicide has been called a way of "relating" and suicide attempts ways of manipulating others. When a therapist finds himself sexually attracted to a patient, his interpretation of the situation may be to make her responsible, and guilty of seductiveness.

The language of psychiatric case records reflects this basically moralistic approach of therapists to patients. In the case study of a woman who progressively deteriorated during therapy, D. M. Kaplan writes:

> Any attempts of mine to interpret vestiges of oedipal matter in her reports were countered by the patient with bitter, derisive protests that I was misunderstanding her and misjudging her whole situation. . . . Her enraged word-twisting assault gave me the impression that she was warning me of the possibility of ideational disorder. . . .[120]

In this passage the therapist reveals his anger at the recalcitrant patient. "Ideational disorder" means psychosis, but it is she, not he, who makes the prediction. Was her "warning" by nature of a threat? I read this case history with feelings of sympathy for a woman victimized by a therapist who does not even call his anger "countertransference."

DEPENDENCY OF THE PATIENT ON THERAPY AND THE THERAPIST

Parallels have been observed between psychotherapy and the brainwashing given Korean war prisoners.[121] Both are procedurally characterized by intensive interviewing concerning personal material and, particularly, "inner feelings" that must be brought to the session by the person receiving treatment. In both situations the person giving treatment is relatively unrevealing of himself, but he interprets the actions of the person interviewed and encourages self criticism.[122] In both, considerable control is gained as the person increasingly comes under the therapist's influence and turns to him for cues and guidelines.

Creating dependency may be considered desirable to brainwashers, but it is never proclaimed as an aim of psychotherapy. On the contrary, when it occurs, it is termed a (temporary) transference neurosis or a neurotic symptom. Yet it is an almost inevitable result of therapeutic techniques. As London observes:

> Sympathetic listening has a strong seductive effect on people in ordinary life situations. . . . Actually unloading to an unexpectedly sympathetic listener will produce . . . strong feelings of gratitude and even affection toward that person. . . . The intuitive recognition of this principle is one of the main things that sends professional confidence men after *lonely* victims who have no one to talk to.[123]

Frank notes that with insight therapies where the objective is to help the patient achieve understanding of her inner feelings and the ability to express that understanding in words and in which the patient expresses herself freely while the therapist maintains a consistent attitude of impartial interest the situation, paradoxically, is one in which the therapist obtains strong persuasive power.

> Since the therapist believes he does not influence the patient's productions, he can regard them as independent verification of the theory . . . the therapist may be tempted to induce patients to produce such material, especially since his theory enables him to conceal from himself the fact that he is doing so.[124]

Patients have suggested that the influence of the therapist is greatly enhanced by his "passivity." Many have told of their efforts to please the therapist and their sensitivity to subtle cues such as facial expressions. Verbal conditioning experiments in which a simulated therapeutic interview was studied found that when the interviewer selectively reinforced certain types of verbalizations with "um hmm," the rate of those types increased.[125] Kubie has observed that the "patient has no escape hatch. [She] is the therapist's captive audience,"[126] although his "performance" is mostly limited to few words, occasional audible (or visible if she is seated, as in most current therapies) shifts in body position, sighs, coughs, grunts, and that most effective "weapon" silence.

To an extreme degree for many patients, and to some degree for all patients, psychodynamic insight therapies foster self-involvement. Schmideberg calls this a "flight from life" in which the person "concentrates on motives rather than consequences, [and] takes more interest in irrational fantasies than in developing better judgment."[127] Former patients often refer to this concentration on fantasies, dreams, and associations in the search for hidden meanings as a kind of "masturbation." As one said:

> While I was in therapy, I had three children, but it was like being half there, in a fog. I'd get up in the morning and go to pick up the baby who was crying, but my thoughts were concentrated on my dream of the night before, what it might "mean," and what my analyst might say about it.

Schmideberg says:

> Free associations presuppose a temporary withdrawal from reality which . . . may further regression, self-centeredness, and concentration on grievances; [patients] are only too ready to regard motivation as an excuse for their behavior. Concentration on mental processes may sidetrack patients from action. They will start discovering motive after motive why they are reluctant to look for a job, instead of getting one.[128]

The self-involvement induced by therapy seems in many patients to produce not only a dependency on the particular therapist, but a need for therapy. Schmideberg talks of "addiction" to therapy. She cites the case of an accountant who spent thirty years in analysis with "leading American analysts." Despite depletion of his economic resources and lack of improvement of the various "anxieties and inhibitions" which sent him to therapy in the first place, he continued in treatment. Schmideberg reports that when she asked if there was anything which "gave him a sense of relief or happiness," he answered, "Yes, associating freely."[129]

It thus appears that patients may in fact be addicts, persons who spend much, if not most, of their life in therapy, often seeing not just one or two, but five, six, even as many as sixteen different therapists over the years. Lately they have also begun to participate in other systematic attempts at personal enhancement or self-understanding such as meditation, macrobiotic diets, astrology, and many others.

PSYCHOTHERAPISTS INTERPRET ONE ANOTHER

Psychotherapists themselves are not immune to interpretation. Schmideberg describes early meetings of the British Psycho-Analytical Society.[130] Dissension was frequently attributed to "personal problems":

> Some members, usually those in a weaker position, are sent for further analysis; others are given, in open discussion or privately, gratuitous analytic interpretations by the colleagues from whom they differ. . . .[131]

She continues:

> Analysts in all countries tend to deprecate the opponent's point of view as "not really analytic," or accuse him of "not having been analyzed deeply enough" or of "suffering from resistance." Such arguments are, of course, unanswerable.[132]

Schmideberg was particularly impressed by the dangers of interpretation when she herself was diagnosed by Ernest Jones as having paranoid attitudes after she, the daughter of Melanie Klein, had ceased to "toe the Kleinian line."

> I was still young and naive, and Jones was very much an authority to me. He had me almost convinced by his logic and manner, when it occurred to me that the letter of mine on which he had based his diagnosis of "paranoid" had actually been drafted for me by Edward Glover.[133]

Schmideberg, who has closely witnessed the behind-the-scenes history of several analytic societies, reports that "they have always presented fundamentally the same pattern."[134]

Accusations of countertransference are a frequent therapist-to-therapist putdown technique. Shepard and Lee give an example in which one therapist concludes that another is a "victim" of countertransference for having postponed treatment of his patient's obesity because, "I figure it's hard enough for her to gain insight about her lack of ego

without suggesting a crash-diet at the same time. . . ."[135]
Shepard and Lee suggest that therapists who wish to avoid
being accused of countertransference should not "admit to
feeling bored, angry, tired, loving, lustful, or depressed" and
"when speaking of a patient, never admit to acting curtly,
aggressively, critically, solicitously, or jokingly."

In a similar, semihumorous vein, Viscott describes the
group therapy sessions participated in by psychiatric residents and staff.

> The point was that everything we did in group was con-
> sidered suitable material for group analysis. Being late for
> a group session was interpreted to mean that you felt neg-
> ative or at least ambivalent about coming to the group or
> someone in the group. . . . Everything we did meant
> something, so said the rules, and interpreting what it meant
> was what the seminar was all about.[136]

The psychotherapist in training is also subjected to interpretation when he undergoes a personal analysis or "didactic" course of treatment.

Not long ago, I participated in a seminar with a group
who were undertaking a study of psychotherapy by having
representatives of various approaches meet with them for an
afternoon to make a brief presentation and answer questions.
I had not been present for the previous sessions; the one I attended was a final wrap-up and evaluation. Several members
of the seminar commented on the "antisocial" behavior of
visiting psychoanalysts who had refused to answer any question that contained a hint of criticism and even went so far as
to retaliate by accusing the questioner of having personal
reasons, including hostility toward the visitor, possibly because he resembled a key figure in the person's life. Interpretation within the treatment context may be viewed by
therapists as a correct and helpful aid to self-knowledge; in
the outside world, it is clearly abusive and accusatory.

The tradition of interpreting those one disagrees with
began as far back as Sigmund Freud himself. In *Freud and
the Americans, The Beginnings of Psychoanalysis in the
United States, 1876–1910*, a fascinating account of the early

days of psychoanalysis, Nathan G. Hale, Jr., tells of Freud's
reaction to a paper by James Jackson Putnam, neurologist
and one of the first distinguished American physicians to accept psychoanalysis: "Freud failed to understand Putnam's
idealistic philosophy. He was fond of Putnam, but somewhat
ungraciously attributed [his] preoccupations to a tendency
to obsessional neurosis."[137]

Many examples of Freud's acerbic interpretations are
found in the recently published correspondence between
Freud and C. G. Jung:

> I can only request that you handle Adler . . . with psychi-
> atric caution. . . .[138]

> Our only lady doctor is participating like a true masochist
> in the Adler revolt. . . .[139]

> And possibly his masochism was only waiting for a good
> whipping. . . .[140]

> . . . The trouble with you younger men seems to be a lack
> of understanding in dealing with your father com-
> plexes. . . .[141]

> . . . I am convinced that his neurosis was speaking for
> him. . . .[142]

When Freud turned his interpretive eye on Jung himself as
their relationship began to disintegrate, Jung protested:

> . . . I can only assure you that there is no resistance on
> my side unless it be my refusal to be treated like a fool
> riddled with complexes. I think I have objective reasons
> for my views. . . .[143]
> It is only occasionally that I am afflicted by the purely
> human desire to be understood *intellectually* and not be
> measured by the yardstick of neurosis. . . . I am forced to
> the painful conclusion that the majority of [psycho-
> analysts] misuse [psychoanalysis] for the purpose of
> devaluing others and their progress by insinuations about
> complexes (as though that explained anything. A wretched
> theory!). A particularly preposterous bit of nonsense now
> going the rounds is that my libido theory is the result of
> anal eroticism. When I consider *who* cooked up this
> "theory" I fear for the future of analysis. . . .[144]

In the six decades since their correspondence ended, hundreds of persons have suffered Jung's fate of being "measured by the yardstick of neurosis" for the human "affliction" of needing respect.

STIGMA

In the fifteenth century, the *Malleus Maleficarum* codified the ancient "demonical model" of behavior aberrations, which "had embraced all conduct that departed from the existing norms and was policed by zealous church and secular authorities. The most outstanding result of this thought model was the Inquisition, a social movement that among other things influenced the diagnosis and treatment of unusual imaginings, esoteric beliefs, and extraordinary conduct."[145] St. Teresa of Avila, one of the first to relate the concept of illness to persons exhibiting signs of insanity, protected a group of nuns from the Inquisition by attributing their behavioral peculiarities to "natural causes," thus implying that the appropriate professional consultant was the physician, not the priest. Although Teresa used the concept of illness metaphorically, it was eventually applied literally.

But mental illness is not like other illnesses:

Persons who are labeled mentally ill are not regarded as merely sick; they are regarded as a special class of beings, to be feared or scorned, sometimes to be pitied, but nearly always to be degraded. . . .

Further, because of the inherent vagueness in the concept of mind, its assumed independence from the body, and its purported timelessness (derived from the immortal soul), there is a readiness to regard this special kind of sickness as permanent. . . .[146]

So says psychologist Theodore R. Sarbin of University of California at Berkeley, who, with James C. Mancuso of the State University of New York in Albany, explored attitudes of the public toward mental illness in an article published in 1970 in *The Journal of Consulting and Clinical Psychology*[147] In their article, they advocate rejection of the entire concept of mental illness. Despite a large and sustained propaganda effort on the part of "mental health movement" advocates, and despite the commitment to psychiatric treatment of its Friends and Supporters, the average person (1) will tolerate and adjust to considerably deviant behavior on the part of persons in the environment, (2) is much more reluctant than the professionals to apply a psychiatric explanation for deviant behavior, and (3) rejects and isolates any person whose behaviors come to be diagnosed as evidence of "mental illness." The label, in itself, has a deleterious effect. As Dorothea Dix, crusader for more humane treatment of incarcerated persons, and Clifford Beers, former mental patient and a force behind the mental health movement, among thousands of others, learned, the "verdict of the ages" is that a person who is once insane is always insane. Insanity is not something one *does*, but something one *is* deep inside, so deeply and invisibly that it can never be completely eradicated once it is discovered.

Those who have tried to believe otherwise are wrong. Negative public opinion is not close to being dispelled. As Shirley A. Star said,

> mental illness is a very threatening and fearful thing and not an idea to be entertained lightly about anyone. Emotionally it represents to people loss of what they consider to be the distinctively human qualities of rationality and free will, and there is a kind of horror of dehumanization. As both our data and other studies make clear, mental illness is something that people want to keep as far from themselves as possible.[148]

That the problem is the label, not the behavior in itself, has been documented in several studies in which actions were described or exhibited with and without a psychiatric label.[149] It was invariably found that extremely deviant behavior was often better tolerated than mildly deviant behavior which had, however, been "diagnosed" as evidence of psychiatric illness. Senator Thomas Eagleton's problem was not depression or even drunken driving; it was the intolerable label of mental illness that had been stuck on him.

Nor are vice-presidential candidates the only persons whose employment future is endangered by psychiatric stigmatization. According to Schmideberg, one man was refused New York City employment because when he was interviewed for the job he had mentioned in passing that he had been in hospital with an "abdominal" complaint, and the interviewer who was hard of hearing believed he had said "mental," and persons with "mental complaints" are barred from City employment.[150] Service records of veterans can adversely affect a person's subsequent civilian career if they include evidence of psychiatric treatment or classification. Psychiatrists have been interviewed by FBI officials for information concerning a person under investigation. Persons who have received psychiatric treatment often feel they have no recourse but to lie about it to a prospective employer, but this means suffering continual fear that, as with the unfortunate Eagleton, this "skeleton" will someday be revealed. Hospitalization is the most difficult to hide. New York State law requires that the diagnosis of every psychiatric patient seen in a clinic or hospital—whether public or private—be on file in the state capital, along with the person's address, race, and other information. A hospital identification number is used instead of the name, although the records of Medicaid patients are more subject to exposure. It has also been found that all other things being equal, including diagnosis, one is more likely to be hospitalized if one is poor.[151] The issue of protection of a person's right to privacy has been raised in various ways by individual states, and is a current matter of controversy.[152]

The stigma exists even among mental health professionals and the Friends and Supporters of Psychotherapy. Although Friends talk fairly freely among themselves, most of them are aware of the negative reaction to anything psychiatric in the mind of the general public. It is not just what a city has to offer culturally that keeps most psychotherapists in the large metropolitan areas; it is only there that visits to a therapist can go unnoticed by other persons.[153] A psychiatric social worker sued a psychiatrist to prevent further distribution of a book in which her life story formed the major case history.

Not only employees, but family, friends, the court, and public school teachers are influenced. In one case, two boys were picked up for loitering, and the one without evidence of psychotherapy in his record was dismissed by the judge. The other boy, who had been seen at a child guidance clinic some years earlier, was sent to a Remand Home for psychiatric observation "in his own interest."[154] Hannah Green, in the novel *I Never Promised You a Rose Garden*, tells of the anguish experienced by Deborah's parents as they tried to come to terms with the concept of their daughter's confinement as a mental patient.

One problem is the absence of a concept of "normality," or mental "health," in psychiatric classifications. There are events in anyone's life which could be used to construct a damaging record. In psychiatric case histories, the record contains not a representative sample of a person's life story, but items of "systematic significance." Furthermore, the very use of psychiatric terminology is pejorative in connotation. Behavioral psychologist Richard B. Stuart notes that "once a negative label has been applied, there is a clear and present danger that the person so identified will be the victim of additional negative inference solely on the basis of . . . having been designated as a deviant."[155] In one investigation, college students administered larger amounts of electric shock to experimental subjects whom they believed had been hospitalized for mental illness than they did to "normal" subjects.[156] Stuart speculates "that once family members are apprised that a troublesome person in their midst has been diagnosed as mentally ill, the same set of negative reactions may ensue."[157]

In a revealing experimental study, institutionalized mental patients who were told that observers knew that they were mentally ill were compared with patients who believed observers thought them to be normal. "Knowing a person knows" was found to have extremely damaging effects. Those patients who were told that observers knew they were mentally ill seemed more tense and anxious, felt less appreciated and found a simple experimental task to be more difficult. Furthermore, impartial observers judged them to be less well-adjusted.[158] In the study in which normal subjects were believed to have been hospitalized for mental illness, this belief led to social rejection, dislike, and more harsh judgment of the subjects' performance in addition to greater willingness to inflict pain on them.[159] Even the staunchest psychotherapy advocates recognize that applying a psychiatric label to a person can in itself be harmful.[160]

In view of the unreliability of diagnostic tests of personality and the pejorative connotations of psychiatric labels, children are usually "protected" from their case records by prohibiting access to them by the persons closest to the child —teachers and parents. But decisions about placement in "special" classes, for example, are made by psychologists and administrators who utilize psychodiagnostic records in making them. It is also common for the flavor, if not the details, of the psychological reports to be communicated to the teachers during conferences about the child.

Access to case records by parents and children themselves is a controversial issue among educators, but even when the law specifically permits such access, it remains difficult to obtain. The principal of the school is a formidable figure to most parents. Even those aware of their rights often elect not to demand them.

Stanley L. Brodsky, a psychologist whose work is primarily concerned with inmates of correctional institutions, has objected to the "selectively" closed file.[161] Brodsky calls for an opening of files to the clients themselves. He discounts the traditional objection that the subjects of the case records would be damaged if exposed to their own case records.

One advantage to open files would be the lessened likelihood of factual error. While serving in the capacity of school psychologist a few years ago, I "warmed up" the interview of a little girl to whom I was charged to give an intelligence test by asking her age. She said seven; her record said eight. Although the school authorities' first reaction was to believe the records, not the child, they agreed to investigate and ultimately found that the child was correct. It was also decided that her "emotional problems," the reason she had been sent for tests, were attributable to incorrect grade placement. A normal seven-year-old was being viewed as a dull eight-year-old. Her school difficulties stemmed entirely from this error.

DIAGNOSIS

The assumption of the leaders in nineteenth-century psychiatry that abnormal behavior is based on organic disease underlies the official system of classifying psychiatric disorder, the *Diagnostic and Statistical Manual* of the American Psychiatric Association. However, instead of being restricted to the few known disease entities that have behavioral effects (i.e., general paresis due to syphilitic infection and phenylketonuria to biochemical imbalance) and to behavioral aberrations strongly suspected to have discoverable biological bases (i.e., primary dyslexia in children, some forms of alcoholism, and the major psychoses), the concepts of mental illness have expanded, and the number of "conditions" listed has proliferated to include virtually any form of deviance or maladaption. Recent accounts report such syndromes as "existential anguish" and "sense of alienation."

In a recent critique of the classification system, Juris G. Draguns of Pennsylvania State University and Leslie Phillips of Vanderbilt University note that etiology, manifestation, and outcome are confounded, making diagnosis inherently uncertain. The categories used are so broad that patients assigned to a given category seldom show all the characteristics by which it is defined. Furthermore, as Draguns and Phillips point out, few symptoms compel the assignment of a patient to a given diagnostic category.[162] Several highly prestigious and influential authorities have recommended their abolition; their uselessness is attested to by the presence of but a single page reference to diagnosis in a recent book on psychotherapy over nine hundred pages long. The fact is that the function of diagnostic categories is largely political.

Before they turned to psychotherapy itself, clinical psychologists often earned their daily bread by making diagnoses by means of various subjective tests and procedures, notably the Rorschach and other projectives. But in 1959 psychologist Kenneth B. Little said:

It is somewhat embarrassing to have to say that the published evidence on projective techniques indicates that they have either zero, or at best, very low positive effective validity indices. Even in those studies with the most positive results, correlations are of an order of magnitude which make predictions for the individual largely a waste of time.[163]

But interest in diagnosis is consistent with adherence to the medical model of psychodynamic psychotherapies. External symptoms are the result of internal dynamics. Projective tests present the patient with a relatively unstructured stimulus such as an incomplete sentence ("If I were only able to—"), an inkblot, or a photograph of two people facing one another. The theory is that the patient will "project" her personality, including her "unconscious,"[164] on to the situation. Hermann Rorschach believed that analysis of the quantitative and objective aspects of the patient's responses to a standard set of inkblots (how many responses, which part of the blot was used, etc.) would lead to clear and unambiguous diagnoses. It was a brave and exciting idea, but it did not work. Good clinical tests fill three basic requirements: they are easy and even pleasurable to administer, they give the patient a sense of the importance of the undertaking, and they are valid. The Rorschach and other projective tests, but particularly the Rorschach inkblot test, meet the first two criteria admirably, but appear to fail on the last. The test has been used hundreds of thousands of times. The number of research reports on it themselves run into the thousands. Clinical psychologists spend as much as two years of training in learning its intricacies. Yet an abundance of negative research has failed to convince many clinicians of its lack of value. The cost to the patient required to take the test can be as high as $300.

There is one thing certain: clinicians liked the Rorschach. In the 1930s and 1940s, tests on intelligence were the primary psychological measuring instruments. By 1960 projective tests with the Rorschach heading the list were the most popular, despite the fact that research had, by then, discredited them. As with therapy itself, the issue is sometimes simply evaded. It is said that the Rorschach is not really a test at all, but a "technique for eliciting information about the personality,"[165] in which case it need not meet reliability criteria.*

After reviewing diagnostic assumptions and categories used by psychodynamically oriented clinicians and finding that their diagnoses have a "high probability of unreliability and invalidity," Richard Stuart said:

> These findings were not in themselves surprising, as it is reasonable to expect that the assessment of an unobservable entity must be a highly variable procedure. What is surprising, on the other hand, is the apparent complacency with which the mental health profession has accepted such discordant results. The same criticisms have been expressed in similar terms for years. Yet practitioners continue to use the same unproductive procedures, ignoring the principle that scientists must constantly correct their methods in the light of experience.[166]

Not only are most practitioners not scientists, they are loath to change any cherished (and lucrative) procedure simply on the basis of research reports. The recent waning of interest in psychodiagnostic test battery results by clinical psychologists has come from gradual changes in training emphasis as psychologists responded to the lure of private practice. Diagnosis was once the psychologist's special domain; treatment, the psychiatrist's. In a team approach, the psychologists administered tests, the social worker dealt with the patient's family,

---

* The unreliability of personality tests, even "objective" ones like the MMPI (Minnesota Multiphasic Personality Inventory), has greatly hindered research progress in evaluation of psychotherapy, since quite a few investigators have based their findings on results of such tests. It has also been found that diagnoses—whether based on tests or not—are likely to be biased. Although many psychologists who are critical of diagnoses of personality testing believe that gross measures such as distinguishing between psychosis and neurosis tend to be reliable, other things being equal those of lower economic status are more likely than more affluent patients to be considered psychotic (see Goldenberg, Contemporary Clinical Psychology, pp. 14–16). In fact, the criteria for many diagnoses are so vague and ambiguous that mental illness becomes whatever a psychiatrist says it is. In many states, it is what any physician says it is.

and the psychiatrist did the psychotherapy. Today, members of all three professions are hanging out shingles.

In addition, negative research findings played a role in decreasing popularity of psychodiagnosis. It has been charged that personality tests, which are essentially subjective clinical evaluations but tend to be cloaked in the prestige of the test, are an invasion of privacy. According to Viscott,

> Rorschach and other projective tests are highly subjective, and . . . their results may also suggest deeper pathology than actually exists. These tests can become a jumping-off point for the clinician who tends to look for evidence to back up the test findings. In this way he may prove the diagnosis of a disease that sometimes does not exist. . . .[167]

The diagnostic process can thus ultimately be harmful to the patient by including prejudices. This is particularly dangerous in the case of children because of the school records. As writer Viki Holland points out, "psychologizers label people with . . . negatively loaded words. Words are being used as weapons, and not much seems to come from the process except grant proposals and bad feelings."[168]

Advantages accrue to the professional who invents a new diagnostic category, but the steamroller tendency to incorporate new labels into the terminology ignores the following facts: naming something does not explain it, transient moods or behaviors do not give reliable information about underlying traits, and a person can be harmed by being given a pejorative label.

Psychologist Anthony F. Donofrio, writing in the journal *Mental Hygiene*, noted the danger of "systematic error" in which a psychologist is biased in his diagnosis by the comments of previous psychologists whose reports are contained in a child's file. What then appears to be confirmation is actually "illusory correlation."

> Misdiagnoses with conformity in language or semantics are rife; the heavy reliance on projective tools whose interpretative validity is very questionable, indeed, distressing. One sees many parents confused and emotionally upset. Some have already been referred to private psycho-

therapists and are seen, later, financially and emotionally drained.[169]

Donofrio, whose concern is mainly for children, although his remarks are generally applicable, distinguishes between "objective" and "projective" tests and finds the former useful when they measure "cognitive or intellectual functioning: attention, concentration, memory, perception, learning and subject achievement."[170] But 170 case records tend to contain little reference to these in comparison with the quantity of interpretive material extracted from the child's responses to "projective" stimuli.*

PSYCHOTHERAPY AS SOCIAL CONTROL

Imagine Friends and Supporters getting married to one another and having children. At the first sign of trouble, off goes the child to psychotherapy. In places like Westport, Connecticut, where people are affluent and many are in "communications" fields, typical high school students see their shrinks after school, and there are more psychotherapists per capita making a living on the locals than in New York City itself. By now, some of those juvenile patients have become adults, and some have protested their former psychotherapy.

Psychotherapy, which once epitomized the politically liberal intellectual attitude, became an object of scorn and derision in the eyes of the liberals' offspring, the so-called "campus radical." It is a tool of capitalism, a means of "social control," an "agent of oppression." Underneath the rhetoric lies accurate appraisal of the process. In *Repression or Revolution? Therapy in the United States Today*, "radical" therapists Michael Glenn and Richard Kunnes discuss the "true function" of psychotherapy:

* It is argued that the situation is changing: many school psychologists would welcome change. But both training programs and practitioners are held back by government regulations. Many state certification requirements and college training programs contribute to an overemphasis on assessment procedures, including the use of projective tests. An awakened public is needed to force change.

In today's rapidly changing world, therapy serves the status quo. It bolsters the power of those who run the country. Therapy distorts reality, and then presents this distortion as the Truth Unveiled, which it presses on people, exhorting them to accept it and *adjust* to what they cannot change.[171]

There is no question that the person who goes to a psychotherapist and learns to adapt to a situation, to adjust herself is less likely to apply pressure outward in an attempt to bring about change in society. Psychotherapy is a distraction from other pressures. In traditional psychoanalytic therapy, the patient may specifically be requested to make no changes in her life situation during therapy. Furthermore, with all psychotherapies, to the degree that the problems reside in the society the psychotherapist is not the appropriate person to solve them. Since psychotherapy is a commercial enterprise, not social action, psychotherapists are not rewarded for leaving their offices to protest societal conditions.

Some writers view psychotherapy as a means of supporting the economic structure of the society. In an article originally presented in 1969 at the nineteenth annual meeting of the Society for the Study of Social Problems, Psychiatric Sociology Division, Nathan Hurvitz listed several ways in which psychotherapy may be harmful, and noted that the medical model may actually contribute to the conditions that it proposes to treat.

> Despite the growing awareness that traditional psychotherapy is no more effective than any other type of therapy, that it may be harmful, that there are serious limitations to the medical model on which it is based, that it is used for reactionary purposes, and that nontraditional and nonprofessional psychotherapy may be more effective in some instances, psychodynamic psychotherapy continues to spread.[172]

According to Hurvitz's analysis, this occurs because psychodynamic therapy is in

> accord with the individualistic and competitive mobility system and the ideology of liberal democracy of American capitalism, . . . [its] latent purpose is to serve as a means

of social control . . . [which] is accomplished through the
ideology and practice of psychotherapy. . . .[173]

In Hurvitz's view, psychotherapy "makes personal problems
of political issues."[174]

By blaming individuals, not social conditions, for their
problems, psychotherapy decreases the likelihood that a force
will be mobilized to change conditions. To be poor is to be a
failure, and to be a failure is a personal problem. Even to
march in protest is to be a neurotic, maladjusted person
whose behavior is the acting out of inner frustrations. For
Hurvitz, it is not surprising that Friends of Psychotherapy
are better educated people:

> This ideology, which is fostered by intellectuals who iden-
> tify with the existing order, permeates the common culture
> and lives of people who do not understand the nature of
> our society, and fosters a "false consciousness" among
> them; it protects the status quo against those who would
> change it; it psychologizes, personalizes, and depoliticalizes
> social issues; it identifies success with personal worth; it
> fosters a concept of adjustment which often implies
> submission; it is used in ad hominem arguments to
> disparage others; it gives credence to idealist, spiritualist,
> and occult concepts that deny a scientific basis for theories
> and practices for solving problems and changing behavior
> and society; and it leads to misunderstanding the position,
> aspirations, and ways of changing the conditions of op-
> pressed . . . groups in America.[175]

Although few welfare recipients or parents of public
school children are among the Friends and Supporters of
Psychotherapy, the social workers, psychologists, and educators who deal with them have been trained to accept psychodynamic assumptions. Thus, the effects of psychotherapy
principles affect them. They are "diagnosed" or otherwise labeled, and their problems are viewed as arising from personal and family conditions.

Psychotherapy, which originally functioned to provide a
rationale for changes in social mores and values, particularly
concerning sexuality, became a "handmaiden of oppression"
by providing an even stronger rationale for not examining

poverty, crime, social protest, or racial prejudice as social issues. These were personal problems. The women's movement has begun to refute this ideology by saying that "the personal is political," and it is no longer accepting the pat answer that problems are personal neuroses. Feminists are seeing the sex caste system itself as the basis for many so-called "individual problems."[176]

It has also been noted that the psychotherapist is neither ethically nor morally neutral.[177] Therapists' values affect their practices and their patients.[178] The therapist can be viewed as a contemporary moralist who decrees what is good and bad in the name of science.[179] When the therapist values motherhood, male dominance, female passivity, heterosexuality, or frequent sexual contacts, it affects his patients directly. When the therapist expresses his values in writing, it affects public policy. Former American Psychological Association president George Albee says of the illness explanation of psychopathology

[It] . . . supports the cultural forces of reaction that delay [necessary] social changes. . . . If mentally disturbed persons suffer from unknown and undiscovered illness, then the strategy for action is to discover the cause of the disease. But if they have been damaged by hostile and evil social environments, then we must change the dehumanizing forces of society.[180]

The social control exerted by psychotherapy is primarily through its ideology and the way that ideology has penetrated social institutions and generally held values of the society. A person who has never and would never visit a therapist—and this is the vast majority of citizens—is still affected by psychodynamic principles when their child is assumed by school personnel to be suffering from a damaging home environment, when a prospective employer insists on a personality test, when a physician adopts an it's-all-in-your-head attitude toward a serious physical ailment, when friends apply labels like "neurotic," "disturbed," or "sick," and when safety valves in the form of clinics and counseling centers inhibit true social reform.

2

Psychotherapy and Scientific Research

THE NATURE OF SCIENTIFIC RESEARCH

Although current society is sometimes criticized for its worship of science, there is also a segment of the population that has expressed negative views about science and "all it stands for." A sociology student who had read a paper of mine said:

You say that psychotherapy is not scientific implying that if it were scientific it would be all right. Science is in fact dangerous. They present a lot of evidence which has damaging and inaccurate political implications. Social sciences support the oppression of women. I agree that psychotherapy can be oppressive, but I would not want to put my life in the hands of any "science."[1]

It is important not to confuse what is often called science—technology, scientists themselves, and the uses to which certain discoveries are put—with the use of scientific methods of inquiry. We need people who are not fooled by sleight-of-hand manipulation of statistical data, who understand that it is as inaccurate to draw a conclusion from one biased observation as from one thousand biased observations, and who know that it is not numbers in themselves but objective and public observation that is the basis of scientific methods.

According to *Webster's Seventh New Collegiate Dictionary*, scientific research refers to "investigation or experimentation aimed at the discovery and interpretation of facts, revision of accepted theories or laws in the light of new facts, or practical application of such new or revised theories or laws." This broad definition applies equally well to laboratory research and to "library" research.

EXPERIMENTATION

There may be some concepts that are inherently difficult for people to grasp—not that they are difficult to one who finally understands, but that the human brain is simply not geared to them. This may be why formalized concepts of experimentation came so late in human history. In medicine, they did not appear until Claude Bernard in the nineteenth century; in social psychology, they came only within the past thirty years; in psychotherapy, whether experimentation can validly be used is still being argued.

Scientific experimentation means more than mere observation; it requires that the investigator actively alter conditions to determine their effects. And it is the most effective way to determine causal relationships. Careful observation can tell us what happened; experimentation allows us to isolate necessary and sufficient conditions. Scientific methods are ways of finding things out with increased certainty. They may sometimes become complicated, but they are not basically mysterious. If science has mystique, it comes from its results, not its methods.

In certain situations, effects are so immediate and dramatic as to be undeniable. Mix chemical A with chemical B, and BOOM! It is fairly obvious that the explosion was caused in some way by the mixture of the chemicals. For the sake of the doubting Thomas who sits on the shoulder of the scientific researcher, *once* may not be quite enough. Maybe chemical A had a little of chemical C in it. Maybe the explosion was the accidental result of peculiar atmospheric conditions. Seems far-fetched, but, still, to be sure, we carefully check every step of the entire procedure and repeat it. BOOM! Maybe just once more, measuring quantities of both chemicals with great care? BOOM! We are now ready to say with as much certainty as scientists ever have that when chemical A is combined with chemical B the result is an explosive reaction.

The scientific work does not end there. Each answer gives rise to endless questions: What are the minimal quantities of A and B necessary to produce the reaction? Can the reaction be altered by changing the proportions of the two chemicals? After the explosion, what substances remain and in what form? Would a similar result be obtained if chemicals D and E were used? And so on, with each question representing an advance in scientific sophistication and each answer an advance in knowledge.

Now, suppose that BOOM! was only *pfft*, a sound easily muffled by a passing automobile or the investigator's assistant's footsteps. In this case, although the addition of A to B may produce a reliable effect, considerably more, and more careful, observations would be necessary before that fact could be clearly established.

Suppose further, that chemicals other than B produce a similar effect on A, and that most ordinary substances are mixtures containing A or B. Discovery of the A-B reaction would be far less likely. A clearly discernible reaction of pure A and pure B is important for clear identification of cause and effect.

If we imagine that A is the patient, B is the therapy, and BOOM! (or Pfft) improvement, we can begin to examine the notion of psychotherapy research. The question is: When B is added to (or "administered" to) A, does BOOM! occur?

The answer to the question, Does psychotherapy help? (i.e., does A plus B = BOOM! or pfft?), can be any of the following, depending on whom you ask.

There is no question about the effectiveness of psychotherapy. I see evidence in my practice daily. My patients tell me they are helped, I can see improvement myself, and they continue to come for treatment, often returning again and again over the years.

The truth is, the effectiveness of psychotherapy has never been demonstrated despite thousands of investigations. The ones that show favorable results are about equal in number to those that show unfavorable results, with the vast majority even of published studies finding essentially no differences.

Psychotherapy means so many different procedures depending on the patient, the therapist, and the circumstances, that any attempt at generalization would be foolhardy.

Whether or not therapy is effective is not the important issue. What *is* important is what happens during therapy; what is the exact nature of the therapeutic process.

The results show that psychotherapy makes some people worse and some people better. The research problem is to be able to identify which is which.

It depends on one's definition of improvement. Mere symptom-relief without any change in the personality constellation itself is of worse than no value. Conversely, important personality changes are often unaccompanied by any obvious signs of improvement. Often a patient feels *worse* just when the greatest progress is being made.

Almost all research studies are deficient in one way or another. For example, they usually employ inexperienced therapists and they do not take into account other sources of help obtained by the "nontherapy" subjects.

Since editors of scientific journals favor studies in which effects are found, studies in which A plus B equal no pffts or BOOMS! are likely to go unpublished, even unsubmitted. Authors have learned to be wary about sending articles to scientific journals reporting on experiments which did not "produce effects." In other words, if a researcher conducts an experiment to determine whether psychotherapy of the mother helps children work in school and finds no differences between groups with and without therapy, the report would be essentially unpublishable. Oddly enough, the editors are less concerned about BOOM! versus pfft differences than about "reliable" effects even when they are small.[2]

CONTROLLED RESEARCH

The notion of scientific control is simply that in order to conclude that X caused Y, other possible influences on Y must be ruled out somehow. If a patient feels better (Y) after psychotherapy (X), other explanations for the improvement must be untenable. In research, this often means using a control group. To illustrate with a more simple problem, let us consider how to find out whether a new drug, Epizone, relieves joint pain. If we give Epizone to many patients who have been in pain for a long time and if for all of them the pain ceases abruptly twenty minutes later, it would seem to be a pretty convincing case for Epizone's effectiveness. But things are seldom that clear-cut. Pains come and go mysteriously even without medication, and drugs have different effects depending on the condition of the patient. Or the improvement might be real, but so small that the other factors could obscure it. In sloppy situations like this, we use a control group for comparison. We administer Epizone to the experimental group only, and we observe both groups to determine whether, in general, the group with the drug shows more relief from pain than the control group. The investigators in a truly controlled study allow no differences between the groups except active ingredients of the drug.

Although individuals in the groups differ from one another, the requirement of a comparison (or control) group is that it not differ *on the average* from the experimental group with respect to such crucial matters as how sick the members of the group were to begin with, or to any other characteristic that affects response to Epizone. If enough people are tested, this is best accomplished by randomly assigning subjects to experimental conditions (i.e., Epizone versus no Epizone). Random, in the scientific sense of the term, means unbiased. The person making the selection does not favor blonds (or persons over thirty, or males, or schizophrenics) in assigning persons to the Epizone group. Because human beings seem unable to help making biased selections even when they very consciously and conscientiously try to avoid it, random decisions are made by scientists through the use of mechanical devices (a crude one is the toss of a coin) or of specially prepared tables of random numbers. (An excellent discussion of the importance of random assignment to experimental conditions and other issues in psychotherapy research methodology can be found in Robert R. Holt's monograph, *Methods of Research in Clinical Psychology*.)

All subjects are given a pill of some kind to rule out the psychological effect called "placebo," in which just the awareness that one is being treated may have an effect. The persons administering the medication are unaware of whether they are giving pills containing or not containing the ingredient in question, and the persons who are observing for effects are not aware which type of pill the patient had been given (a procedure called "double blind"). Such careful efforts to eliminate sources of contamination, or "confounding," were gradually developed, many of them very recently, as their need was discovered. In too many earlier cases it could not be determined whether experimental results were due to real effects or experimenter bias of some kind. The double-blind method has demonstrated that the effects of expectation, or placebo effects, can be powerful enough to be completely responsible for the fact that a drug or other treatment appears effective.[3]

Controlled research on psychotherapy is not nearly as simple as the situation described above. But controlled research is needed to determine whether the reports of good effects are due to high expectation and/or biased observation, or to specific, nonplacebo processes that occur in the course of treatment.

THE SCIENTIFIC STATUS OF
PSYCHOANALYTIC THEORY

The most general characterization of a scientific proposition or theory is that it is subject to test by observation. Is there a conceivable way, even complicated, expensive, and untried, of verifying the assertion, or, conversely, is the assertion stated in such a way that a test is inherently impossible? For the most part, psychodynamic theory is untestable. Although Freud postulated stages of normal psychosexual development as universal, failure to find evidence of them in a given individual is not taken as disproving the theory, or even as disproving that they occurred in that individual. As has been repeatedly observed, psychoanalytic theory is immune to falsification, and hence is not a scientific theory at all.

The "intrapsychic" mechanism, "reaction formation," in which thoughts or feelings that are intolerable are repressed while their converse are expressed,[4] allows any observable behavior to be compatible with the theory.* This problem plagues general analytic theory. It also characterizes difficulties in the consultation chamber. When a patient protests against an interpretation it can lead the therapist to believe in it more firmly.

Psychoanalysis is bad science because its techniques do not utilize repetition of observation. Those in the psychoanalytic tradition claim as validation for their theories insight and understanding. But, as Naomi Weisstein expressed it, "insight, sensitivity, and intuition . . . can confirm for all time the theories one started with. . . . Clinical experience is not the same thing as empirical evidence."[5]

Aside from the problem of subjective methodology and a theory which can incorporate virtually any experimental result, attempts to subject some of the most basic and widely accepted Freudian ideas to experimental test have tended to be unsuccessful. Psychologists at the University of Rochester found, for example, that dreams associated with greater

* As in formal logic, if a proposition and its converse are both asserted, anything can be "proven."

emotionality were recalled better than those which were more neutral. By most interpretations, Freud's concept of repression would lead one to expect the opposite.[6]

And, as Charles Sheridan says in his textbook *Fundamentals of Experimental Psychology,*

> If clinical intuition were enough without scientific controls, bloodletting would be a well-founded procedure, for centuries of clinical judgment support it. Many an astute fellow went through life convinced that his bloodletting was an effective means of treating various diseases (even though at the time of the bubonic plague estimates of the amount of blood in the human body were so far exaggerated that people were literally bled to death). Of course the patients sometimes died, but they sometimes got better. No treatment is foolproof, after all! The trouble with the method of the bloodletting of the physician was that he had no *objective criterion* of the effectiveness of his treatment—or at least he failed to put it to an objective test. . . . Eysenck has pointed out that the psychoanalysts are doing the same sort of thing today. They are convinced, on the basis of their clinical experience, that their therapy works, but they have not done the necessary experimental tests which would establish that they are correct. . . .[7]

Many therapists have recently claimed that psychoanalysis is not really a therapy, but a laboratory for research on the human psyche. As Weisstein even more succinctly expressed it, "Some laboratory."[8]

There is one testable deduction from psychodynamic theory: if a patient exhibits a symptom, removal of that symptom will not cure the underlying trouble. Therefore, a symptom-removal therapy is not only basically ineffective, but dangerous (as in the case of simply reducing the fever of an infected appendix with ice packs). Other symptoms will eventually emerge. But the evidence overwhelmingly fails to support this prediction of "symptom substitution." In fact, the opposite seems to be true. Removal of a symptom may initiate positive cycles of functioning and of social interaction.

Allen Bergin and others have repeatedly likened the current state of psychotherapy to that of medicine in the 1850s, saying that both therapy and therapy research are "primitive." But he implies we should "bear with it" and continue to study individual cases for the purpose of collecting "insights." What such an approach does, however, is fog the distinction between therapy and research about therapy. We are actually much more sophisticated than we were a century ago about our ability to make scientific tests. Therapy itself may be primitive, and, as medicine once was, equally likely to help or to harm, but the idea of rigorous tests and the procedure for making such tests are part of current scientific psychology. It is neither scientific naïveté nor procedural difficulties that for decades prevented psychotherapy research. In addition to endless equivocation about the results of studies, there was a strong disinclination by practitioners to conduct research or even to allow it to be conducted by others.

RESISTANCE TO RESEARCH BY PSYCHOTHERAPISTS

> There is increasing reason to believe that the attitude toward psychotherapy research held by the majority of practicing clinicians is not only indifferent as many have long feared, but uncooperative; and by inference, antagonistic.
>
> RICHARD L. BEDNAR AND JEFFREY G. SHAPIRO, "Professional Research-Commitment: A Symptom or a Syndrome"[9]

Refusal to conduct research studies, or to cooperate with the research efforts of others, has been so characteristic of psychoanalysts and of the psychodynamic therapists that it is fair to say that psychotherapists have had a tradition of resisting research. Freud himself relied solely on the revelation of clinical insight. For him, treatment *was* research, but only in the sense of subjective "discovery," not as experimental test.[10] Long before Freud's death in 1939, the descriptions of glowing success and phenomenal cure frequent in the early days had become rare, and the very goals of the procedure had begun to be expressed not as cure of specific disease but as personality reconstruction or redevelopment. The reaction of the psychoanalytic institutes to their lack of success was to cease any publication of treatment summaries, to become increasingly uncooperative with and even resistant to research designed to determine the effect of therapy, and to place the goals of therapy inside the patient where they were not subject to direct observation. As Schmideberg said, "Analysts . . . [accept] the tenets of analysis as 'truth' in a pseudo-religious way by trying to fit their patients to the preconceived theory and by taking for granted, without substantiating it, that this 'truth' is necessarily healing."[11]

Uncertainty among themselves about the value of insight therapy helps to explain some peculiar events. In the twenties and thirties, psychoanalytic institutes published summaries of treatment results, a practice that was subsequently discontinued.[12] The door of the consultation room was closed to the outside world and not even in the case of an analyst in training did anyone other than the participants themselves directly observe what went on. Analysts were particularly active in resisting the objective examination of treatment. In 1932, the New York Institute of Psychoanalysis would not allow one of its members to make sound recordings of the analytic hour.[13] When, in 1961, psychoanalyst William V. Snyder attempted to subject his own analytic work to critical analysis, his colleagues called the effort "heroic."[14] Case presentations were heavily weighted with interpretation and summary, with little direct quoting of the patient. Textbooks did not encourage the systematic recording of therapeutic events; some even discouraged note-taking.

Private practitioners have been the most resistant. A recent review of psychotherapy research revealed that in twenty-five years, only fifteen studies had employed a private practice setting. When 16,000 independent therapists were invited to participate in a large-scale investigation of psychotherapy, less than 1 percent of them agreed to assist.[15] As Stream and Blatt found:

> Proponents of both long and short term therapy are so dogmatic about their own orientation that research be-

comes limited because therapists feel it is unnecessary to explore an area about which they have so little doubt.[16]

The suggestion has been articulated that therapists' resistance may be based in their disinclination "to face the realities of the effects or noneffects of psychotherapy."[17]

One researcher who analyzed psychotherapists' attitudes toward research efforts found hostility that resulted from the new status hierarchy in which the researcher achieved ascendance over the therapist, and a "threatened loss of self-esteem following removal or lowering of accustomed defenses which operate when the therapist works in privacy."[18] Without research, of course, psychotherapy practice is based almost exclusively on the rather shaky foundation of clinical lore and intuition.

Resistance to research is accompanied by a parallel resistance to criticism. Melitta Schmideberg, among the most outspoken of the original insiders, recently provided a description of the interpretive atmosphere of professional psychoanalytic meetings. To speak disrespectfully of psychotherapy was prima facie evidence of one's own ill health. This attitude was partially overcome only in the sixties, but as late as the early seventies analysts in a face-to-face seminar claimed to have been personally attacked by polite, but penetrating questions. Millon notes that "despite questions concerning effectiveness, proponents of each technique were not only convinced of the utility of their cherished procedures, but prospered and confidently inculcated each new generation of fledgling clinicians. Disputes among 'schools' of therapy were evident, of course, but they were handled by verbal polemics rather than by empirical research."[19] Schmideberg said that in psychoanalytic meetings, phrases which allowed no argument or objection, such as "the analysis indicated" or "the material proved," were commonly used. Dissenters were "not really analytic," or the suggestion was made that the person had not "been analyzed deeply enough."[20]

George W. Albee, in his presidential address to the American Psychological Association in 1970, suggested a basis for the resistance of the professional to research. He pointed out that there are fundamental differences between the function of the practitioner and that of the scientist.

> A primary one involves self-criticism and mutual criticism. *Science* is open and its knowledge is public. Any discrepancies in knowledge are debated openly. One of the hallmarks of science is its insistence on public disclosure of findings. . . . In sharp contrast, a *profession* must jealously guard its secrets! . . . If the knowledge of the professional, his techniques and his skills were available to anyone . . . a profession would disintegrate.[21]

Albee suggests that psychotherapists today are not unlike professionals throughout the ages. He cites Veblen according to whom the first professionals were the Egyptian priests of the Nile, and he comments:

> [The priests] discovered that the flood of Nile coincided with the juxtaposition of certain stars. Immediately, they had powerful knowledge of great value to their society and, like professionals ever since, they kept their knowledge *secret*, thus preserving the prestige of their profession, their credibility, and their godlike qualities.[22]

Psychotherapists may act like the priests of the Nile, but the "secret" they protect is questionable.

DOES PSYCHOTHERAPY HELP?

> The American Psychoanalytic Association, who might be supposed to be prejudiced in favor of their own specialty, undertook a survey to test the efficacy of psychoanalysis. The results were so disappointing that they were withheld from publication.
>
> ANTHONY STORR, "The Concept of Cure"[23]

Psychodynamic psychotherapy has always had its critics. Their complaints were based on philosophical, religious, moral, theoretical, and plain common-sense grounds.[24] Although there were some reports of attempts to evaluate therapy scientifically as early as the 1930s, it was in 1952 that se-

rious scientific criticism really began. In that year the
influential British psychologist Hans J. Eysenck presented his
"challenge," an article in *The Journal of Consulting Psychology* called "The Effects of Psychotherapy: An Evaluation."
In it, Eysenck announced that the scientific literature contains no evidence whatsoever that psychotherapy is beneficial
to those who receive it.[25]

How did people respond to Eysenck's paper? In 1971,
Allen E. Bergin stated:

> It is slightly amazing to find that 18 years after his
> original critique of therapeutic effects, Professor Hans
> Eysenck is still agreed and disagreed with more than any
> single critic on the psychotherapy scene. . . . The out-
> pouring of praise and invective, and of claims and counter-
> claims, has been an extraordinary phenomenon. . . .[26]

Bergin continues:

> He has been a prime stimulant, if not irritant, pressing the
> field toward rigorous examination of its assumptions and
> procedures. For thus dramatically calling these issues to
> our attention, he is to be congratulated and not con-
> demned as so many have been inclined to do. It is time,
> after all, that this field provide publicly verifiable evidence
> that its costly treatments have effects.[27]

In 1961, Alexander Astin published "The Functional Autonomy of Psychotherapy." An educational and child psychologist himself, Astin stands somewhat removed from the politics and economics of psychotherapy. Its undeniable truth,
and Astin's wit and irony, have made this article very popular among psychologists. "Functional autonomy" was the
psychological term for a habit which continues after its initi-
ating circumstances are gone. The habit has become self-
propelling, or "functionally" autonomous. Astin observed
that although psychotherapy began as a "service for troubled
people who asked for help," it continues despite lack of evidence of efficacy. After the first surge of disappointing research results, research in psychotherapy itself took a turn
which may have seemed reasonable enough to psychotherapists, but which those who ultimately pay the bills

might not have agreed with had they known what was going on. With the efficacy of therapy undemonstrated, Astin said,

> psychotherapy should have died out. But it did not. It did not even waver. Psychotherapy had achieved *functional autonomy*.
> The development was of especially profound significance for practitioners who, at last freed from the petty demands of having to serve their clients, were now able to engage in hot squabbles about how psychotherapy should be done, and even hotter ones about who should do it. . . .[28] Now that everybody agreed that the evidence was no good, psychotherapy was vindicated.[29]

Astin reported that Rosenzweig, in 1954, replied to Eysenck in "a crushing attack," that "neither was there any good evidence that psychotherapy *hurt* anybody."

In recent years, criticism of psychodynamic psychotherapy as ineffective or worse has increased to such a degree that standard clinical psychology textbooks include statements that "those who rise to the defense if not to the support of analytic therapies . . . are unable to adduce empirical evidence favoring [their] efficacy"[30] and that "There is no demonstrated relationship between the acquisition of insight and clinical change"[31]; and even that "the idea of cure in psychoanalysis is analogous to the cure of physical disease ought to be finally discarded."[32]

In the field of child psychology, a similar disenchantment is occurring. According to Donofrio, "several studies conclude that child psychotherapy has not proven its effectiveness."[33] In 1966, Shepard and his associates at the University of London carefully selected fifty school children so that they matched the symptom picture of fifty children receiving clinic therapy. After two years, the percentage of improvement was almost exactly the same in the two groups. A summary of many studies of children who had been studied after they had received psychotherapy concludes that "the present evaluation of child psychotherapy, like its adult counterpart, fails to support the hypothesis that treatment is effective."[34]

From their study of patients at the General Infirmary at Leeds, England, British psychiatrist Harold E. R. Wallace and social worker Marion B. H. Whyte conclude that "psychotherapy has little effect on the outcome in psychoneuroses. . . ."[35] And even practicing analyst Anthony Storr admits that "the results of the psychoanalytic process are genuinely unpredictable."[36] Finally, California psychologist Nathan Hurvitz states:

> Since World War II there has been a growing concern about mental health and a greater acceptance of psychotherapy as a means of treating "mental illness." However, there are serious questions as to whether the many psychotherapists who practice in various settings according to psychoanalytic or psychodynamic theories and concepts play a significant part in alleviating the widespread mental health problem that exists. . . . There is no agreed-upon, objective evidence based on experimental studies that use appropriate measures and control groups which indicate that any school or method of psychotherapy based on psychodynamic principles, theories, or concepts helps people to overcome disordered, inappropriate, or deviant behavior that is presumed to have a psychological basis any better than any other school or method or any more than their own life experiences. . . . Testimonials are not evidence— whether they are offered on behalf of psychotherapy, prayer, or voodoo.[37]

Hurvitz, like Astin, questions the persistence of psychotherapy in the absence of evidence. He concludes that there is a "latent" purpose of social control, which is served by psychotherapy. This viewpoint has also been suggested by Kate Millett, Seymour Halleck, and a number of other writers. The effectiveness of psychotherapy as social control is not solely dependent on its working as a therapy. It can control by discouraging people from seeking solutions that do work, solutions that might be disturbing of the social, economic, or political status quo.

RECOVERY WITHOUT TREATMENT

The main argument of the Eysenck challenge was that people in control groups improve spontaneously without treatment, given enough time, and the amount of time required is approximately the same as the time required for therapy. Eysenck presented the results of a study in which severe neurotics were given sedatives, tonics, suggestion, and reassurance, but not psychotherapy. Recovery, in this case, was defined as (1) a return to work for at least five years, (2) no further complaint or only "slight difficulty," and (3) successful social adjustment.[38]

Of the 500 subjects:
45% were recovered after one year
72% were recovered two years later
82% were recovered three years later
87% were recovered four years later
89% were recovered five years later

In other words, almost 90 percent of these persons who had been totally disabled for at least three months were cured without treatment five years later.

From this study, and from one conducted by Landis in 1937, Eysenck arrived at a figure of 66 percent "spontaneous recovery" within two years. He then examined the results of nineteen other studies concerning the effects of psychotherapy and reported as follows:

	Percentage improved
Patients who received psychoanalysis	44
Patients who received eclectic psychotherapy	64
Patients who received custodial care, or treatment by a general practitioner	72

These figures include psychoanalytic patients who broke off treatment, about one-third of those who began. When those patients are discounted, both psychoanalytic and eclectic treatment rises to approximately the same level. A number of other studies obtained similar rates of recovery without treatment.

Not surprisingly, the issue of recovery without treatment became a controversial one within the profession. If two-thirds of all patients recover spontaneously, the proportion of patients who recover after receiving treatment should be higher than that for psychotherapy to be judged helpful. In some clinics, improvement rates were much lower, as low as 30 percent or even 20 percent. Does this mean that therapy has somehow obstructed a natural healing process? If 66 percent improve without treatment, and a given therapist or clinic shows a 20 percent rate, it can be concluded that the treatment is actually harmful!

Psychotherapists have attacked the issue of recovery without treatment in several ways. First, they have appealed to additional studies and reanalysis of earlier studies. It has been demonstrated, for example, that there were errors and arbitrariness in Eysenck's procedures which affected his overall conclusions. Psychologist Allen E. Bergin's 1971 analysis of "new" evidence from fourteen studies yields a median rate of improvement without treatment of about 30 percent, although he admits that those studies, too, "have weaknesses."[39] Bergin would not like to see the 30 percent figure used as a baseline. A higher figure would be needed for persons who enter therapy with anxiety and depression; a lower one for "obsessives," and persons with psychosomatic ailments. Anxiety and depressions, the reasons most often given for entering psychotherapy by the persons this book is mainly about, have a well-established tendency to go away by themselves in time.

But maybe not quite by themselves. The second major reaction of psychotherapists to the spontaneous recovery issue is to assert that the patients who improved without treatment really did receive treatment. Spokespersons among psychotherapists have claimed that those who do not receive treatment from professional psychotherapists improve because they have received psychotherapy from a non-mental health source! Psychologists and psychiatrists have undergone years of rigorous training in the use of standard and accepted techniques, and their procedures are both expensive and time-consuming, but when patients for whom they and their treatments are unavailable get better at a rate equal to those who receive their services, it is because those persons were actually "treated" by nonprofessionals—clergymen, physicians, friends, beauticians, and bartenders. Or, they may have been helped by association with self-help groups such as Alcoholics Anonymous. There is no reason to assume that people are not helped by nonprofessionals, but it is untenable to then go back and argue that therefore psychotherapy has some special curative efficacy above and beyond that provided by such contacts.

Faced with clear evidence of improvement without "treatment," psychotherapists have found treatment under every rock. The "control" subjects were helped by "untrained therapists." For example, a popular and successful male college student came from an extremely "disturbed" home in which every member of the family besides himself had been hospitalized for severe mental illness. His history was "carefully scrutinized." It was found that he had spent much of his time as a grade school child with another, "nonpathenogenic," family and it turned out that the mother in that family had actually been "prototypic":

> [She] influenced more than one stray lad toward security, resilience, and accomplishment. It is difficult to deny the potent therapeutic impact of this woman. . . . While there are probably few like her, she represents a dimension of socially indigenous therapy that may be more significant than is usually recognized.[40]

It has even been suggested that these persons may actually be more effective as a group than professionals,[41] since lay therapists are selected for effectiveness while professionals are selected on the basis of academic credentials or professional political standing. This conclusion suggests new avenues of research and new possibilities for training: study how the nonprofessionals do it, and select candidates on the basis of their personality rather than grades in school. To the troubled person seeking help, there are clearly practical considerations. Why pay $50 an hour to a psychiatrist when one can get a whole evening with a bartender for less than $20? Or see a physician for $25? Or go to a beauty parlor or barber shop and come out with a haircut as a bonus?

Of course, if patients in a control group differ significantly from treated subjects then they are inadequate for comparison and the research is faulty. If, for example, those who are more seriously "disturbed" are selected for treatment in a clinic, and their rate of improvement is compared with persons not as ill to begin with, it is not valid to conclude that therapy was ineffective. Incomparability of the control group vitiates the case for spontaneous remission. It is essential that the two groups be selected either through random assignment or careful matching, and some of the reported studies did not use these methods. They are therefore rightly open to question. Some of the criticism of Eysenck's article runs along these lines.[42]

If an investigation is conducted in a clinic which has a waiting list, it is possible to compare patients in treatment with those who wanted treatment but could not obtain it, a technique used by psychologists Barron and Leary in 1955. Although they did not use random assignment, they measured the two groups and found them generally comparable in age, sex, education, and diagnosis. The therapy patients did not improve more than the waiting list controls. But the authors concluded, not that therapy was ineffective, but that "the use of waiting-list controls in investigation of changes in therapy may be complicated by therapeutic factors involved in the initial intake evaluations and decisions. . . . The use of additional 'nonwaiting-list controls' is suggested for future investigations on the effect of psychotherapy."[43] Astounding as it may appear, this conclusion attributes therapeutic effects to being placed on a waiting list!

In a similar vein is a passage by Jerome D. Frank in which he discusses the rapid improvement often exhibited by patients in therapy for less than ten sessions:

> If the psychotherapist lifts his gaze from the subtleties of the therapeutic interaction to encompass the patient's life situation, he will find that the improvement he attributes to his maneuvers often coincides with major changes in the patient's pattern of life—divorce, reconciliation, changing homes or jobs, departure from the home of a burdensome relative and the like. These changes coincide too often with psychotherapy for the relationship to be fortuitous.[44]

The situation may have been ripe for change at the time the person entered psychotherapy. This might even have been a part of the reason for seeking help. Although Frank admits that the mechanism is probably the "morale-boosting" that results from any "supportive personal contact," the real life changes which produced the improvement are indirectly attributed to psychotherapy itself, supposedly making therapy worthwhile.

The final, and, in many ways, the major attack by psychodynamic psychotherapists who say that "spontaneous remission" statistics are not sufficient evidence for concluding that psychotherapy is ineffective, has to do with symptoms. In essence, the argument runs as follows: The loss of symptoms is not a cure. In fact, it can mask underlying worsening of the disease. To measure improvement in symptoms is therefore fallacious to begin with.

CRITERIA FOR IMPROVEMENT

When it comes to evaluating research on the outcome of psychotherapy, decisions must be made concerning the criteria by which improvement is said to be detected. Not surprisingly, this can be a very ticklish matter. Psychodynamicists are unlikely to regard mere symptom removal as evidence of improvement, or lack of symptom removal as evidence of failure. And since the aims of psychotherapy tend to be vague or expressed in subjective terms, whether the aim has been attained is difficult to assess. It is not surprising, therefore, that much of the reaction and criticism of outcome research is expressed in terms of failure to utilize appropriate criteria.

Some of the measures commonly used are

Therapist ratings
Test scores
Patient questionnaires
Judge's ratings of clinical records
Self-rating by patients

Interviewer and observer ratings
School discipline records
Objective symptom change
Changes in income[45]

But therapists' ratings are by far the most prevalent. Not only is the therapist as a "committed participant"[46] likely to be biased in favor of seeing improvement in his patients, but it has been shown that therapists are likely to see more improvement in patients who functioned at a high level anyway at the beginning of treatment.[47] In view of these biases it is doubly remarkable that few studies have found unequivocally positive results.[48]

Some psychotherapy researchers have taken the position that it is really not necessary to study psychotherapy effectiveness:

> The question of cure is ultimately a philosophical one, since we know too little of the nature of man [sic] to be dogmatic about what constitutes the minimum requirements for psychological health; and the term "cure" is in any case meaningless when we come to consider the manifold problems of the human condition, and the difficulties we all have in living.[49]

> In analysts' offices all over the country thousands of patients every day see and feel the cause-and-effect of psychoanalysis. . . .[50]

> In raising the question of the validity of therapy, we might just as well question the justification for living or inquire whether man [sic] would be better off without a nose. . . . The task of the psychotherapist is not to achieve "objective improvement." . . .[51]

To the believer, no criterion of success is needed; whatever sign of failure is presented remains unconvincing. Freud himself set the pace when he stated that psychoanalysis can only be criticized by psychoanalysts since critics who had not submitted themselves to years of clinical evidence were incapable of making a judgment. The trouble is that in the course of collecting those clinical data, objectivity is likely to be lost along the way.

Perhaps it is not surprising therefore to find a recurrent emphasis on not doing studies that attempt to test the overall efficacy of psychotherapy. Bergin actually recommended a "moratorium" on "gross" studies of the general effects of treatment. Kenneth Mark Colby agrees with Strupp and Bergin that it is meaningless to study vague questions such as "the effectiveness of psychotherapy."[52] Steven Lee Weiss, writing in the *Journal of Consulting and Clinical Psychology,* notes that critics of research have maintained that adequate evaluations of psychotherapy have not been made. They say that the question Does psychotherapy have positive effects? is "too simple to answer meaningfully."[53] Strupp, Bergin, and others feel that for the global question of whether psychotherapy "works" should be substituted questions such as what specific kinds of therapy have what specific effects with what specific patients under what specific circumstances.[54] Answers to such complex questions are not available at present.

Most studies which have yielded "evidence of effectiveness" have done so only at a "pfft" level of magnitude. Such results may be interpreted as encouraging to psychotherapists but it is doubtful whether patients and clients[55] of psychotherapy would be willing to make the emotional and financial investments it entails if they were fully aware of the findings that have come from these attempts at scientific validation.

Would the average patient be content to wait for the answers? Would she be likely to agree with Hunt? He says that until such research is conducted "we're justified in continuing to use what techniques are available to us. After all, the cure rate for lung and stomach cancers by surgery is estimated at only 5 to 15 percent, but no one suggests that such operations be dropped."[56]

In their attempt to refute research-based criticism of psychotherapy, psychotherapy advocates have even gone so far as to virtually denounce experimental research. A number of writers have advised that attempts to evaluate psychotherapy be abandoned in favor of "naturalistic methods" in which changes that take place outside of therapy are studied. Such observations may be helpful in suggesting areas for study, but they are usually far too subjective and uncontrolled to answer specific questions, even questions of overall effectiveness. What we really have here is an attempt to escape from scientific research and its findings.

Another tactic is an escape to research that avoids the main issues. In 1960, Julian Rotter, in his *Annual Review of Psychology,* stated: "Research studies in psychotherapy tends to be concerned more with some aspects of the psychotherapeutic procedures and less with outcome . . . to some extent, it reflects an interest in the psychotherapy situation as a kind of personality laboratory."[57] The studies referred to are the so-called process investigations. Examples of the procedures that such studies might use are:

Give a questionnaire to patients coming to a clinic for psychotherapy asking what they expect to get out of treatment and relate that to diagnosis, socioeconomic level, age, education, or any other variable.

Using tape recordings, compare the number of comments made by the therapist at the beginning, in the middle, and toward the end of therapy.

Compare the language patterns of psychotic and neurotic patients.

Determine the socioeconomic and ethnic backgrounds of psychotherapists and the kind of training they receive.

Compare the techniques actually used by psychotherapists of various "schools" by viewing videotapes of actual therapy sessions.

The results of such investigations are of limited value.

Because research is inherently difficult, it is also expensive. A "little" study easily runs into tens or hundreds of thousands of dollars by the time such costly items as professional consultants and computer time are included. Most of the cost is borne not only by psychotherapy's Friends in the "mental health" movement but also by the general public through

universities and government agencies. The profits to therapists are rarely redeployed to research on effectiveness.

As far as the psychotherapy researcher's cry for more
specific research is concerned, those decisions are better
made by funding agencies, and by the researchers themselves, in the context of the failure to find overall positive
effects. Maybe some forms of psychotherapy are helpful to
some types of persons under certain conditions. Who can say
it would not be useful to know what kinds, what types of
persons, and what conditions? To say one did not want to
know is like denouncing motherhood and apple pie. But if
the purpose of the research is to prop up a profession sag-
ging under the weight of its own ineffectiveness in a desper-
ate last-ditch effort to find a rationale for its survival, we
might prefer to put our research dollars elsewhere.

Joseph Wolpe, originator of one of the behavior therapies,
took Strupp and Bergin to task for their essentially anti-out-
come-research position:

> The burden of [their] statements is that psychotherapy is
> too complex for questions about its efficacy to be simply
> put and simply answered. This has long been the main
> premise of those who have argued against the feasibility of
> rigorous research and who have looked for pretexts for ig-
> noring unwelcome data. Bergin and Strupp are, of course,
> in favor of research and cannot be accused of ignoring
> data, but their attitude to some of it is very much
> influenced by this "complexity" bugbear.[58]

All too many psychotherapists seem to agree with Hussain
Tuma, one of Bergin and Strupp's consultants, who said:
"Answering Eysenck's challenge should remain if at all only a
possible side issue, not an important goal."[59]

DETERIORATION IN
PSYCHOTHERAPY

In 1966, Allen Bergin suggested a possible explanation for
the results of the many studies which found overall ineffectiveness. Bergin's idea was that psychotherapy was not really
ineffective; average results that looked like ineffectiveness

were produced by combining data on subjects whom therapy had helped with data on those whom it had harmed.

Bergin's paper did not introduce a new term or a new concept. Freud said that psychoanalysis can be harmful under several specific conditions, e.g., with schizophrenics, or if incomplete. The idea had grown, too, that certain therapists had harmful effects on many patients.[60] But there was little in print on the subject. Most studies of effectiveness used no category below "ineffective." Bergin's paper brought the term "deterioration effect" into more general use; the idea that therapy harms began to be talked about more widely and openly among professionals and researchers.

In Bergin's own view, he had "solved a controversy." He examined the data from some previously published studies and found that the variability in the treated groups was greater than in the control groups: as the result of psychotherapy some patients got better, and some got worse. This was, in his words, "a direct and unambiguous refutation" of the oft-cited Eysenckian position of therapy ineffectiveness. Psychotherapy was not weak; it was powerful; it had power to heal and power to harm. The problem now simply lay in finding out how to tell which result would occur with a particular patient.

In 1971, Bergin cited evidence that deterioration exists among patient populations,[61] and is more frequently found in treated than untreated groups. He said that some patients would deteriorate anyway, the therapist being unable to arrest or reverse the process, but that there are also cases in which patients "have already attained a neurotic equilibrium that is upset by the therapist, resulting in the initiation of a new cycle of deeper deterioration."[62] Because several years had passed since he had first brought up the topic of deterioration in therapy, Bergin had had time to receive correspondence from therapists and from patients who told of their personal experiences. They provided him with "rich detail" regarding the process of therapist-caused deterioration.

I have found some of these examples most disturbing, perhaps because I have been too naive regarding the way life is. Apparently there are many areas of error and malpractice that are regularly covered up by practitioners in every field. It seems to be an all too common procedure to ignore these incidents, no matter how serious the consequences may be for the patients involved. Indeed, I hope that one of our suicide centers might do a careful study of the possibility of therapist-precipitated suicides. In general, deterioration of various kinds is much too common to be ignored.[63]

The physician's first duty is not to harm. Patients helped and patients hurt by psychotherapy may balance out statistically, but the moral issue cannot be so easily disposed of.

By 1967 the following statement was typical: "Psychotherapy may be harmful as often as helpful, with an average effect comparable to receiving no help."[64] And, in 1970, behavior therapist Richard B. Stuart reviewed research literature and stated:

> In summary, it can be said that the patient who enters psychotherapy does so not without a distinct risk of deterioration or of simply wasting [her] time and money. . . . the weakness in the psychoanalytic approach . . . has spawned most of the current psychotherapeutic approaches. . . . The adverse evidence is particularly compelling because the treatments have been carried out with patients drawn from the "more favored" groups of the society, who are presumably most free of situational stress. . . .[65]

In 1973, psychologist Herbert Goldenberg, in his textbook *Contemporary Clinical Psychology,* made the following comment in a footnote:

> The so-called *deterioration effect* (Bergin 1970) is beginning to be considered with increasing seriousness as therapists face up to the fact that psychotherapy can do harm as well as good. While most studies follow the custom of reporting their results as percentages improved or unimproved, it would be helpful, although understandably personally difficult, if the proportion harmed by psychotherapy were included.[66]

During the years in which I was collecting material for the possible writing of this book, I gave talks on the subject of psychotherapy to a number of meetings of various feminist organizations. I discovered that my audiences contained many Friends and Supporters of Psychotherapy. Although a substantial minority were still in therapy, and some of them were angry at me for my critical approach to the subject, many others were women who looked back on their therapy with regret and were gratified to hear me criticize what they themselves had found an odious influence in their lives. I obtained lengthy tape-recorded interviews with twenty-one women who volunteered to talk about their therapy. Most of the women in the sample were to some degree identified with the women's movement, and no claim is made for representativeness of this sample to the population of all women in private treatment. On the other hand, the therapist behaviors they describe and, in some cases, the iatrogenic deterioration which occurred during their therapies, are similar to those described in the professional literature itself. Furthermore, in only three cases did the therapist's behavior deviate from that which would generally be considered professional, or from relatively standard, traditional, psychodynamically oriented practices.

The women were white and middle class. They lived either in the city or the suburbs. Twelve were from the New York City area, two from London, and one from the suburbs of Oslo, Norway. All but two had completed college, one was an M.S.W., one an M.D., and three were working on other graduate degrees. Eight were married, eight divorced (or about to be divorced), and five had never been married. Ages ranged from 21 to 52 years; median age was 38. Number of therapists seen by the subject and members of her family ranged from one to 15; average number of therapists was five; only two of the women had been treated by just one therapist. Total years in treatment ranged from less than one to seventeen; average number of years in therapy was eight.

Although the focus was entirely on private treatment, four of the women had been hospitalized one or more times. For these women, therapy began in the hospital and later continued privately. The remaining seventeen women entered therapy for one or more of the following reasons:

Reason for Entering Therapy	*Sample Response*
Depression and general unhappiness No. of subjects-10	"I was in my early twenties and very depressed. Nothing was working out. I was overweight and unattractive." "I was disgusted with myself and my life. Nothing was happening and I was very lonely."
Family and/or marital problems No. of subjects-11	"My husband and I were not getting along at all and something had to be done about it." "My son had become involved in serious thefts." "I did not enjoy sex with my husband and it made him very angry if refused."
Strong encouragement from others (e.g., friends, newspapers, physicians, school personnel, etc.) No. of subjects-20	"My guidance counselor was the first to suggest it." "All my friends were in therapy it seemed, and whenever I talked about the trouble I was having with Karl, they always recommended therapy." "The way people talked, anyone not in therapy was simply out of it." "I read in the newspaper where the columnist recommended therapy for someone who sounded like she had the exact problems I had."

Reason for Entering Therapy	Sample Response
Self-improvement No. of subjects-13	"It wasn't that I really had problems—I was too shy and still am—but I went into therapy more to find myself than to be cured." "I wanted to maximize my potential—I saw therapy as a way of helping me develop my personality so that I would be stronger."
Specific symptoms No. of subjects-4	"I was afraid to go anywhere alone" (also alcoholism, drug dependency)

Most of the women gave at least two reasons for entering therapy. In four cases, it was the troublesome behavior of another member of the family as well as social pressures that led the woman *herself* to enter therapy. In twelve of the sixteen married and divorced women, their husbands also saw therapists, but in only two cases was the husband the primary or initial patient. In most cases, the husband visited a therapist only in conjunction with his wife's or child's therapy or, when he received treatment for "his own problems," it was for a shorter period of time (an average of one and a half years). This finding is consistent with the assertion that women constitute the bulk of private psychotherapy patients.

For nine of the women in this sample, the women's liberation movement seems responsible or partly responsible for a change in their attitude toward psychotherapy. Four of the women attributed their leaving psychotherapy directly to the women's movement. Others who had already left therapy before becoming involved in the women's movement said that the movement had changed them so that they would never go back into therapy.

Of the nineteen women who expressed wholly or partially negative reactions to their psychotherapy, the following therapist attitudes and behaviors were held responsible:

1. Encouraging guilt feelings. Eight patients were told that their guilt feelings were beneficial because they provided the motive force for staying in therapy and working to overcome their illnesses.

2. Use of the medical model. Twelve women who in retrospect saw themselves as confronted with environmental pressures and realistic problems were labeled and treated as "neurotic," "incompetent," and mysteriously "ill." Her problems were "symptoms" whose causes resided in her own inner pathology.

3. Blaming the patient for failing to improve. Therapists were reported to say such things to patients as "You don't want to get well," "You like to be unhappy," or "You are unconsciously encouraging your child's (or husband's) negative reactions." Such statements led the women to a further state of dependency and despair since they were, in fact, trying their best to cope. Nine of the women reported that their therapists had made such statements.

4. Keeping the woman in therapy through the use of threats. Psychotherapists were frequently (eight out of twenty-one cases) reported to have said, "You are too sick to quit treatment," or "Without therapy, you would be unable to function," or "You would be a wreck in two months if you broke off now."

5. Allowing the woman to continue in therapy for many years without improvement. This was true for at least fourteen of the twenty-one women studied. Even one of those who felt her therapy had been helpful viewed the last three to five years (out of eight) as of decreasing benefit, and wished that she had terminated treatment at least two years earlier than she did.

6. Failure to refer the woman elsewhere, to end treatment, or to change methods despite lack of improvement and even deterioration on the patient's part.

7. Allowing or encouraging emotional dependency. Six of the women indicated their dependency through such statements as, "My life depended on what Dr. X thought of me."

8. Holding biases with respect to material presented by the woman. Accusing her of inventing, imagining, fantasiz-

ing, or lying about things that ran counter to the therapists' theories and values was described by five of the women.

9. Sexual seduction, attempted seduction, or accusing the woman of trying to seduce the therapist. Actual intercourse was reported by two of the women. Attempted seduction is more difficult to determine since it can be relatively subtle and fused with the very frequent suggestion by the male therapist that the female patient is consciously or unconsciously sexually attracted to him. Fourteen of the women in the sample reported discussions concerning the possibility of sexual attraction between patient and therapist.

10. Failing to help with real problems. Ten of the women complained about their therapist's failure to assist with their daily problems. The therapists were described as unresponsive to such problems as heavy household responsibilities, ill-treatment by the husband, or sex discrimination on the job. Five of the women felt that the therapists' viewing such problems as resulting from the woman's neurosis had only increased the difficulties they had in dealing with them.

11. Failing to give status to societal and environmental pressures as sources of difficulty. With only two exceptions, the therapists focused almost entirely on the woman herself, rather than on the situation in which she found herself.

12. Directing or interfering with her major life decisions. Although the traditional psychoanalytic techniques used by most of the therapists call for relative lack of direction, seven of the patients felt that they were given explicit or implied advice about life decisions. The women were very sensitive to subtle and perhaps unintended value judgments held by the therapists.

13. Showing more interest in sexual fantasies, dreams, and childhood events, than in current problems. This is not unexpected according to psychoanalytic theories and principles, and it was complained of by ten of the women.

14. Holding and expressing patriarchal values. Since most of the women in the present sample held feminist

views at the time of reporting, they were especially sensitive to such expressed views as, "Woman's place is really in the home, you know," and, "The value of a college education is to be able to talk to her husband's friends." Fifteen of the women felt that their therapists held patriachal viewpoints.

15. Tending to see more pathology in women than in men. Therapists often blamed the woman herself and other females, especially the patient's mother, for her "sickness" and those of other family members and overlooked or excused even very deviant behavior on the part of males.

16. Failing to respect confidences. Four of the women in the sample complained that what was told to one therapist came back to them through another even though permission to exchange information had not been requested of the patient. The women felt that their relationship with the therapist was biased because of this.

17. Being cold, impersonal, and nonsupportive. Seven of the women made such statements as: "No matter what I said, it wasn't enough, or it wasn't right," "I waited for some positive sign from him that something I did was good, but he only reacted to the negative, and I became more and more depressed," "I left every session in tears."

The women described several negative patterns of behavior on their parts induced by psychotherapy:

1. Overdependency on the therapist was described by twelve women.

2. Having life decisions later perceived as wrong ones greatly influenced by the therapist at the time. These were particularly likely to involve school, marriage, and career in such a way that traditional women's roles were supported. This was complained of by seven of the women.

3. Ten women described a therapy-induced egocentric passivity in which daily events were experienced as unimportant. As one woman said, "I went through the motions of caring for my baby, but my mind was preparing for the next session—analyzing my dream of the night before and wondering how the therapist would react to it."

4. Therapy often interfered with relationships between friends and family members. Nine women made explicit reference to this phenomenon.

5. The financial burden of psychotherapy led to years of social and material deprivations to some degree for all of the women; to a serious degree for nine of them. One woman, for example, paid $15 each week out of a $50 paycheck, which left no money for social activities, new clothes, or even an adequate diet.

6. Ten of the women felt that their continued expectation of help from psychotherapy led them not to try solutions on their own. In some cases, they were specifically requested by the therapist to not attempt to deal with their problems through any major change such as divorce, marriage, or a change of job. Looking back on it, the women felt that their lives might have been more satisfactory if they had more actively sought solutions to some of their problems on their own.

7. Fifteen of the women regarded their psychotherapy as one of the many cultural forces that isolated them psychologically from other women. All but three of the women viewed the women's movement as, among other things, a change in female society from one of mutual distrust to one of open acceptance of one another. For these women, psychotherapy was at least partly a matter of paying someone to listen to them, a need that largely or completely dissipated when they began to be able to speak openly to other women in consciousness-raising groups and, especially, to discover that other women experienced similar frustrations, doubts, conflicts, and guilt of their own. Thus, they no longer perceived themselves as uniquely "neurotic," the only one on the block accused of frigidity, penis envy, or unwomanliness.

Schmideberg notes that psychoanalysis often encourages a "flight from life" by concentrating on motives rather than consequences, and by showing more interest in irrational fantasies than "developing better judgment," or being able to react to important matters in a normal and human manner. A patient is induced to "regression, self-centeredness and concentration on grievances," and sidetracked from action. Interpretations, "dwelling unduly on the past or on unreal fantasies," and failing to remove symptoms are some of the ways in which therapy produces ill-effects.[67] Furthermore, deterioration continues and may increase in a self-perpetuating manner when its occurrence undermines the patient's confidence and self-esteem.[68] Analysts often do not recognize deterioration, or may even interpret it as a sign of progress (development of the "transference neurosis"). They tend to handle its manifestations through interpretation, and, according to Schmideberg,

> when the situation gets out of hand they often resort to panic measures, get rid of the patient—sometimes in a very brutal manner—without consideration for what is to happen to [her]. I know of two patients treated by leading analysts for twelve and twenty years respectively, who eventually were sent by their analyst for lobotomy.[69]

Schmideberg cites several cases of persons who came to her for treatment after years of unsuccessful therapy with psychoanalysts. She usually found such patients difficult to help because "their realistic situation" may have "deteriorated, sometimes beyond repair," and because "they have been made to feel that analysis is the only worthwhile therapy, and that there must be something quite specially wrong with them if it cannot help them as it has helped others."[70] She describes some of the difficulties faced by analytic patients in a passage in which being in therapy is compared to being imprisoned:

> Every type of therapy that isolates the patient from and overprotects [her] against ordinary life has effects almost like those of having been "institutionalized." Normally we make hundreds of small decisions daily, and occasionally important ones, as a matter of course, and we cope with innumerable anxiety-provoking situations. We take the dangers of the traffic or the rudeness of shop assistants for granted; expose ourselves to anxiety when applying for a job or taking an examination. It is well known that a [person] who has spent years in prison or some other institution often becomes terrified of traffic or is unable to make the simplest decision. Years of analysis may produce similar

effects, interfering with normal decision-making, and the
readiness to expose oneself to displeasure or anxiety. The
patient develops a sort of "mental hypochondria." Having
been isolated from life for years and unused to handling
situations, [she] suffers from anxiety, and tends to attribute this largely realistic anxiety to irrational factors, and to
believe that it indicates a deep-seated abnormality which
can be cured only by further analysis. Thus the situation is
a self-perpetuating one. Patients must learn gradually to
stand on their own feet, yet many analysts do not encourage such step-by-step efforts sufficiently, sometimes because they themselves are not realistic enough. Occasionally
an analyst even warns a patient against stopping "prematurely" adding that if he fills the patient's vacancy, he may
not be able to take [her] back.[71]

It is also "extremely hurtful," according to Schmideberg,
when psychotherapists do not react in a normal and human
manner to matters of deep importance to the patients.[72] The
fear that their actions may be the result of countertransference or that they will lose "objectivity" with some of their
patients has led to such extremes as failure to express any
sign of commendation for a patient who finally achieves a
difficult real goal, or failure to express sympathy or condo-
lence to a patient who has lost a close relative. Since this aloof
behavior occurs in a person the patient feels dependent on, it
can have disastrous results. Although therapists may claim
that the patient is not reacting to them, but merely "bringing
material into" the therapy session, many patients have told of
the importance of the therapist's behavior in determining
their feelings about themselves and their real life decisions.
When the therapist does not react to what the patient tells
him, the message conveyed to the patient is that what seems
important to her really doesn't matter.

SUICIDE

To most people's minds, the inadequacy of the treatment
procedure is never more apparent than when a patient com-
mits suicide. The therapist was unable to prevent the ex-

treme act from occurring. Often he was unable even to predict it. Suicide rates for patients in private therapy are not
available, but there is reason to believe that it is not a rare
event. Rogow, in *The Psychiatrists*, says:

> Of course, all analysts and psychiatrists have had patients
> who committed suicide or who became psychotic because
> an underlying psychosis was exposed by the analysis or
> therapist, but it is probable that these unfortunate results
> would have obtained had these patients not sought help.[73]

But a patient goes to a doctor for safety, not for increased
threat. The "calculated risk" involved in psychodynamic psychotherapy is not usually explained to the patient.

There is evidence that certain psychotherapists may contribute to the likelihood that their patients will commit suicide. In *The Lay Analyst*, a novel supposedly based on fact,
which describes psychotherapy from the viewpoint of a
friend of many Friends and Supporters of Psychiatry, Anne
Richter tells of two women whose suicides were attributed
by their acquaintances to specific behaviors of the psychotherapist they shared. Otto Kernberg, then medical director
of the famous Menninger Clinic in Topeka, Kansas, one of
the most respected treatment centers in the world, announced at a meeting of the Society for Psychotherapy Research that some therapists' patient suicide rates were consistently higher than those of others, and suggested that
therapist behavior was at least partially responsible for the
differences. Michael Rotov, Deputy Medical Director of the
Trenton State Hospital, has written of twenty cases from two
psychiatric hospitals over a ten-year period in which a particular section of one of the hospitals was found to account for
a disproportionate number of suicides, again giving the implication that staff behavior was a causative factor.[74]

Merton J. Kahne, Research Psychiatrist at M.I.T. and clinical associate at Harvard Medical School, published an article
on suicide among patients in mental hospitals. He described
the reactions of the psychiatrists when a patient kills herself.

> Their repetitious expressions of guilt and self-recrimination
> are accompanied by acute dread and awareness of the si
> lent accusation of colleagues. These alternate with unsub-

tle suggestions that other persons bear equal or greater responsibility for what happened. Such behavior, occurring against a background of frenetic staff conferences, reports, investigations, and hospital policy revisions, provides disagreeable reminders of the thinness of the social veneer which supports one's professional activities. . . .[75]

The patient's suicide was taken personally: "The suicide is almost always taken by the therapist as a direct act of spite against him. . . . Many therapists refer to the event as being 'fired.' "[76]

The psychotherapists studied by Kahne, members of a hospital staff, were in a very public situation:

The sudden necessity to prepare a rational statement, for evaluation by his colleagues, of the complex social and psychological events in which he and his patients were involved is commonly experienced as intensely traumatic and characteristically results in patently superficial formulations, often couched in complicated psychological jargon which strains the listener's credulity.[77]

One of the factors that Kahne found to be associated with suicide by patients was the therapist's "capacity to relate to them as reflected in measures of social distance and the attention he pays to his patients' social milieu."[78]

Psychiatrist Erwin Stengel has little hope for suicide prevention through individual psychotherapy and sees it as a public health problem. Prevention should be aimed not at individuals, but at the "suicideogenic" processes in the social environment.[79]

In "Suicide Precipitated by Psychotherapy: A Clinical Contribution," Dr. Allan A. Stone, also of Harvard Medical School, indicates that the issue of whether psychotherapy can precipitate or contribute to a suicide was not dealt with in hundreds of articles on suicide published in the psychological journals during the preceding ten years. As possible explanation for the omission, he lists "anxiety over malpractice suits, reluctance to wash professional linen in public, and finally, the difficulty of attributing any result to psychotherapy, good or bad."[80] Recognizing the difficulties involved in asserting the existence of cause-and-effect chains in "the area of behavioral science," Stone nevertheless offers "[his] own clinical impression that psychotherapy, whether it cures or not, often has a powerful impact which can be either benign or malignant."[81] In his article, Stone delineates specific ways in which psychotherapy is able to precipitate suicide through malignant effects.

In 1972, Dr. Donald W. Light, of Princeton University, published an article in the *American Journal of Sociology* titled "Psychiatry and Suicide: The Management of a Mistake," in which he noted:

> Even though it is a recognized risk, [suicide's] finality arouses feelings so strong that the suggestion of failure and of a mistake cannot be ignored. Emergencies such as suicide differ from regular error in that they throw into doubt the efficacy of the profession.[82]

During a two-year study, Light was able to observe the effects of five suicides from the time each was made known until the case was closed several months later, and to conduct interviews with psychiatrists and other staff members. Like previous investigators, he found the reactions of the patient's psychotherapist included anger and a sense of betrayal.[83] One psychiatrist said: "She fought me all the way, and I guess she finally made her point."[84]

Therapists also feel guilt because of the "stark way suicide highlights certain weaknesses inherent in the work situation."[85] There is, for example, no psychiatric diagnostic category of suicide. Suicides occur in all categories. Thus, there is a dearth of information which can be drawn on in the staff discussions trying to deal with the tragedy and its implications.

More difficult than the sudden and unexpected suicide is the case of the patient who has given many warnings prior to the act. One psychiatrist had said of a patient just prior to her suicide attempt that she was "not suicidal." Another said the same thing of a patient who had just killed himself.[86]

Even more frequent than such striking denials are the actions through which the psychiatric profession reasserts itself by having the last word. This takes place most effectively in the "suicide review" held by a medical committee several months later. Even when a mistake is recognized, it is frequently concluded that the suicide was in fact inevitable. The main function of the suicide review conference is as

a ritual designed to reaffirm the profession's worth after a deviant act has cast doubt upon it. . . . The main feeling is one of being impressed by the reviewer, a reaffirmation of how fine psychiatry is; for in its darkest hour, a clear lesson can be drawn by a model of the profession (the reviewer), implying that, had the best men in psychiatry been handling the case, it would not have happened. In sum, the review of a suicide is temporarily harsh, then, uplifting because of the display of psychiatric wisdom which has arisen from an act of ultimate failure.[87]

Some of the therapist behaviors that were associated with patient suicides were also those more likely to be exhibited by psychoanalysts or psychoanalytically oriented psychotherapists. These include allowing a "symbiotic" transference to develop,[88] failing to relate to the patient's real situation,[89] negative countertransference, or even "excessive empathy."[90] It has also been suggested that interpretations of "suicidal elements" in a patient's dreams, associations, or fantasies risk the danger of actually suggesting the idea to a patient.[91]

EVIDENCE OF EFFECTIVENESS

On the other hand, there are many people who have been to psychotherapists and who maintain with strong conviction that their therapy helped them. Can their experiences be denied? Positive results have also been obtained in some research investigations. What about those? The following is a list of reasons why a person might feel she was helped or why she might be inclined to say she was helped.

1. The therapy really helped. The skill of the therapist acquired during his training and study was utilized in the treatment process and that skill, as exhibited in the therapist's behavior, produced real change in the patient which she experienced as positive benefit which would not have otherwise come about.

2. The therapy really helped. The therapist's behavior

during the sessions was responsible for real change in the patient which she experienced as positive benefit which would not have otherwise come about. But the things that the therapist did that were particularly helpful were not the result of his training and study; they were, rather, the result of his being an intelligent, warm, and sympathetic human being. He helped, but training had little to do with it.

3. The therapy helped. The therapist's behavior during the sessions was responsible for real change in the patient which she experienced as positive benefit which would not have otherwise come about. But the particularly helpful things that the therapist did were not the result of his training and study, but because he elected to depart from his training and engage in practices that were in fact antithetical to those prescribed by his trainers. He helped in spite of, not because of, his training and credentials.

4. The therapy seemed to help. The patient experienced real change which she felt would not otherwise have come about, whereas, in fact, the change was due not to therapy but to other positive changes in her life situation. She thought it was due to the therapy because it was all happening at the same time.

5. The therapy seemed to help, but, in fact, not only was it *not* responsible for the positive changes she experienced, but she would have changed more had therapy not held her back to some extent. While it did not prevent positive change, it retarded it. And yet it seemed to be helping.

6. No improvement occurred. The patient became dependent on the therapist, however, and believed that she would not have been able to get along without him. She became convinced that had she not been in therapy, she would have become worse and therefore she was grateful for therapy and claimed that it had helped her.

7. She got worse. She was convinced, however, that her deterioration would have been more acute had she not been in therapy. She felt therapy had saved her life, although it had been unable to prevent her from suffering.

8. She was not helped but she had spent a fortune and

five years of her life in having to concentrate on inner motives rather than what was happening around her. To admit to herself or to anyone else that it was all of no benefit was more than she could bear. She *believed* she was helped although she did not really feel helped.

9. She was not helped and she knew it, but the time and cost had been so enormous that she saved face with family and friends by pretending to be helped.

It is not easy to tell which category a person is in from what she says. It is not even easy to tell which category one is in oneself. But only if the first category contains a great many people is professional psychotherapy supported. There is a good deal of evidence that this category may contain the fewest cases of all.

Uncertainty has plagued the insight therapist to some degree since the beginning of psychoanalysis, and increasingly since the 1960s.[92] There is a theme of pessimism and cynicism found in many works, even those of ardent exponents of psychotherapy. The therapist is, after all, the ultimate believer. After a certain point, his material benefits, important as they may be in an absolute sense, provide limited compensation, especially for psychiatrists, who tend to earn less than physicians in other specialties. He has identified his raison d'être with the therapeutic process. If it is in fact damaging or ineffective, or if he, individually, personally, and, unlike what he believes to be the case with his colleagues, is ineffective, then his life has been a failure. Expressions of doubt have grown more pervasive over the last two decades, since scientific evidence of ineffectiveness has begun to accrue and therapists have been urged to subject their techniques to criticism based on considerations other than whether or not they followed the proscriptions of traditional practice. Uncertainty about the profession as a whole is probably easier to live with than questions about one's personal abilities. Their extreme defensiveness concerning research, and their refusal to subject their own work to criticism even among colleagues in the analytic societies (perhaps especially there) suggests that therapists have always been uncomfortable about the therapeutic enterprise.[93]

A FINAL NOTE

Our review of outcome studies goes back to the 1920's. The more we examine this material, the more evidence we find of deterioration effects among patients as a result of inept psychotherapy of the type reported in recent articles.

ALLEN E. BERGIN AND HANS S. STRUPP, *Changing Frontiers in the Science of Psychotherapy*[94]

Although there is no question that psychotherapists differ, to attribute the harmfulness of psychotherapy to occasional inept practitioners takes the profession as a whole off the hook. Other attempts to defend psychotherapy, while not denying that ineffectiveness and harmfulness occur, involve criticism of particular training institutions, of certain *kinds* of therapy, of criteria used by the critics (it has even been claimed that what is seen as deterioration is really a form of improvement),[95] and of other aspects of research methodology. It has also been said that the therapy may not actually be damaging to the patient but simply unable to counter strong deteriorative processes, i.e., without the therapy, deterioration would have been even worse.[96] Furthermore, whenever patient evaluations are involved reports of harmfulness may be interpreted as exaggeration, as an expression of "deep transference," in which case complaints about therapy are part of the process of cure, or as the result of a therapy prematurely terminated. In the last instance, the ill effect is admitted, but the responsibility for it is placed on the patient's shoulders not the therapist's. This is a common ploy, but insufficient in itself to explain why some therapists have worse results than others.

In a remarkable but typically Freudian turnabout, Otto Kernberg, a highly influential and well-known psychoanalyst, has actually managed to hold the patient at least partly responsible for therapist-induced harmfulness. He spoke of a kind of "collusion" between the "poor" or "damaging" therapist and the "masochistic" patient who has "a deep need" to destroy her chance to survive. When such patients continue

to accept treatment from destructive therapists, they are involved in an inevitable process. Such patients cannot be
helped in any case.*

Another example of psychodynamic blaming of the patient
is given by Florence Rush in an article on the sexual abuse of
children. Rush shows how Freudian theories of infantile sexuality have been used to excuse the perpetrator of the sexual
offense and to blame the victim:

> He (Freud) noted that the majority of children could es-
> cape from the sexual situation if they wished and he main-
> tained that the silence shown by some children following
> seduction, could be explained in terms of their own feeling
> of guilt in yielding to forbidden attraction. . . . [experts
> in child study] noted that the most striking feature of sex-
> ually assaulted children was their unusually attractive per-
> sonalities. This was so noticeable that the authors fre-
> quently considered the possibility that the child might
> have been the actual seducer rather than the one in-
> nocently seduced.[97]

Rush found that in addition to blaming the child victim of
sexual abuse, psychodynamic writers blamed other innocent
persons in the child's environment, especially the mother,
even when it was the father who committed the acts. Rush,
like Hurvitz, views the role of the psychotherapist as one of
social control. Sexual abuse of children serves a function similar to that of rape, in which the powerless are terrorized into
accepting domination. Society, represented by psychiatry,
helps rationalize the process.

---

* This suggestion appears transparently vicious, foolish, and ut-
terly self-damning on his part. But in his mind, the "collusion theory" was a "contribution to psychoanalytic theory."

3
Somatopsychic Illness

TYPES OF SEVERE "MENTAL DISORDERS"

Before Freud, psychiatry was dominated by the "somatic" conception that all emotional and behavioral disorders were caused by physical pathology of the nervous system or other physiological systems or organs. This view was greatly encouraged by the discovery of the relationship between syphilitic infection and psychotic behavior. But the physical bases for other severe mental syndromes eluded detection. The psychoanalytic contention that psychoses have no organic base promised some hope in a time of discouragement. It was ultimately agreed that there are two major categories of severe mental illness: the organic conditions and the "functional" psychoses. For several decades, the majority of mentally ill persons in hospitals—those diagnosed as "schizophrenic" or "manic-depressive"—were assumed to be psychologically malfunctioning, not organically impaired. Such deviant behaviors as the immobility and mutism of the "catatonic," or the hyperactivity of the "manic" were interpreted to be symbolic representations of intrapsychic conflicts resulting from traumatic events in the patient's early life.

This medical model is both inappropriate and abusive as it is applied to normal (or, as psychiatrists and Friends refer to them, "neurotic") private psychotherapy clients. It is even more insidious in denying the organic base of these often very severe conditions, which are very likely physically determined.

Recently, the conception of purely functional psychosis has eroded. Manic-depressive, or "affective" psychoses had in fact long been believed by some psychiatrists to be organically based. In 1965, S. H. Kraines presented the paper "Neurological Theory of Depression" at the American Psychiatric Association meeting. He stated:

> The manic depressive syndrome is a self-limiting disease manifested primarily by alterations in mood, rate of intellectual activity, somatic symptoms, and secondarily by psychopathology. Clinically, this syndrome appears to be physiologic in origin, neurophysiologic evidence suggesting that it may result from hypothalamic pathology.[1]

Although some investigators have maintained that neurotic and psychotic, or "endogenous," depression lie on a continuum, the weight of opinion favors distinguishing between them. In a manic depressive psychosis, there may be mood swings or, more commonly, a predomination of either mania, which may or may not be euphoric, or depression. Psychotherapy has not been demonstrably effective for this, and many patients do not need and do not want any form of psychotherapy or psychoanalysis. Research findings strongly suggest hereditary transmission of the condition.[2]

Manic depressive patients have played a role in the development of the mental health professions. Most notable was Clifford Beers, whose book *A Mind That Found Itself*, published in 1908, described his own experiences as a hospitalized patient. It led to a movement for "mental hygiene" and reform of mental hospital abuses. For thirty years, Beers was secretary of the National Association of Mental Health, an organization dedicated to providing public support for research in mental illness and to a campaign for removing some of the ancient stigma with which mental illness has been associated.[3] More recently, Fieve's famous patient, producer-director Joshua Logan and his wife, Netta, have spoken publicly[4] about Logan's affliction over many years in which he experienced the "highs" of the manic phase, the lows of depression, as well as "prolonged periods of normalcy." Fieve has been credited with the discovery of lithium carbonate as a treatment and as a prophylactic agent, the first, he says, "available in psychiatry." While not helpful to all patients,* lithium has achieved "dramatic relief in the manic phase and appears to prevent onset of the depression phase."[5] Logan, who has been taking the medication several times a day for four years, has reported feelings of hopefulness about his life and his work as a result of the preventive treatment.

"Schizophrenia" is the diagnostic term applied to the largest category of hospitalized mental patients. One quarter of all mental patient beds throughout the world belong to persons so classified.[6] Common, often severe, more often so mild it goes unrecognized, it is also baffling. Absence of expression of emotionality, poor insight, the feeling that thoughts are being broadcast aloud to others, free and spontaneous flow of incoherent speech, and bizarre, nihilistic, and widespread delusions are some of the criteria on which a diagnosis of schizophrenia is based.[7] There are many theories, and much controversy; nothing one could say about it would not be disputed in some quarter. There are those who would abandon use of the term as a diagnostic category altogether, claiming that the criteria are not only vague but favor certain social groups over others, and that stigmatization has evolved around the very term. At the other extreme is the belief that schizophrenia (or the "schizophrenias") is a genetically transmitted biochemical disease treatable by physical methods such as diet and medication.[8] In the middle are those willing to use drugs as an adjunct to psychotherapy,

* Diabetes and low-salt diets are contraindications, and the blood lithium level should be monitored regularly to prevent undesirable side effects.

but whose essential position is that the major etiological influence is psychogenic.

New Jersey psychiatrist Jack Ward, an opponent of psychodynamic psychotherapy for schizophrenia, said, in "Doctors Speak on the Ortho-Molecular Approach," that most of his colleagues have developed a closed mind to the biological approach.

We're trained that almost everything is on an emotional basis. To oversimplify what we are taught about schizophrenia, we were taught that something goes wrong with the mother-child relationship, commonly before the ages three to four, something happens to the family and this is compounded over and over again: . . . the way to treat schizophrenia is to go and dig into [her] background to find out what the original problems were to try to correct these.

I had a very interesting time treating schizophrenics this way. Fascinating. Unconscious material is very interesting tracking it all down. Interpreting symbolism can be rather gratifying if the patient agrees with you. . . .[9]

Under the assumption that schizophrenia is experiential in origin, it follows that the family, most particularly the mother, produced the condition through behavior. Thus mothers of young schizophrenic children are typically induced to come into psychotherapeutic treatment themselves. It also follows from the concept of psychogenic causation that "the talking cure" is the appropriate treatment. Therefore nonmedical therapists, including American psychoanalysts, who although they are physicians eschew the practice of physical medicine, are appropriate professionals for dealing with this major mental derangement. In other words many psychotherapists (social workers, psychologists, psychoanalysts) may have a professional interest in adopting one theory of schizophrenia causation over another. I do not imply that vested interests in the narrow sense are the sole determinants of a scientific position; I do aver that such interests produce biases of varying degrees of tenacity.

Humphrey Osmond, Director of the Bureau of Research in Neurology and Psychiatry at the New Jersey Neuro-Psychiatric Institute, observes in his article "The Medical Model in Psychiatry" that seven current models of schizophrenia causation and treatment exist in addition to the psychoanalytic or psychogenic. In the *family interaction model,* the family, not the individual, is taken as the unit. Where a family contains a schizophrenic individual, that person has been "selected" by the others as a kind of scapegoat, to "act out the family pathology." Proponents of the *social model* view mental illness as a reflection of a sick society: "They see mental hospitals as some sort of shelter for people too battered to live in the jungle outside—in fact, as asylums. In this particular model, the remedy is the reform of society."[10] Osmond calls the position of Erving Goffman and Thomas S. Szasz the *conspiratorial model:* the patient is a victim, unwillingly locked up by family, hospital staff, and other agents of society. The *moral model,* in sharp contrast, holds that the mentally ill are "wayward." Focus is on behavior and on changing it, not on inner experience. The behavior may be labeled sin, irresponsibility, or deviance. In this model, Osmond lumps together behavior-modification programs with those based on religion. R. D. Laing, the charismatic British psychiatrist, has provided a model in which the status of the schizophrenic experience is actually elevated above that of normal persons. As Osmond describes it, "Laing uses fragments of three models, psychoanalytic, conspiratorial, and a new one of his own, which we have called the *psychedelic model* [my italics]."[11]

The last two models are of probably the greatest importance. The most common model, the one compatible with and usually used jointly with the psychogenic or psychoanalytic models, Osmond calls the *impaired model:*

> In the impaired, something is wrong with the person that makes [her] different from other people; [she] may be called disabled, handicapped, impaired, or crippled, or [she] may be given a more specific label that reflects [her] disability; blind, deaf, paralyzed, addicted, insane, mentally deficient. . . . In the impaired model, the person is expected to behave as much like a normal person as possible.[12]

Osmond himself prefers the *medical model* in which the individual is treated by others as ill in a specific, treatable way. What he recommends is a return to the nineteenth-century concept of "somatic" underlying factors, the one overturned when Freud arrived on the scene at the beginning of this century.

New York psychiatrist Allan Cott agrees:

> Many years of close consideration of the available evidence, including experiences in my own work, have caused me to doubt that faulty interpersonal relations will appear in the textbooks several decades hence as a significant factor in the cause of mental disorder. The absence of clearcut evidence does not show that the "functional" hypothesis is incorrect, but only that it has not been demonstrated *even once*.[13]

Furthermore, considerable evidence has accumulated to indicate biological processes are correlated with, and are likely responsible for, schizophrenic symptoms. Psychiatric geneticist F. J. Kallmann, who has been studying the genetics of schizophrenia for over forty years, theorizes that schizophrenia is caused by a mutant recessive gene which produces metabolic deficiency.[14] Much of his evidence comes from studies in which the identical twin of a schizophrenic patient showed a much higher likelihood of developing a similar condition, even if not reared in the same family, than did a fraternal twin or ordinary sibling. At present, the genetic picture has by no means been clarified, but the existence of hereditary factors is undeniable.[15] In a study of the offspring of schizophrenic mothers, it was found that incidence of the child having the disease was increased for individuals who were likely to have been subjected to anoxia, or oxygen deprivation, at birth.[16] These findings suggest that a predisposition, rather than the illness itself, is inherited, but they clearly support the concept of an organic basis. Although the much-sought chemical test of schizophrenia has not yet been identified,[17] physiological correlates, such as electroencephalograms among others, reveal "schizophrenic" characteristics.[18]

The medical model which stigmatizes normal persons as psychologically "sick" is, in Osmond's terms, an impairment model. Persons who turn up in psychotherapists' offices with complaints of anxiety, depression, or interpersonal difficulties are labeled "sick," but not really allowed to play the role of an ill person. They are in fact held responsible for their illness as well as for the course of treatment.[19] To view schizophrenics and others suffering from severe "mental" illness as organically impaired and treatable is not to denigrate them. Patients are relieved at the thought that they are *physically* ill, not merely because it implies treatment possibilities but because it removes some of the moral burden.

DOES PSYCHOTHERAPY HELP PSYCHOTIC PATIENTS?

Freud did not believe that psychoanalysis was an effective treatment for psychoses.[20] One of the most characteristic symptoms of schizophrenia is "flatness of affect" and emotional withdrawal from other people, so Freud and other psychoanalysts judged the schizophrenic incapable of the intense transference relationship required for successful psychoanalysis. In *This Stranger, My Son*, Louise Wilson tells the story of her psychotic son. The Wilson family discovered that in fact private practitioners often accept schizophrenic patients for treatment. They also discovered that psychotherapy does not prevent a downward trend in the patient.

There is evidence that psychotherapy may help accelerate the process of deterioration or retard spontaneous remission. When psychotherapy is effective, it tends to be a type of psychotherapy that bears little similarity to traditional methods. The Professional Committee of the Schizophrenic Foundation of New Jersey, four psychiatrists who advocate the use of antischizophrenic drugs and vitamin therapy, wrote in 1970:

> Attempts to treat patients with a serious degree of schizophrenia by means of talking therapy have been dismally unsuccessful. This conclusion is based on the fact that when this approach is adopted, specially trained psycho-

therapists, who probably have to have a certain kind of personality make-up themselves, are needed; the amount of time and persistence required are forbidding, and the results are dubious.[21]

Psychoanalytic explanations of schizophrenic symptomatology have been offered in profusion, but such interpretations are only given after the fact, not predictively. It is one thing to look back at the babyhood events described by the mother of a schizophrenic and declare that, for example, the illness "was clearly precipitated by the birth of the little sister when the patient was sixteen months old," but quite another to be able to prescribe methods of infant care that will prevent the illness, or even be able to look at the family interactions in a particular case and judge that a specific child will become ill.

Journalist James A. Wechsler is another parent who published the story of his schizophrenic son and of the attitudes toward the parents held by the many therapists—eight major ones, and many interns, residents, and other temporary or "minor" therapists in hospitals—who treated Michael before his suicide at age twenty-six.[22] While Tony Wilson showed symptoms of abnormality almost from babyhood, Michael Wechsler's illness was not evident until adolescence. Several of the therapists totally excluded the parents from communication. Sadly, this was particularly true of the first psychiatrist, who, being first, was able to set certain patterns, and the last, who saw Michael for a long session the very afternoon of the day he took his life and subsequently denied the possibility of "deliberate" suicide until the note was found. Using their need to establish a relationship of trust with the patient as justification, the therapists clearly "took sides," and supported son against parents, even in irrational demands. The parents were shocked at the outset by the first therapist's flat refusal to see them or even to speak to them on the telephone. Wechsler, clearly a fringe member of Friends and Supporters, writes from an anger and bitterness that is essentially at a personal level. Although he grew increasingly disenchanted with psychotherapy as Michael progressively worsened during years of expensive and evidently useless treatment, the psychotherapy "mystique" and authoritarianism hindered effective parental action. Both the Wechsler and the Wilson fathers were persons of high status; Wilson was a surgeon, Wechsler, a famous journalist. One can only wonder what further abuses are experienced by families who do not command respect on the basis of their position in society.

Although psychotherapy was hailed as a promising treatment for schizophrenia and manic-depressive psychoses in the 1950s,[23] by the 1970s, the picture had changed considerably. In *Treatment of Schizophrenia* published in 1968, Philip R. A. May of the Neuropsychiatric Institute of the University of California declared that medication, not psychotherapy, is responsible for any improvement that occurs. Others have said that such psychotherapy techniques as the couch and free association are not only inappropriate but dangerous with psychotic patients. Even those who feel that psychotherapy can be helpful say it depends on the technique used and on the therapist's experience and personality.[24]

Everyone needs others to relate to, and the need is more perceptible in times of trouble. Psychosis is a troubled time for the patient, and for the patient's family. It is tragic that the abusive interpretive methods of psychogenic therapists have so often been applied.

The use of the major tranquilizers or antipsychotic drugs began about twenty-five years ago and has steadily increased.[25] Such drugs appear not to produce real cures, since the differences between patients given drugs and those not given drugs decreases over time. Furthermore, long-range toxic effects such as hypotension, drowsiness, weight gain, impotence, extreme sensitivity to light, and others have been observed.[26] Proponents of the "ortho-molecular approach" make strong claims for the efficacy of large doses of niacin and other vitamins with minimal or no side effects,[27] and electroconvulsive shock therapy still has many supporters, including patients who have undergone the treatment.[28] It appears that the days of psychotherapy as treatment of choice for psychosis are limited. Psychiatrist Karl Bowman has in fact recommended that psychiatrists think beyond "psychogenic" disturbances and cases amenable to psychotherapy: the case load of psychiatrists should be broadened to include, and ultimately be limited to, "somatopsychic" medicine in which behavioral and emotional symptoms are attributable to physiological causes.[29]

THE MOTHER OF THE SCHIZOPHRENIC PATIENT

The psychoanalytic assumptions that neurosis and other forms of mental illness result from interpersonal events in the person's childhood led naturally to consideration of child-rearing practices. Social psychologists, anthropologists, and other behavioral scientists relate the "national character" of a country or culture to its child-rearing customs, and psychotherapists, especially psychoanalysts, become instant experts in child psychology. Pediatrician Benjamin Spock, in his famous book on baby and child care, attempted among other things to guide parents away from psychically harming their children. The Friends and Supporters of Psychiatry are especially concerned about inducing "complexes" in their children.

This assignment of causation to childhood became a basis for derogation of women, in their roles as mothers. Whatever degree of responsibility for the condition not placed on the patient herself is attributed to her mother. "Deficient" mothering has been related to hostility, resentfulness, rebelliousness, sexual problems, depression, and virtually any other form of psychopathology. It is quite usual for a woman to take her child for treatment only to be told that it is she herself, not the child, who has the problem and who needs therapy. In some cases, the guilt thereby induced by those looked to for help has had tragic consequences.

Nor is this attribution of blame to the mother limited to psychoanalytic theory. Anthropologist Gregory Bateson and his associates in California viewed the mother as the direct causal agent in the psychosis schizophrenia.[30] A schizophrenic person is one who has been unlucky enough to have a schizophrenogenic (or schizophrenia-causing) mother! Psychotherapists were fascinated by the theory. For at least two decades its pernicious influence was widespread, and mothers of mentally ill children suffered the double pain of the sick children and of being themselves blamed for the sickness.[31]

Schizophrenia-inducing mothers, according to Bateson, place their children in a "double bind": they demand affection, then reject the child who attempts to display it. They "send out" simultaneous messages of love and hate, placing their children in impossible situations from which the only refuge is escape to a fantasy world of mental illness. But the mother is herself the one placed in a double-bind situation by the theory and the therapist who espouses it. Since she is judged to be at once accepting on the surface and rejecting underneath, any behavior on her part "fits" the theory. Overt display of affection indicates her "seductress" side, but failure to show affection is construed as evidence of her more basic rejection. Unsurprisingly, the famous double-bind theory turned out to be elusive when researchers attempted to study it. Not only unproven, it is unprovable, since it involves subjective interpretations of behavior.

Psychoanalyst Lewis B. Hill devoted a full chapter to "mothers of schizophrenics" in his book *Psychotherapeutic Intervention in Schizophrenia*. Hill objected to the term "schizophrenogenic" as a "bit of name-calling without proof." But despite his nonalliance with Bateson (who is not, after all, a psychoanalyst), Hill gives the impression that a mother interviewed by him would be little better off than if she were seen by one of Bateson's followers.

Here are some descriptions of "these mothers" by Hill:

. . . their anxiety, guilt, and sense of incompetence are such that they can tolerate the situation only if they convince themselves that they are in command and if they take over and direct the conversation in an effort to keep it away from those subjects which they do not dare to discuss. Another [possibility] is that these women are vain or, if you prefer, narcissistic and are actually more concerned with the impression which they are making of themselves than they are with the realities concerning the patient.[32]

. . . these mothers are devastatingly, all-loving of their child who is schizophrenic. This love is idealized, romantic, and unrealistic and leads to extensive denial of anything they observe in the child contrary to their fantasies concerning him.[33]

. . . these mothers love their children not only excessively but conditionally.[34]

It is certain that the majority of mothers of schizophrenic patients have shown considerable moral sadism. . . .[35]

. . . not far beneath the surface she freezes when anything unpleasant is mentioned. She holds one at arm's length, being quite critical, demanding and long-suffering out loud.[36]

. . . most of these mothers are described by the family as obsessively concerned about cleanliness. . . . A few report that they discontinued nursing because they found it pleasurable.[37]

. . . they actually have no awareness of the reality of their children. . . .[38]

True, she was overconcerned, ambitious, and interfering with his affairs in an effort to promote his interests. . . . Unfortunately, these mothers are not capable, as a rule, even after the patients have long been ill, of grasping the facts of the situation.[39]

It is unsettling when one's child displays deteriorative symptoms of depression, social isolation, outbursts of rage in which violence against others is threatened, irrationality, excessive fears, sleeplessness, aberrant eating patterns, or any of the other symptoms characterized as schizophrenic. The first visit to a psychiatrist usually comes after many years of attempting to cope with the situation on one's own. Schizophrenia strikes all levels of the population, and for most, the psychiatrist is a last resort, turned to in desperation. The child has been difficult to manage, and parents have typically alternated between the two basic modes of reaction: patient understanding and attempts to retaliate and to gain control. Sometimes, meeting disruptiveness in the child with punitive parental action is deliberate, sometimes it is reactive. Nothing seems to work. But the psychoanalytic assumption that schizophrenia is psychogenic and environmentally produced implies that something could have worked, that the child's illness was caused by the parents' behavior and often exclusively by the mother's.*

When the mother talks to the psychiatrist, there is no behavior on her part which will be construed as faultless. If she is calm, she may be considered "unfeeling" or as "denying reality." If she shows signs of emotional upset, she is "long-suffering," "narcissistic," "unable to control her impulses," or "acting out." If she is well-groomed, she risks seeming "narcissistic" and too concerned with the impression she is making on the psychotherapist. If she expresses affection for her sick child, she is "overconcerned," "excessive in her love." If she tries to explain how she tried to be a good mother, she may be considered "obsessive" about cleanliness or even "morally sadistic." Furthermore, his viewpoint does not lead the psychiatrist to attempt any real relationship with her, since she is "not capable" of understanding the situation.

In Louise Wilson's book about her schizophrenic child, this dialogue occurred in an interview between the parents and the child's therapist after the husband had described the child's behavior. The psychiatrist turned to the mother and said:

"Have you anything to add?"

"No," I said, "my husband has told you everything, except maybe that I would just like to add that I am so baffled by what has happened to our child. We have a good home, doctor. Believe me, we have."

"Why do you feel it necessary to tell me that? No one has said you haven't," he responded quietly enough.

I was hotly embarrassed. "I mean," I explained, "that it might help you to know that Jack and I haven't got any problems between ourselves that would upset a child. We never fight—"

* Although schizophrenics' fathers are often described as weak or inadequate, the blame still rests on the mother, since it was due to her faulty personality that this was the man she "chose" as her husband.

"You never fight?" he repeated.

I was tripped up, and tangled in my own words. "Not seriously, that is . . ." I tried again, "I just mean there isn't any reason that I can see, nothing wrong with our home that would have made Tony so unhappy," I finished, annoyed with myself. Dr. Maxwell looked steadily at me. "Nothing wrong that you are aware of. But no child is born with problems. It is always something in the home. In some way he has been damaged in your home."[40]

In fact, a comparison of families with and without schizophrenic sons, made by Joan Huser Liem in the *Journal of Consulting and Clinical Psychology*, strongly suggests that any consistent communication patterns within the families of schizophrenics are more likely the *result* of the patient's behavior than the *cause* of the illness![41]

4

Professionalism

SOURCES OF PSYCHOTHERAPY

It has been noted that if Freud had not continued to let his patients be considered "sick" and his treatments "medical" but had instead adopted the more logical position that psychoanalysis was a *social* enterprise, he would not have been able to support his family.[1] By developing psychoanalysis in the context of private medical practice, he charged his patients fees. He did not have foundation grants or a university salary. Income from his writings came only later in his life. In his book *In the Name of Mental Health*, psychiatrist Ronald Leifer says:

> The only way in which Freud could obtain access to the subjects of his study and also earn a living was to avoid tampering with the popular definition of his patients' problems and his professional activities as medical.

In spite of his willingness to define psychoanalysis as a medical *practice*, the evidence suggests that Freud was more interested in science and money than in helping people. Freud's use of the medical model, which defined him as a physician and his patients as ill, did not serve a scientific or a medical purpose. It served the social and economic purpose of permitting him to have socially justified access to intimacy with persons who would pay him a fee to be the subject of his scientific inquiries.[2]

It has continued to be convenient to use the medical model for psychotherapy. Leifer observes an "ironic aspect" of the professionalization of psychotherapy within medicine:

> One of the functions of the medicalization of psychotherapy is to regulate and control its practice. Psychiatrists, however, are unable to agree on a definition of psychotherapy. . . .
>
> How can a professional group regulate an activity it is unable and unwilling to evaluate? The answer, obviously, is that it cannot. There are no acceptable standards of psychotherapeutic performance as there are, for example, standards of adequate surgical performance. This is due in part to psychotherapy's being conducted in private. . . . But there are so many varieties of psychotherapeutic theory and technique that therapists themselves have no established standards by which to judge the effectiveness or harmfulness of their activities.
>
> The only standards that psychiatric groups have attempted to establish for psychotherapy are the credentials of those who practice it. . . . As a result psychotherapy is not regulated.[3]

Provided he has the degrees and the license, whatever the therapist does is understood to be treatment: "He may sit silently, mumble inanities, give advice, moralize, dispense drugs, issue threats, administer electric shocks or give his patients affection and support."[4] All is psychotherapy.

Although psychotherapy professionals are mostly thought of in the context of private practices, their services are also obtainable in social service agencies, "child guidance centers," teaching hospital clinics, and various types of group practice. The Community Mental Health Act of 1963 led to the establishment of many community mental health centers which must provide a "comprehensive and coordinated range of services" in order to be eligible for federal funding. The

National Institute of Mental Health designated five types of essential services to be provided by community mental health centers:

1. Inpatient Care. The center is in part a small psychiatric hospital located in the community.

2. Outpatient Care. The center is also a psychotherapy clinic.

3. Partial hospitalization. Patients not in need of full hospitalization are able to live at home and spend their days at the center, or, depending on the individual situation, to be employed in the community but receive night care at the center.

4. Emergency care around the clock for patients needing hospitalization.

5. Consultation and educational services to community agencies and professional personnel (this last is vague, and in some cases has been interpreted to mean no more than consultation to community professionals and agencies with regard to individual cases or programs).

The establishment of these community centers has been hailed as a "revolution." In his textbook *Contemporary Clinical Psychology*, California psychologist Herbert Goldenberg stated that the community mental health programs are "likely" to reach low-income groups, train nonprofessionals, explore new methods of therapy (e.g., group therapy, family therapy, crisis intervention), focus on prevention, increase interdisciplinary and collaborative approaches among various types of professionals and community agencies, educate the public, and study the distribution and risk of mental illness in the community.[5] It is also in fact unlikely that they will do anything not in the interests of the mental health professions.

In addition to whatever else the community mental health movement may do, it is intrinsic to its design that it perpetuates a medical orientation to the treatment of the vague, ill-defined "diseases," treatable by the vague, ill-defined methods of psychotherapy. Most centers are headed by psychiatrists. They are an expansion of the realm of the psychiatric profession and, to a lesser degree, that of other mental

health professionals. Some critics have claimed that: a primary function of community mental health centers is social
control;[6] because they are state bureaucracies they are ill-
equipped to attack problems of racism, poverty, poor housing, and other social conditions generally assumed to be
among the causative factors in mental illness; some needed
services are not offered even by the most "comprehensive" of
facilities;* "reaching out" to the working class communities
and ghettos will in many cases add another strike, the "mentally ill" stigma, against groups already burdened by oppression from numerous sources;** and that, despite pressures
and disguises reluctance to utilize the services of the mental
health professionals or to associate oneself in any way with
the psychiatric profession is so pervasive and so deeply
rooted in the history of the culture that ultimate failure of
the centers is inevitable.

Columbia University sociologist Charles Kadushin, in *Why
People Go to Psychiatrists,* states that outpatient programs in
community mental health simply will not work:

> The relationship between community psychiatry and the
> community at large appears at first glance to be a rela-
> tionship between an unorganized mass of potential clients.
> But nothing could be further from the truth.[7]

A person's potentiality as a client does not result from psychiatric need:

> The Friends and Supporters of Psychotherapy are more
> likely to seek treatment than others. They go mainly for
> help with "psychoanalytic" problems, which tend to be
> less bizarre and less obvious than other psychiatric symp-
> toms.[8]

* For example, psychiatrist John D. Kysar notes that long-range
treatment of chronically ill children would not be provided (Kysar,
"The Two Camps in Child Psychiatry: A Report from a Psychiatrist-
Father of an Autistic and Retarded Child," p. 108).
** Community mental health centers often use members of the
poverty community itself to bring clients to the center. These representatives (paraprofessionals) operate in neighborhood offices
which may disguise from potential clients some of the social implications of applying for what they do not always realize are psychiatric services.

Thus, centers designed for the whole community will be utilized by only a segment of it, and not the segment originally defined as the target population.

In a report issued in 1972 by members of Ralph Nader's Task Force on the National Institute of Mental Health, and vigorously attacked by the psychiatric profession, psychiatrists were advised to limit themselves to functions in which their medical training is utilized for the treatment of medical illnesses, and to give up the practice of psychotherapy. According to the report, community mental health centers, in addition to providing facilities for persons who are psychiatrically ill, should help individuals with "problems of living" such as securing adequate housing and employment.[9] I think that these functions are in fact separate and best not housed under the same roof. Local psychiatric facilities for psychiatric inpatients reduce the isolation associated with large and remote state hospitals, but the "comprehensive" care of the community mental health centers has had the unfortunate consequence of expanding the medical model to areas in which it is unwarranted. This model implies that sickness of the individual is the basic cause of the problem, a stance clearly in opposition to recognition of the societal roots of "individual" problems.

Community mental health centers, existing by the good graces of public policy and public money, are unlikely to help with basic social problems, and terribly likely to serve as another "lid." According to Hurvitz, "this movement accepts the society which established it and by enabling the society to maintain itself, perpetuates the problems it was planned to abolish."[10] He cites an article in the *Los Angeles Times* about a center to be set up in a black ghetto and paid for by state, federal, and private sources: "The medical director of the projected center is reported as saying that the 'center will help people live in their surroundings of continual crisis,' an objective that institutionalizes present evils."[11] Private psychotherapy has personalized the condition of middle-class white women, whose problems are often based on sexist discrimination and prejudice, and has prevented or muted attempts to alter those social conditions. In the same way, bringing psychotherapy to the ghetto may do no more

Defining a "Profession"

	Medical Doctor	Law	Clergy	Psycho-analysts	(Ph.D.) Clinical Psychologist	Agency Social Worker	(M.S.W.) Social Worker In Private Practice	Nurses	College Professors	Police	Plumbers	Librarians
Special Training or acquisition of special skills	yes	yes	yes	yes	yes	yes	yes	yes	yes, but not in teaching	yes	yes	yes
Special title or garb	"doctor" yes	"counselor" infreq. no	"rev." "father" yes	"doctor" yes	"doctor" yes	no no	no no	infrequently ("nurse") usually	no	"officer" yes	no no	no no
Legal sanction	yes	yes	in some respects	not for analysis	current struggle	no	no	yes	no	yes	no	in-creasing
Monopoly of needed services	yes	yes	no	ro	no	no	no	to some degree	no	yes	largely	no
"ethical" codes	yes	yes	varies	yes	in-creasing	varies	yes	yes	some	yes	no	no
Autonomy of practitioners (private practice)	yes	yes	not usually	yes	yes	no	yes	rarely	no	to some degree	yes	no
National organization	yes	yes	various	yes	yes	yes	yes	yes	yes	yes	union	yes
Mystique	yes	yes	yes	yes	yes	some	yes	yes	some	yes	no	no

than "quiet restive neighborhoods" and offer the ideology of individual solution to social problems.[12]

WHAT MAKES IT A PROFESSION

Although special training is basic to many professions and occupations, only medicine meets all the listed criteria of a profession, as shown in the accompanying Table. The physician is distinguished from others by his title. In the hospital, his dress—white coat and stethoscope—set him apart. In his own office, he stands out against the uniformed underlings who surround him. Sociological surveys have indicated his discomfort when such visible clues to his identity are missing.[13] He is quick to identify himself as a "doctor" in social situations, although for other reasons he may be loath to reveal himself in public situations.

The medical profession has through its political activities (it maintains one of the most active lobbies in Washington) been awarded a total monopoly on the "practice of medicine," an undertaking which consists virtually of any activities over which it appears feasible and profitable for physicians to claim sole rights. Because of this monopolization, many essential services are not available to persons who require them. It has been conjectured that if nurses, policemen, teachers, parents, recreation workers, and others were trained in certain medical procedures, thousands of lives would be saved annually. But proliferation of medical skills would not serve the interests of a medical profession which has effectively propagandized to prevent the encroachment of outsiders on its selected domain.

The autonomy of individual practitioners in private practice and the "ethical codes" which protect the profession from the public are traditionally available to medicine and law. Teachers at all levels work for institutions; only private tutors operate independently, and they are used mostly in special situations or as supplements. Nurses do not work autonomously; they work under a physician's supervision. While there is a small market for private detectives, law-enforcement agents operate in a highly structured hierarchical organization. Librarians need libraries, and most libraries are publicly owned or are operated as a department of a larger institution.

But doctors are autonomous. Private practice, the most lucrative and exploitative mode of service distribution, has until recent decades been considered the "most ethical" form of practice. Organized medicine has imposed obstacles to any other structure. Physicians who attempted to operate jointly to engage in group practice or to participate in prepayment or other forms of insurance plans were effectively opposed by the entrenched ideologies and enforcement policies of the American Medical Association. It was not until the 1960s that some segments of the public began to recognize the prevalence and severity of abuses perpetrated by the powerful hand of organized medicine. Not much has been done yet to correct the situation. The physician maintains his mystique among most patients. His authority is legally secured; his services are needed, and they are not available elsewhere. The use of the male pronoun is especially applicable here. Not only are more than 90 percent of M.D.'s male, but female physicians tend to enjoy a much lessened degree of mystique.

Many psychotherapists are physicians, but physicians do *not* have a legalized monopoly on psychotherapy. Nonphysicians can be jailed for performing surgery; they cannot be arrested for performing psychotherapeutic counseling. Because other professions than medicine engage in psychotherapy, the issue is fraught with contradiction and confusion. Interprofessional disputes are rife. Territorial claims overlap.

Medicine might have been able to convince the public that psychotherapy was a purely medical function three or four decades ago, but physicians themselves were not convinced then. To many of them, psychotherapy has always seemed somewhat silly, if not sinister. Lately, however, psychiatry has scored important victories over its competition in other professions through legislation which permitted welfare or other government agencies to reimburse *only* for psychotherapy services performed by physicians or under the supervision of physicians. Although some insurance companies cover psychotherapy by psychologists and social workers, the powerful Blue Cross and Blue Shield companies restrict their reimbursements to physicians. Psychotherapists of varying professional backgrounds differ little in actual practice, but the establishment of psychotherapy as an independent "fifth profession"[14] is unlikely when powerful societal agencies like government and major insurance companies indulge in such regulations. The various psychotherapy professionals are in competition with one another, and the physicians are winning.

Of the four major types of professional psychotherapists, all are called "doctor" except subdoctoral social workers. Questionnaire responses by patients and former patients indicate that most patients are aware of therapists' professional backgrounds and make distinctions among them (distinctions which tend to be fictional since psychotherapists from different professions practice in much the same way).[15] As already noted, the columnist Ann Landers, for example, has urged the public not to trust any but a medically trained person. The medical profession itself engages in a kind of double-talk which clarifies nothing except their insistence on their own ascendance:

> The official view of the medical profession [is] that all [nonmedical therapists] should practice only under the direct supervision of physicians. Doctors feel that their long years of medical training, plus the very fact that they chose medicine as a vocation, have imbued them with a desire to cure, to heal; whereas nonmedical analysts, because of their background in the behavioral sciences have an intellectual approach which may underestimate the human need.[16]

The arrogance of the medical profession and its financial investment in public relations has resulted in an enviable public image. In this country, no calling is more prestigious. Nonmedical psychotherapists, especially those called "doctor" and using doctorlike office settings and medical terminology receive some of the respect bought by AMA money. They may not have quite the prestige or receive quite the income of the medical doctor, but they are close behind.[17]

PROFESSIONAL IMPERIALISM

A low degree of intellectual curiosity among those who are attracted to psychotherapy has been mentioned frequently, and not only by researchers. It is "mysterious," they have said, that in view of its prestige and financial rewards, good students do not enter psychotherapy in larger numbers. The prestige of psychotherapists is greater among its Friends and Supporters, but psychiatrists are at the bottom of the prestige totem pole among physicians, and practitioners are ill-favored among many colleagues in nonmedical allied areas such as experimental psychology and sociology. The general public is often distrustful of psychiatry and all it stands for. While there is awe associated with the very title "doctor," terms like "real doctor" or "*doctor* doctor" are commonly used to differentiate the doctor who practices physical medicine from the psychotherapist.

The prevalence of the M.D. degree among psychotherapists whose treatments are exclusively verbal and interpersonal and the fact that it is a requirement for psychoanalysts are products of professionalism. This exclusivity has been one of the factors held responsible for the absence of creativity among psychoanalysts in particular. According to Dr. F. C. Redlich of Yale University, analysts create

> a tightly controlled shop through a careful system of educational supervision and control. One could almost speak of censorship. The boundaries are tight. There is little room for the doubter, the critic, the maverick.[18]

The rejection of the analyst without a medical degree, the "lay analyst," ultimately undermined the medical profession's hold over psychotherapeutic practice in the United States. It is ironic that by failing to extend their domain beyond medicine, M.D.'s allowed alternative psychotherapies to develop among nonphysicians. Thus, clinical psychologists, social workers, marriage counselors, members of the clergy, and educators began to practice psychotherapy, often with a psychodynamic, even psychoanalytic, orientation.

HOW TO BECOME A PROFESSIONAL PSYCHOTHERAPIST

There are several routes to becoming a professional psychotherapist. Psychoanalysts in the United States are almost all M.D.'s. After their medical training and three years of psychiatric residency, they attend a psychoanalytic institute for two or more additional years of training. For most psychoanalysts, this postresidency training lasts for four or five years; for as many as 10 percent, it goes on for nine years or more.[19] Psychiatrists are also M.D.'s. Those who do not become psychoanalysts typically spend two years or less in postresidency training. Clinical psychologists complete a year or more of "internship," usually in a mental hospital, prior to the doctorate and as part of its requirements. Their period of postdoctoral training tends to be longer than that of psychiatrists, but shorter than that of psychoanalysts. They are not M.D.'s but are "doctors" because of their Ph.D.'s. Social workers, in contrast, tend not to undertake postgraduate training. Furthermore, their final degree is usually the Master's in Social Work (M.S.W.) which is obtained after two years in graduate school. There are social workers with doctorates, however, and this seems to be becoming more usual.

In *The Fifth Profession*, William E. Henry, John H. Sims, and S. Lee Spray observe that "the entrants into any of these four systems who finally do become psychotherapists are highly similar in social and cultural background. They come from a highly circumscribed sector of the social world, representing a social marginality in ethnic, religious, and political terms."[20] Despite their segregation in different institutions during training, psychoanalysts, psychiatrists, clinical psychologists, and social workers "become with time increasingly like their colleague psychotherapists in other training systems. The marks of the professional training route which remain upon them seem to reside far more largely in residuals of professional separatism than in views of the patient or in ways of relating to [her]."[21]

Most psychotherapists, whatever their professional background, are these days engaging in the private practice of psychotherapy on a fee-for-service basis. With the possible exception of the psychoanalyst, they are also sitting beside one another in "continuing education" workshops and seminars for training in new techniques and approaches.

Comparing the professions of law and medicine with that of psychotherapy, one finds several major differences: (1) Law and medicine each have only a single professional route to practice. Specialization occurs after a period of unified training. Psychotherapy, on the other hand, has at least seven routes; among ones not already mentioned are the clergy, psychiatric nursing, and education (e.g., guidance counseling). These involve widely disparate training modes and professional identities which, however, tend to converge in very similar professional behaviors in actual practice. (2) While the professions of law and medicine have required relatively clear and strict criteria for licensing, psychotherapists have as yet been generally unsuccessful in obtaining similar legislation. (3) Although public demand undoubtedly influences medicine (the recent clamor for acupuncture is an example) and law, the influence of the public on psychotherapy is much greater. (4) The most fundamental difference is that however much the evils of professionalism may interfere with the provision of services by physicians and lawyers (and such interference is considerable),[22] there are objectively determinable services which practitioners of law and of medicine provide. This is not true of psychotherapy. Reliable evidence of effectiveness has not been found, and its very goals are vague if not controversial. Professor Perry London, of the University of California, observes that "neither having different kinds of tradesmen plying the same craft nor calling it by different names offers the wealth of confusion or requires the delicacy of distinction that is demanded by the very number of psychotherapeutic schools and styles proclaimed by its practitioners, by now so acclimated to multiplicity that they see no ironies in it."[23] At present, there are probably over seventy accepted ways of "doing" psychotherapy in use by professional therapists. London further states:

> Now if this plenitude of treatments involved much variety of techniques to apply to different persons under different circumstances by different specialists, there would be no embarrassment of therapeutic riches here, just as there is not within the many specialties of medicine or law or engineering. But this is not the case, and psychotherapeutic "systems" (or "orientations," as they are often glibly called) speak more to epithets than entities, and more to the perspective and labels of their founders than to the facts of human behavior. One hardly goes to a psychoanalyst to be cured of anxiety and a nondirective therapist to be treated for homosexuality, as [one] might to a cardiologist for one condition and a radiologist for another. Nor does the same doctor use Freudian therapy for psychogenic ulcers and Rogerian treatment for functional headaches, as a physician might use medicine for one ailment and surgery for another. On the contrary, being a certain kind of therapist has little bearing on treating a certain kind of problem, but refers rather to the likelihood of treating all problems from the vantage of a certain system.[24]

Like law and medicine, psychotherapy tends to be practiced by prestigious individuals, most of whom operate in private practice which, with success, is highly lucrative. Because such professionals relate directly to the public, their public image is closely related to their financial success. Generally, physicians and most lawyers have found it safest to keep a low profile and to depend on intraprofessional associations to provide them with clients through referrals. "Public appearances" if successful, can boost a practice, however, and are therefore engaged in by professionals who feel they can handle them. Professionals, like politicians, are very careful of their behavior in public situations. Every member of the public is a potential client or one who may refer a client to them.

The degree to which professional training is a kind of indoctrination has often been remarked on. According to Strupp, the effects of therapy can not be accepted at face value in proving anything about the effectiveness of the method itself. It is my personal observation that all great therapists I have known have a profound faith in the utility of their therapeutic operations, to the point of fanaticism. Analytic training, at least in part, is designed to remove the ambivalence and the doubts in the trainee. Once he becomes a "true believer" he is considered to be a first-rate therapist.[25]

Personal therapy is required for psychoanalysts and obtained often, although less frequently, by other psychotherapists. It has often been described as a primary indoctrination method. According to one psychologist, the main function of the personal analysis during psychotherapy training is "personal validation of the unconscious" in which the student suffers a "narcissistic wound" considered essential to knowing the nature of the processes involved. The training psychoanalysis or "didactic" therapy is not viewed as necessarily making the trainee a healthier person.

The view of this therapy most often presented to the public is that it prevents the therapist's problems from interfering with his treatment procedures. "Once he has been analyzed," according to Hunt, Corman, and Ormont, "he can listen to his patients objectively and judge the nature of their problems and his thinking will be less likely to be colored by his own unconscious tendencies, craving or distortions."[26]

In sharp contrast to this idealistic and traditional view is the contention that training analysis is dangerous and possibly related to the high suicide rate among psychiatrists. Viscott suggests that personal therapy involves hazards of mutual involvement between personal and professional life. Patients and former patients I have interviewed have said that there were things they never told their therapist out of embarrassment, or because of their wish to give a good impression. This tendency is likely to be exaggerated in training analysis in which, unlike the ordinary relationship between therapist and client, the therapist is in a strong position for affecting the student's vocational future. As Viscott's character, Stanley, said,

"Well, I don't want to appear too upset or disturbed in analysis or they'll throw me out of the Institute. I was only given a conditional acceptance to the Institute and they postponed their decision whether I can begin the seminars or not until the end of this year, depending on how my personal analysis goes."[27]

One can only conjecture how the practicing psychotherapist feels about himself after having been through a "false" therapy in which he covered up, instead of exposed, his personal difficulties. Such problems may explain the fact that a substantial proportion of therapists return to personal therapy as many as four times. Henry, Sims, and Spray found that 37 percent of all psychotherapists "had therapy" more than once; 20 percent of psychoanalysts and 24 percent of clinical psychologists from their sample undertook personal therapy three or more times.

The various psychotherapy professions differ in training. In the following examination of some of the issues in training my focus is chiefly on clinical psychology and, to a lesser degree, on psychiatry.

No less an authority than Carl Rogers has suggested that training may not be of much importance to the student of whatever school or system. It is not which theory one attaches oneself to but the degree of faith in one's chosen theory that is most important. The most effective therapists are those with the greatest faith in what they are doing, according to Rogers.

Glenn and Kunnes criticize training methods for their authoritarianism. They complain, as did former psychoanalyst Melitta Schmideberg, that disagreement with authority may be treated as psychopathology in the trainee. They say:

Once in training, therapists live in a closed-guild system, apprentices to masters. They are steeped in the myths of hierarchy and status as obvious values and are taught new manipulative techniques and "professional" skills, which will enable them to one-up patients. They are given a special identity, dependent on their practicing the craft like their elders. Imitation then becomes the clue to gaining status and prestige.[28]

The "scientist-professional" model in psychology, in which equal emphasis is placed on research and on practice, has been reaffirmed again and again at national conferences. Its critics have pointed out that the goals of scientists are not only different from those of professionals, but are in fact incompatible.[29] Science is an open and public enterprise, while professional practice depends on secrecy and mystique. In his 1970 presidential address to the American Psychological Association, George Albee considered establishing separate schools of professional psychology, or even abandoning clinical psychology altogether as an academic field.

Many therapists place experience far above classroom training in importance, and a frequent criticism of research in psychotherapy is that inexperienced therapists administer the treatment.[30] But stories of highly experienced and prestigious figures who consistently damage their patients are circulated in the halls of conventions, and when psychotherapists discuss their most successful "cases," they often describe "innovations" in technique in which the rules of training have been ignored.

As evidence accumulated that therapists could induce deterioration in patients and that good therapists did not differ from bad in training or years of experience, researchers began to think in terms of therapists' personality characteristics. The following traits are generally considered to be most helpful: nonpossessive warmth, positive regard for the patient, accurate empathic understanding, unconditional acceptance, permissiveness, genuineness.

Psychologist Charles B. Truax has written about the relationship of the therapist's "interpersonal skills" to the outcome of therapy. He has also reported success in teaching empathy, warmth, and genuineness to lay personnel in a relatively short period (100 hours of training). According to Truax,

> [The important] skills are learned, either overtly or covertly, in early, formative interpersonal situations other than psychotherapy, and that focused training capitalizes on what may often have been past incidental learning. . . . To the degree that some persons are inherently helpful, and by that we mean that they have been rewarded for

being helpful from their early, formative years onward, we would expect that these skills have been built upon and reflect fairly permanent personality characteristics.[31]

The "therapeutic" personality traits of persons in an individual's natural environment have been cited as a possible explanation for "spontaneous" improvement or deterioration. For example, a study of college students and their roommates found that an "understanding," "warm," and "genuine" roommate improved a student's grades. Conversely, having a roommate lacking in these traits led to poorer academic performance.[32]

Truax estimates that

> only one out of three people entering professional training have the requisite interpersonal skills to prove helpful to patients. Further, there is no evidence that the usual traditional graduate training program has any positive value in producing therapists who are more helpful than nonprofessionals. In short, current procedures for selection and training are indefensible.[33]

He and others have called for personality screening for psychotherapists before training, and for changes in training procedures so that those with undesirable personalities are weeded out. Candidates for psychotherapy training should not be selected merely on the basis of their academic performance. As things stand now, however, psychotherapists can reach the very pinnacle of success even though they may be not helping at all or actually causing harm. Once credentials are obtained, professional success often depends more on professional politics than on effectiveness. Colleagues have described some therapists in print as inadequate people, motivated by morbid curiosity and a need for power over other people's lives.

Yet no one has suggested a practical way of eliminating the harm done by incompetent highly credentialed psychotherapists. The fundamental ethic of professionalism places the welfare of the profession above all other considerations. Client welfare is related to the reputation and image of the profession and hence to its welfare. This has been true in medicine and law to a degree. However, psychotherapy, with its vague or unstated goals, does not have their measurable effects. Its harmful professional is traditionally untouchable so long as he does not physically harm or sexually interact with his patients. Since there are now professional therapists who are openly espousing patient-therapist sex and other treatments involving physical contact, even these protections are no longer certain.

CLINICAL PSYCHOLOGY

The separate discipline of psychology began as a laboratory science in the nineteenth century. In the first decade of the twentieth century, the forerunners of today's clinical psychologists began to practice in the field of psychological testing. Psychologists gave intelligence and performance tests in the child guidance centers that were opened for the first time in the second and third decades of the century, but treatment of the mentally ill was considered the exclusive domain of psychiatry, and psychologists worked mainly in university clinics. Both world wars bore significant responsibility for the development of psychology as an applied science. Suddenly, during an emergency situation where need took priority over scientific precedence, psychologists were pressed into service. In World War I, psychologists developed and administered intelligence tests, Army Alpha and Army Beta, for readers and nonreaders respectively, and rough group tests of psychological maladjustment. Over the objections of certain academicians who wanted to keep psychology a pure science, clinical psychology was organized as a subdivision of the American Psychological Association.

During the interval between the wars, psychologists began to encroach more and more on the physicians' sphere of diagnosis, especially in the use of mental tests. The antagonism between psychology and psychiatry over this issue has never been resolved. In the 1930s psychologists adopted the Rorschach and other personality tests which took them further toward true clinical work. They "saw patients." Toward the end of that decade psychoanalysts who came to this country to escape the Nazi holocaust began to have an impact. Although psychoanalytic institutes here were open only to physicians, the opposition of Freud himself to the policy of excluding lay practitioners was well known. Psychologists studied psychoanalytic techniques outside the institutes and eventually set up psychoanalytically oriented institutes of their own.

It was after World War II that clinical psychology received its biggest boost. Coincidental with a rise in need for psychological services, Carl Rogers gave psychology a form of therapy all its own in his 1942 book *Counseling and Psychotherapy*. In it he described a nonanalytic type of counseling which emphasized the present emotional state and dispensed with some of the medical terminology. His technique was eventually called "client-centered" psychotherapy. Among its advantages was a commitment of its advocates to psychotherapy research, and a reduced likelihood of the iatrogeny that results from the interpretation, transference, and authoritarianism of psychoanalytic methods. Rogers stressed nondirective "reflection" of the client's feelings as the major therapeutic strategy. The postwar era was characterized by a great demand for psychotherapy services, and many clinical Ph.D. programs were assisted by aid to universities from the United States Public Health Service. Thousands of psychologists worked for the Veterans Administration. Treatment of former soldiers shifted clinical emphasis from the intelligence and achievement measurement of children to the personality testing of adults.

The stage was set for the beginning of the present era. As Goldenberg reports,

> [Many psychologists] found the practice of psychotherapy more personally and professionally rewarding than testing, to say nothing of its increased financial compensation. They enjoyed the status, responsibility, and independence of being a doctor. But they were risking censure from their nonclinical colleagues who were becoming alarmed at this swift venture into full-time professional work, as well as from psychiatrists who were also critical of "upstart" clinical psychologists who weren't content to "know their place."[34]

The response to these attacks was increased professionalization: clinical psychologists pressured state legislatures for the
passage of certification and licensing laws; the American
Board of Examiners in Professional Psychology was established to provide regulation within psychology; and a Code of
Ethical Standards of Psychologists came into being.[35]

Professional ethics are contradictory. In the eyes of the
public, they safeguard the client. Their real purpose is also to
safeguard the profession itself, even at the expense of the client.[36] In an early version, medicine's ethical code actually
forbade patients from communicating their evaluations of
physicians to each other. If a patient was severely ill-treated,
the code attempted to prevent the patient from reporting
that ill-treatment to friends, relations, or other potential patients. While no codified restrictions are placed on patients
today, there is a strong residual feeling that there is something "not nice" about downgrading a physician. (Patients
usually refer to physicians and therapists not by name but as
"the doctor" or "my doctor," whether praising or com-
plaining. Complaints are often expressed in the plural: "The
trouble with doctors is that they. . . .") Ethical codes in
medicine and psychology restrict behavior by practitioners
which would encourage overt competition. While this is por-
trayed as protecting the clients, the result is the inability of a
client to obtain evaluative and comparative information from
other members of the profession and, therefore, the protection of incompetent doctors. In the face of public scrutiny, the
reaction of professionals is to close ranks. The most unethical
thing a doctor can do is criticize another doctor in public.

This is why the statement by the medical director of a
world-famous clinic that "of course" they could not publish
evidence that certain therapists were harming patients
seemed wholly reasonable to his professional audience. The
only verbalized reaction his remarks elicited was the comment that they, too, knew of famous and successful therapists
who were harmful to their patients.

In the 1970s, psychologists of what Goldenberg calls the
"fourth generation" ". . . spend much of their time as psychotherapists; today there is little or no challenge to their
right or competence to do so."[37] But dissension between ap-

plied and scientific psychologists has, if anything, intensified:

> Private practice of psychotherapy by qualified psycholo-
> gists is approved by the American Psychological Associa-
> tion but is still controversial. Academicians are concerned
> about (and perhaps somewhat jealous of) the practitioner's
> income and freedom from responsibility to publish his find-
> ings or conduct his work scientifically.[38]

The professionalization of clinical psychologists has increased. A study conducted in 1969 found private practice to
be the "single most frequent setting for clinical psychologists."[39] At the same time, psychologists' research in psychotherapy has found no evidence that the psychodynamic-
"medical" model is helpful, and it has also come up with
some grim suggestions that for some patients, and with some
therapists, it can be decidedly harmful. Conflict between
researchers who are aware of its shortcomings and who do
not benefit from it financially, and practitioners who do
benefit from it financially and have traditionally minimized
the importance of scientific research is inevitable, especially
when the two are members of the same national organization, the American Psychological Association. Thus, for all
his prestige and economic satisfactions, the clinical psychologist stands posed between two enemies: physicians who
challenge his right to treat the "sick," and scientific psychologists who challenge his techniques.

These evils in psychotherapy practice are analogous to
those of any profession which manages to stake a claim to
needed services, to monopolize those services, and to indulge
in economic exploitation as the result of such monopolization.
When this is clear and conscious, it is called corruption.
When the service monopolized is vague, insubstantial, and
controversial, it is easier to find excuses such as psychiatrist
Otto Kernberg's idea that patients with a "will" to self-injury
seek out harmful psychotherapists. It is doubtful that the
public would accept the theory of "collusion" as an acceptable alibi for inaction by other professionals. Few patients realize the degree to which they "bear responsibility" for their
"neuroses" in the minds of their "doctors" and in the traditions and professionalism of psychotherapy practitioners.

LENGTH OF TREATMENT AND PSYCHOTHERAPY AS A "LABORATORY"

As conducted by Freud and those who worked with him, early psychoanalysis was usually of a few weeks' or months' duration. It was not until later that analyses of several years' length began to occur. In his very popular and influential book *Persuasion and Healing, A Comparative Study of Psychotherapy*, Jerome D. Frank says that, "within wide limits," duration of treatment seems to depend largely on the therapist's theories of how much treatment is necessary rather than on the patient's condition.[40] Despite the fact that there is no evidence favoring long-term treatment, Frank continues,

> psychotherapy has tended to become increasingly prolonged in settings where there are no external obstacles to its continuance. . . . At one university counseling center the average number of sessions increased from six in 1949 to thirty-one in 1954. It is hard to believe that the lengthening of treatment reflects changes in the severity of patients' or clients' illnesses. More probably it reflects certain changes in the therapist's attitudes produced by increasing experience.[41]

Joseph D. Matarazzo, Professor of Medical Psychology at the University of Oregon Medical School, says that "the psychotherapy interaction [is] an excellent setting in which to do research on basic, person-person processes (i.e., on the subject matter of general psychology)."[42] Such sometimes unending experimentation by the therapist, his patient's romantic attachment to him, his own passivity or unwillingness to let the patient go during years of treatment keep patients on the couch for five, ten, fifteen years, or longer. When circumstances prevent continuance with one therapist, the patient herself may go on to seek a second, or even a third.[43] In the last paper he ever published, *Analyses Terminable and Interminable*, Freud expressed concern about the long durations that had by that time become common.[44] Arguing for a more

focused type of treatment than psychoanalysis, Viscott states:
"The process of psychotherapy is too long and expensive as
it is now, and there usually isn't enough time to discuss all
the real problems. The theory that work expands to fill the
time available for it is especially true in psychotherapy."[45]

Clinical psychologists and psychotherapy researchers Kenneth I. Howard and David E. Orlinsky concede that personal
distress brings the patient to therapy. But they still view it as
a kind of "education" which "is tutorial in form and often
requires remedial work to correct the dysfunctional interpersonal and emotional patterns learned in the course of family
and peer group socialization, but . . . characteristically includes more advanced work as well (intimacy, spontaneity,
self-disclosure, etc.)."[46]

Psychotherapy as education is perhaps more palatable than
psychotherapy as a research activity—at least *some* gain is
promised the "patient." But the image of therapy for most
people who enter is still that of treatment. They come because they are troubled; they assume the psychotherapist has
therapeutic skills, and the trappings of medicine in which it
is linguistically clothed support their assumption.

The question that arises here is whether the Friends of
Psychotherapy, or the patients as individual patients, have
any awareness that the patient role has been subtly shifted
from sufferer in need of help to that of student or guinea pig.
One woman patient who always assumed her therapist "knew
exactly what he was doing" was shocked when she learned of
the disorder and confusion in the field. "If psychotherapy is
research, not treatment," she said, "therapists should be paying the patients!"

LICENSING, CERTIFYING, AND THE
AWARDING OF DIPLOMAS

The American Psychological Association does not grant the
right to private practice to everyone holding a degree. Its
Ethical Code regards as "qualified for independent practice"
only those psychologists who

(a) have been awarded a Diploma by the American Board of Professional Psychology, or (b) have been licensed or certified by state examining boards, or (c) have been certified by voluntary boards established by state psychological associations. Psychologists who do not yet meet the qualifications recognized for independent practice should gain experience under qualified supervision.[47]

Ostensibly, licensing laws have only one purpose: to protect the public from unqualified practitioners.[48] Such laws have been passed in about half of the states, usually as the result of pressure from state psychological associations. Many other states have certification laws.

In actuality, legal sanction is an important step in the process of professionalization. The ceremony establishes the identity of the in-group and clearly distinguishes such persons from "nonprofessional," or "unsanctioned" persons. As Goldenberg states:

A license is a permit to practice clinical psychology, including psychotherapy. To be certified as a psychologist means only that the title "psychologist" may be used by those so certified, but does not restrict others from offering the identical services so long as they do not hold themselves out to the public for a fee as "psychologists."

Both types of laws

recognize the profession's status and respectability . . . [and] protect the public from untrained, unqualified practitioners whom the public had no other way of differentiating from qualified ones.[49]

Obviously, from the point of view of the profession, licensing is preferred. It conveys greater power to its members, since it establishes a monopoly over services. This battle was won for medicine decades ago.

During the early 1970s, the New York State Psychological Association waged a battle for licensing that is said to be "unequaled for sheer drama."[50] Since New York is the "psychotherapy capital of the world," what happens in New York affects a larger proportion of therapists and patients than any other single area. I will examine this recent contest, and what it illuminates about the nature of professional imperialism, primarily through statements concerning the bill proposed by state legislator Peter Biondo.

Biondo's bill was strong. It granted control over the mental health field solely to the professionally credentialed: medical doctors, psychologists with Ph.D.'s, registered psychiatric nurses,* and social workers with masters' degrees. It was supported mainly by the New York State Psychological Association (NYSPA) according to which state legislation was the only reasonable answer to the quackery and abuse visited on the unsuspecting and naive public by "unqualified" practitioners. A few years earlier, NYSPA had stopped an attempt by psychiatry to monopolize the practice of psychotherapy in the state. Now the psychologists were taking a bold step of their own. The stakes were high and time was precious. Professional identity was crucial to attainment of reimbursement for services by insurance companies. It was politically unfeasible not to include medicine, nursing, and social work; it was also essential that action take place as soon as possible. Writing in the New York newspaper, *The Village Voice*, Michael C. Johnson said:

> Prestige, power, money (in the hundreds of millions), and professional survival are the stakes in the fight. . . . [The Biondo Bill] is a weapon of war. By it the New York State Psychological Association (NYSPA) is attempting to equalize itself to the psychiatric establishment, eliminate most . . . non-traditionally trained therapists, and become a major beneficiary of proposed national insurance plans. Thus the goals of the bill are to . . . gain power and control, and make money.[51]

In a letter to the *New York Times*, Harold Riegelman, who chairs the New York City Advisory Council on Alcoholism of the Health Services Administration, said,

---

* A low-paid mostly female group totally omitted in *The Fifth Profession*, but actually responsible for the treatment of more seriously mentally ill patients than any other group.

The Biondo bill is an ill-conceived attempt to use a correctable abuse as a smokescreen to gain a destructive monopoly for a small professional group of clinical psychologists who are ill-suited and unneeded in a critically sensitive area of community service.[52]

The "correctable abuse" was the practice of psychotherapy by noncredentialed persons, some of them defrauding the public with false academic degrees.

It was an issue that made good copy, and it served to put certain politicians in the public eye. After defeat of the Biondo bill in the New York State Senate, Morton Schillinger, NYSPA Executive Director, helped create a publicity campaign to expose abuses by nonprofessionals and bogus degree holders. Over a hundred newspaper and magazine articles were reproduced by NYSPA and distributed to its members as addenda to the organization's official newspaper. The attack was strong:

Because of loopholes in the law, as revealed last week by *The News* . . . unlicensed "psychotherapists" and "psychoanalysts" can use potentially dangerous modes of therapy without any state or professional associational control.[53]

Scores of unlicensed entrepreneurs and unaccredited institutions [were] administering "psychotherapy" and other potentially dangerous and untested modes of treatment for up to $50. an hour.[54]

In the same article, Allen Williams, the executive director of NYSPA at the time, was quoted as saying:

Some hard evidence has accumulated which shows that as many as 8 to 10 percent of those treated psychologically by untrained persons may be permanently or semipermanently damaged.[55]

(This is an interesting statement since estimates of the proportion of patients damaged by credentialed psychodynamic psychotherapists often run higher.)

Kenneth B. Little, executive director of the American Psychological Association, justified licensing because

Those with the proper training are ruled by a code of ethics, and are able to treat and diagnose and are aware of allied medical problems. Someone who is untrained can easily precipitate psychotic episodes and then would not know how to take appropriate action.[56]

Such statements are essentially scare tactics. The code of ethics, while stated in terms of patient welfare, is actually designed to protect the profession, sometimes at the patient's expense. Treatment is unproven. Diagnosis is often worse than useless because of the stigmatization it involves; Karl Menninger and Carl Rogers, among many others, have recommended that it be dispensed with. The warning that "psychotic episodes" can be precipitated by people who do "not know what they are doing" has been issued again and again over the past seventy years to protect the therapist's monopolization of treatment. The tremendous authority vested in the highly trained and licensed professional makes it more likely that if harm is to be done, it will be he who does it.

The professional societies are very poor at self-policing, as abundantly demonstrated in the case of physical medicine. Basically, they are concerned with what shows. More attention may be directed to the problem of a doctor with a neon sign in his yard than to a possible case of unnecessary surgery. The claims that professionals are the only ones able to watch over professional activities is propaganda designed to put controls over practice in the hands of those with vested interests in maintaining a favorable public image for the profession. Public statements about "years of intensive training," "ethical codes," and "highest qualifications" give a particularly false picture of a field in which nobody really knows much about what goes on, or what training is appropriate, or how to distinguish a good therapist from a poor one. But the political difficulty of unseating credentialed professionals is so severe that one psychologist has stated he hopes the field will eventually be handled completely by nonprofessionals who can be better selected and retrained, because they are not autonomous authorities.

The scare campaign thus badly confused the issues, as do most propaganda campaigns. The existence of "diploma mills," "phony degrees," and sexual abuse by "unlicensed" persons have nothing whatever to do with the issue of licensing. Protection of the public from charlatans, quacks, or frauds does not result because "properly trained professionals" are the only ones to be licensed. The issue is not licensing per se. The issue is limiting the right to practice to those who have undergone extensive training when the relevance of that training to effectiveness is dubious, when there is a greater demand for services than can be met by those who would meet licensing requirements, and when experts have recommended the adoption of techniques pioneered by nonprofessionals.

The limited type of licensing sought by professionals would also push the price of psychotherapy services even higher than the present near-prohibitive level. A major goal of any professional in-group is to limit membership, enabling the pie to be sliced in bigger pieces. For decades the AMA severely restricted the number of persons who could receive medical degrees, perpetuating a shortage that drove up the cost of services. Psychologists are currently fighting for similar exploitative powers.

After the Biondo bill was defeated, psychologist George Frank of New York City commented in a letter to the American Psychological Association newspaper, the *APA Monitor:*

> The greatest objection to the Biondo bill was that it rendered unto Caesar (in this instance, psychology) more than that which was Caesar's. In the first place, in spelling out what a psychologist could do, all manner of therapeutic intervention was included, from expertise in psychodrama and sensitivity groups to marriage counseling, family therapy, marathon groups, and psychoanalysis, in addition to traditional individual and group therapy. . . .
>
> To compound that particular error, psychologists were given the authority to supervise the (I must add: legitimate) professionals performing these activities. . . . Making individuals who are not qualified in such techniques supervisors of individuals who are qualified, did not make sense.[57]

Frank was not impressed with the issue of "bogus degrees":

> Yes, it is a shame that in order to appear legitimate in-
> dividuals will purchase a degree. Unfortunately that phe-
> nomenon exists in every profession. However, a Ph.D. in
> Clinical Psychology must, also, be considered a bogus de-
> gree, when the psychologist attempts to extend the area
> of legitimate expertise to areas in which they are not
> qualified.[58]

Many of the abuses by practitioners described in inflam-
matory terms in the press are committed by those very persons who, had the Biondo bill passed, would have stepped
into the protection of a license.

Finally, as Carl Rogers and others have cautioned,
certification and licensing can have adverse effects on the
practices and development of the profession:

> As soon as we set up criteria for certification—whether for
> clinical psychologists . . . for psychoanalysts, or, as I
> heard the other day, for psychic healers—the first and
> greatest effect is to freeze the profession in a past image.[59]

Nor does Rogers accept the notion that licensing in any way
assures competence:

> There are as many *certified* charlatans and exploiters of
> people as there are uncertified.
>   If you had a good friend badly in need of therapeutic
> help, and I gave you the name of a therapist who was a
> Diplomate in Clinical Psychology, with no other informa-
> tion, would you send your friend to him? Of course not.
> . . . So, certification is not equivalent to competence.[60]

The New York psychologists tried for the big prize and
lost due to opposition to their attempt at monopolization
from within their own profession and from those nonprofessionals who would be directly affected. Psychologists in other
states have met with varying degrees of success, usually neither trying for nor obtaining the degree of control the Biondo
bill would have provided. To the professional, licensing restricted to persons holding the designated credentials is crucial.

INSURANCE

Now that national health insurance seems to be coming down the pike, the issue of licensing has become particularly urgent for clinical psychologists. . . . They are anxious to establish their legitimacy as an autonomous profession so that when the jumbled pieces of the current health scene finally form a coherent pattern, they won't find themselves out in the cold—which is to say, subordinate to the medical profession.

CONSTANCE HOLDEN, "Psychology: Clinicians Seek Professional Autonomy"[61]

The licensing issue is among other things, a step toward insurance coverage. Insurance companies are wary about covering the services of clinical psychologists who cannot clearly be differentiated from nonprofessionals and other psychologists. The American Board of Professional Psychologists uses the diplomate for this purpose, and are also developing a National Registry of Health Services Providers in Psychology which would list psychologists who had met their criteria for inclusion.

In most states, Blue Cross-Blue Shield, particularly important since they make up about 40 percent of all health insurance coverage, have failed to cover psychologists unless they work under a physician's supervision. If the "Blues" were induced to reimburse patients for psychotherapy by psychologists, it would be because they viewed psychologists as *medical* personnel. This would in fact represent the self-image of many clinical psychologists themselves.

The position of the clinical psychologists was stated by Jack Wiggins, a private practitioner from Cleveland, and a former chairperson of the American Psychological Association's Committee on Health Insurance. Responding to claims of those who oppose including psychotherapy in health insurance from fear that it would increase insurance rates, Wiggins claimed that "experience has shown that prepaid mental health benefits are inexpensive and cost about $1.00 per month per person."[62] He said that critics of insurance coverage are inconsistent since they have raised no voice in opposition to Veterans Administration programs and other subsidized projects which involve mental diagnosis and treatment. He also questioned "cost-effectiveness." Wiggins asserted that many patients who go to medical doctors go for conditions with "psychological components." If these are not treated, money is wasted. He cited one company insurance program that "found a 55 percent reduction in corporate medical payments after mental diagnosis and treatment became available." Another study found that "people who receive psychotherapy tend to increase their incomes. . . . Psychotherapy not only restores people to health, but would actually pay for itself in National Health Insurance!" Finally, Wiggins noted that the Supreme Court included psychological well-being in its definition of health.

> Therefore, it would be unconscionable if mental health services, including psychotherapy, were not readily and directly available to the public in National Health Insurance. Current insurance contracts frequently favor hospital treatment over outpatient care. Actuarial data reflect this as over-utilization of hospital services and under-utilization of psychotherapy. Substantial savings in human suffering and in health care costs can be achieved if psychotherapy is routinely available in health insurance contracts.[63]

Wiggins's position is predicated on assumptions which this book seriously questions: that psychotherapy is definable, that professional training is necessary, that it is generally helpful when standard techniques are used, and that it is reasonably considered a medical service.

In the same issue of the *APA Monitor*, a case against health insurance coverage of psychotherapy was given by Lloyd Humphreys, a professor of psychology and education at the University of Illinois. Flatly disagreeing with Wiggins's contention that inclusion of psychotherapy could reduce insurance expenses, Humphreys notes that 25 percent of medical disbursements in Sweden goes for treatment of mental and emotional problems. Furthermore, demand and need differ. Working-class people do not present themselves to psychotherapists as often as better educated groups. Demand is highest among members of the mental health professions themselves and among the social circles comprising their Friends and Supporters. Two consequences are: (1) "the added costs attendant on the inclusion of psychotherapy . . . would be borne very heavily by those least able to pay"; (2) as job security in blue-collar workers increases, so would their demand for psychotherapy:

> Assessment of need is very difficult because diagnosis is uncertain, psychotherapeutic techniques are of uncertain validity, the duration of psychotherapy is uncertain, and judgments concerning recovery are, therefore, uncertain. Under these circumstances the demand for psychotherapy can grow in an almost limitless fashion. . . .
>
> Considering the combined uncertainties previously listed, and the present delivery system for psychotherapy, which very largely involves private practice, there is no question that the demand for psychotherapy will skyrocket if the costs are hidden in prepayment plans. The only question with respect to demand is, how long it will take various subgroups in our population to catch on.[64]

Because what psychotherapy is, who is equipped to practice it, and who needs it anyway are all so undetermined, Humphreys opposes insurance coverage paid for by the general population. He recommends the formation of plans for psychotherapy that are separate from those of medical treatments: "Those who wish it, think they might need it, can pay for it."

George Albee, former president of the American Psychological Association, went a step further to ask:

> Would it not make more sense to lobby *against* the coverage of mental illness at all levels and by all groups? It is increasingly difficult to keep secret the fact that "mental illness" is *not* an illness after all, . . . almost everyone knows by now that emotional distresses are not diseases.
> If we were to argue and to lobby against all health in-

surance coverage for psychotherapy we would preserve our competitive position with psychiatry, while at the same time being true to scientific reality.[65]

At the other extreme was the pro-professionalization "Report on Psychology in a National Health Care Plan" presented to the American Psychological Association's Board of Professional Affairs in 1971. Among the dreadful consequences of failing to include psychology in a national health care plan, the report lists "arbitrarily limited" mental health services to the public, psychology's loss of an "effective voice as an independent health profession in decision making and program planning," a possible decrease in funding for research, loss of support for training institutions, reduced in come to psychologists, lowered status for psychology, and loss of any insurance coverage now available. Coverage would bring, among other happy results "leadership roles for psychologists," emphasis on prevention, funding for research and training, and better services for more people. Obviously, inclusion of psychological services in insurance policies is a very partisan issue. The general public gets to hear little more than rhetoric, although it will ultimately bear the cost, financial or any other kind, for whichever policy is adopted.

In a letter to the *Monitor,* Bill McChonochie, a psychologist who described himself as a "new member of the profession," also criticized the trend toward professionalism. He complained that the image of the profession as projected in its own newspaper was of "professionally disenchanted, self-indulging money grubbers."[66] McChonochie was annoyed by the actions and statements of men who organized the Council for the Advancement of the Psychological Professions and Sciences (CAPPS).

CAPPS, an independent political group whose leadership consisted of psychologists in private practice, came into being in 1971, and immediately initiated vigorous activity aimed at establishing professional identification in Washington and credibility with lawmakers. According to CAPPS, lawmakers tended to be ignorant about psychology as a profession. CAPPS aimed to have psychologists enjoy the same rights and privileges as psychiatrists. Its organizers wanted psychologists to be identified with psychiatrists rather than with paraprofessionals in the public eye and in national health insurance legislation. In 1973, CAPPS initiated a "multimillion-dollar lawsuit" against Blue Cross-Blue Shield. In a letter to psychologists requesting contributions to the "cause," Robert D. Weitz, who chaired CAPPS's executive committee, pleaded:

> To you who have not yet responded to the first appeal, again I ask for your support. The "class action" suit against the "Blues" is being undertaken primarily to establish the principle that the public shall have free choice and direct access to professional psychological services. We wish to do away with the Blues' present requirement for compulsory medical "supervision" of psychologists and medical "referral"—practices which are obviously unethical, unnecessarily costly to the public, and degrading to the profession. The autonomy of psychology is at stake. Your financial support of the suit is still needed. I urge you, in your own best interest to write out a check immediately. . . .[67]

Requested support from the American Psychological Association was not available since the Association has set up its own political action group after some bitter correspondence and angry confrontations between the two organizations. This, in the last analysis, reflected the basic and inevitable conflict between persons committed to a search for scientific understanding, and who do not profit economically from psychotherapy, and those who further their own financial interests through professionalization at the expense of other concerns. Many predict an ultimate separation between the two, and the establishment of separate professional training programs away from the heavy emphasis on science and academia of present clinical psychology programs.

Clinical psychologists operating in accord with the highly criticized medical model of psychodynamic "illness" today stand on shaky ground both professionally and scientifically. They will undoubtedly continue their activities until the public itself turns its back on them. Without the medical model, without the professionalization that partakes of mystification and exploitation of the public, applied psychologists could in fact serve truly important functions, particularly in assisting other professionals and members of the general public in the utilization of psychological knowledge. But as former president of the American Psychological Association George Albee has pointed out, such "giving away" of psychology uses methods exactly opposite from those which protect a professional elite. Psychology would take psychotherapy away from nonprofessionals; psychiatry would capture it for itself alone. Professional psychologists are fighting for inclusion as autonomous providers of service under national health insurance. Psychiatrists, as represented by their national organization, have gone on record recommending that all mental health services be under medical supervision. The *American Psychiatric Association Guidelines for Psychiatric Services Covered Under Health Insurance Plans, Second Edition,* states:

> Covered psychiatric services should include such services rendered by licensed physicians; as noted earlier, it is recommended that whenever possible, the services of a psychiatrist should be utilized. . . . Services of other mental health professionals should also be covered when these services are carried out with the meaningful collaboration of a physician and under his supervision or with his authorization.[68]

The result of such a policy is a "pseudoshortage" of professional personnel which leads to higher fees for services. It is another example of artificially created scarcity of services provided through professional territorialism. Although professionals other than psychiatrists and nonprofessionals have been found not to differ from psychiatrists in psychotherapy effectiveness, the psychiatric profession's proposal would allow total control of mental health services by psychiatry. Others could work only under medical "supervision," which, in fact, usually turns out to mean simple fee-splitting. Psychiatrists see many patients briefly, or may simply give their signatures on the case records. For this "service" they receive fees many times greater than the social workers, nurses, or nonprofessionals who provide any actual service the patient receives. This is abusive in physical medicine; it is inexcusable in psychiatry. In their article, "Mental Health Coverage Under a National Health Insurance Plan," psychiatrists Robert L. Taylor and E. Fuller Torrey of the National Institutes of Mental Health point out that duration of patient service varies with the ability to obtain profits rather than with patient need. They cite evidence that hospitalization is not only *not* beneficial in the majority of cases, but that when the money is available, psychiatric hospitalization, in which goals and criteria of improvement are vague, may be unnecessarily prolonged. Furthermore, insurance coverage for psychiatric hospitalization has led to admissions of persons with less severe disturbances, especially women and young persons. Just as a well-equipped army is said to be itself a cause of war, empty beds and insurance coverage are themselves causes of hospitalization. I have already discussed the stigmatization that results from a background of psychiatric treatment. It is greatly intensified when there has been hospitalization.

FEES

In a 1973 study, patients and former patients reported that they paid higher fees per session to psychotherapists with M.D.'s ($34) than to those with Ph.D.'s ($26), higher fees to Ph.D.'s than to therapists with only a master's degree ($14), higher fees to male therapists ($30) than to women ($18), and higher fees for psychoanalysis ($30) and "eclectic" therapy ($32) than for "supportive" therapy ($20).[60] Since the study included university counseling centers and clinics which charge very low fees and sometimes do not charge at all, these averages are lower than they would be if only private practitioners were included. The old "standard fee" of $25 per hour is now a standard of $50.* The private female patient must be in a position to pay, or have someone

---

* The high fee from the patient's point of view yields a low income for psychiatrists relative to other M.D.'s. Among psychological service providers, those in private fee-for-service practice report the highest income (see Alan Boneau, "Private Practice Pays Handsomely").

else pay, as much or more for long-term "intensive" psychotherapy as for a college education.[70]

Psychologist Norbett L. Mintz, of the United States Public
Health Service, wrote in 1971 that psychotherapists tend to
be defensive on the subject of the fees they charge their patients:

> It is remarkable how little has been written on this subject
> [of fees] and how infrequently it is presented in a formal
> manner in training programs. I have reviewed the indexes
> of several dozen books dealing with such issues as the
> training of psychotherapists, the practice of psychotherapy,
> the technique of psychotherapy, etc. Most often there was
> no listing for the subject of patient fees, nor for other fi-
> nancial transactions with the therapy situation.[71]

Mintz finds a significant relationship between the development of private-practice psychotherapy "in societies whose
economic basis overexaggerated the importance of a market-
place economy, the sanctity of personal property, and
the privateness of one's financial dealings," and the attitudes
of psychotherapists toward their financial transactions with
patients. Freud's idea was that money is linked subcon-
sciously with sex, and therefore prudishness about the subject is expected, but Mintz notes that psychotherapists who
answered questionnaires were not particularly reluctant to
talk about sex itself. In one cited study more therapists found
it conceivable that they might more openly express anger toward a patient (90 percent) or deliberately stimulate her sexually (50 percent) than either loan money to a patient or ask
for advance payments as a way of borrowing (less than 25
percent). In a letter to Hans Strupp, Kenneth M. Colby also
wondered about the silence of psychotherapists on the subject of money:

> Most psychotherapy is paid for. Yet no one considers
> money as a relevant variable. I believe it has many non-
> trivial implications for what happens in therapy. Therapists
> among themselves talk about sex freely. But when money,
> fees, incomes of therapists, etc. come up everyone has a
> good (but uneasy) laugh. The fact that it is *not* dealt with
> in research means to me that there is something there we
> are not honestly facing.[72]

These recent reactions of Mintz, Colby, and others contrast with the treatment of fees in the traditional literature. It is not that the subject was never discussed. When clinicians talked about fees, it usually was in the context of the psychogenesis or underlying dynamic of the patient's complaints, or about missed-session policies. Or they presented the elaborate rationalizations which have been developed, especially by psychoanalysts, often given in loftily moralistic tones. From the patient-aimed book *The Talking Cure* comes the following dialogue:

> TEACHER: Could a poor teacher like me afford to go to a psychoanalyst?
>
> ANALYST: Money *is* a weighty consideration, but the fees most analysts charge are not large, considering the training involved. Analytic training alone, after the student's graduate degree, costs between $15,000 and $20,000, and sometimes as much as $35,000, because the personal training analysis and the supervised or control analysis must be paid for by the student and are always done by experienced, and therefore expensive, psychoanalysts.[73]

When the teacher observes that the average analysis would cost about $10,000, and wonders whether she could afford that on her salary, the psychoanalyst's reply is a remarkable extension into fantasy. As usual, he begins by answering a question with a question:

> Why do you feel it necessary to pay for treatment out of your income? After all, you wouldn't hesitate to dip into your savings for an operation, if it was necessary. Ordinarily, we prefer analysis to be paid for out of income, rather than savings, yet this is not a rigid rule. It can be viewed as an investment, as a college education is, which will pay dividends for the rest of your life, and you could consider borrowing the money for it, from a member of your family, perhaps, or a friend.[74]

The paying of fees is considered to be an aspect of therapy itself with positive benefits to the patient. In the *Archives of General Psychiatry* George M. Burnell writes that

One of the rationales of many psychiatrists who are charging patients a "reasonable, but substantial" fee is that it gives the patient the "opportunity" to participate actively in [the] treatment program. This argument, despite lack of scientific proof, is felt to be so valid that it is still carried over to patients seen in publicly supported clinics. Further justification by some clinicians lies in the old adage "Therapy is more likely to benefit the patient if it hurts a little."[75]

Burnell cites figures that indicate the rise in fees: in 1960, 20 percent of psychotherapists charged $30 or more per session; by 1968, 56 percent charged that much. Some therapists justify high fees by the respect they create for the therapist. It has also been said that the "suffering" the therapist is exposed to by his patients requires adequate compensation.

Psychiatrist Richard D. Chessick, who manages to be both an advocate and critic of psychotherapy, contrasts the errors of a novice with the "mature" behavior of the experienced psychotherapist. In an unusually open discussion of some of the more thorny problems that arise in relation to paying for psychotherapy, Chessick said the "ominous" message "that psychotherapists are, in a sense, prostitutes"[76] who sell themselves to patients is contained in the title of Schofield's well-known book, *Psychotherapy: The Purchase of Friendship*. Chessick does not agree, as some have suggested, that patients should be "manipulated" by therapists who "do them a favor" by charging a low fee or "accelerating the therapy" through an unusually high fee. (Acceleration of therapy, if it is possible, seems a justifiable goal. A higher per-session fee but a shorter duration might cost less in the end, and less time.) Chessick continues:

The mature psychotherapist does not sell friendship. . . . He sells his time and the professional skill acquired by virtue of his training and ability. If he tries to sell anything other than this professional skill he is, in my opinion, engaging in narcissistic countertransference acting out.[77]

These are frighteningly strong words in the psychoanalytic lexicon. Countertransference may also be a problem if the therapist charges a very high fee to his wealthy patients.

Chessick thinks that fees should be discussed with patients frankly. But a therapist should not undertake to treat a patient who cannot afford the fee except in a clinic situation, because "countertransference problems begin to pile up" later on in treatment when there are others on the waiting list who would yield more financial return.

The least disturbed patients, those who benefit least from therapy, pay the highest fees. Often, such patients regard their therapy not as treatment for illness but as a facilitator of "personal growth." They are also the preferred patients, the ones from whom the therapist derives "greatest satisfaction." According to Cornell University research psychiatrist Arthur K. Shapiro, "the profit motive has been conspicuously unexplored and may be a significant determinant of the therapist's interest in the treatment, patient, and results."[78]

The fees can themselves adversely affect the patient in several ways. Patients may be forced to live a restricted existence because of the large dent in resources made by therapy. This can limit or prevent such pleasures as entertainment, education, children, and even marriage. Fees can also lead to professional corruption. Viscott tells of a psychiatrist who gives all his insured patients electric shock treatment: the costs are "covered" by the policies, and the treatments consume very little of the therapist's time.[79] As a young psychiatrist just out of residency, Viscott began private practice by taking over the schedule of another psychotherapist: "I studied my appointment book during my first free hour and figured out that if I just followed my schedule I would net over eleven hundred dollars after all expenses! That was just my first week!"[80]

Freud spoke of "shame" as a reason for the therapist's reluctance generally to discuss money matters. Schofield has suggested that maybe this shame is because "the sale of friendship" is more prevalent than can be comfortably acknowledged publicly.[81] But "selling friendship," if it occurs, is probably among the least of psychotherapy's sins.

5
The Mad Ride

PROFESSIONAL VARIETIES

Although every member of the reading public must surely have some awareness of the current multiplicity of "orientations" to psychotherapy by professionals, up to this point I have not differentiated among them. Therapists very often describe their approach as eclectic: any treatment which "works" in a particular situation for a particular patient may be tried. Or "although my orientation is basically psychoanalytic, I am not rigidly attached to any one system." Therapists sometimes make sharp *theoretical* distinctions, but usually they do not even do that. Research has again and again failed to find methods, techniques, or even results consistently based on a therapist's espoused school or system. Therapists do differ from one another, but their professional training, their credentials or lack of credentials, and the theoretical positions they adhere to are poor indicators of the real differences.

The purpose of this chapter is to provide at least a glimpse of the current scene and its profusion, without attempting full descriptions or analyses of theoretical positions or details of practice. The well-known psychiatrist Roy Grinker said that "psychiatry rides madly in all directions."[1] But, in fact, most psychotherapy professionals in private practice still (1) protect "the profession" as the source of credentials through "ethical codes," membership in professional societies and organizations, and in their behavior before their clients and the public;* (2) deemphasize or altogether ignore social contributions to the individual's problems and assume personal causation;[2] and (3) belong to professions without true regulatory functions and therefore enjoy essential unaccountability.

A quarter of a century ago, it was said that there were thirty-six distinct therapeutic systems used by traditionally trained and credentialed professional psychotherapists.[3] In 1966 Saul I. Harrison and Donald J. Carek, in *A Guide to Psychotherapy*, listed sixty-nine methods, and Carl Rogers recently estimated that the number exceeds a hundred. In fact it is even more than that, if minor variations and combinations of techniques are included.

Perhaps vagueness in theoretical approach is not surprising in a field where vagueness of methods and objectives prevails. "Eclectic" has one advantage. New methods are continually being presented directly to the public in books, magazines, and through the electronic media. To commit oneself to a particular method might rule out a method popular in the public eye.

Routes from the discovery of a psychotherapy technique to its widespread use are given in the following diagram. In the old way, some time elapsed between the discovery of a method and its general acceptance and widespread use. During that time, the profession had an opportunity to further elaborate and evaluate the innovation. In the new way, the "system" is presented directly to the public, creating a demand long before scientific research or even clinical evaluation by the originator or by others can be conducted. Thus

* Some therapists who reach their clientele directly through popular writings are exceptions. Such persons are not dependent on referrals from colleagues.

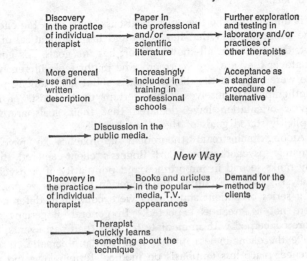

Old Way

| Discovery in the practice of individual therapist | → | Paper in the professional and/or scientific literature | → | Further exploration and testing in laboratory and/or practices of other therapists |

| → | More general use and written description | → | Increasingly included in training in professional schools | → | Acceptance as a standard procedure or alternative |

| → | Discussion in the public media. |

New Way

| Discovery in the practice of individual therapist | → | Books and articles in the popular media, T.V. appearances | → | Demand for the method by clients |

| → | Therapist quickly learns something about the technique |

psychotherapy has become an "anything goes" situation in which claim to professional status depends increasingly on credentials, no matter how irrelevant the training on which they are based. It is understandable that this era of supermarket psychotherapy is also one in which pressure for licensing has escalated. Everything else about psychotherapy is vague and undefined. Credentials have become the only available handle on the situation, the only thing that gives it structure.

Therapists differ in technique, theory, and goals. According to Goldenberg:

Freud's ultimate goal for his patients was simply the ability to love and work. The client-centered therapist . . . seeks to promote the client's growth, maturity, spontaneity, and creativity by helping [her] release [her] natural inner resources and potential. Sullivan's followers, who stress the importance of interpersonal relations in normal development, see as their goal each patient's ability to integrate all parts of [her] self-esteem (including all parts previously rejected as the "bad me"), to reduce [her] loneliness, and to reach out and try to become closely related to others. . . .[4]

It is unusual for the therapist to discuss goals with the client. She assumes either that her goals and his are identical or, if not, that he, as an all-knowing seer, has *the* goals. His goals, whatever they are, are "correct." She might feel differently if she were aware of the disagreements about goals among psychotherapists themselves. Only certain psychologists of behavior orientation have declared that their goals are the explicitly stated goals of the client herself.

Among mainstream theoretical approaches to psychodynamic psychotherapy, Carl Rogers's client-centered therapy ranks second in importance and popularity after psychoanalysis.* When Freudian and Rogerian therapists' responses to a series of patient statements were compared, differences were not as great as expected.[5] In general, Rogerians are more concerned with immediate feelings than past events, involve the client in less intense and less "problematic" transference, place less emphasis on medical terminology and diagnosis, engage in scientific research, and stress counselor qualities of empathy, acceptance, and positive regard for the client. The goal of therapy is self-actualization, or growth, which can best be achieved in a permissive, nonjudgmental counseling relationship in which the therapist reflects back the client's feelings. This acts as a catalyst to the development of the client's inherent potentialities.[6] Rogers urged his followers to refrain from "directive" behaviors such as advice-giving and making psychoanalytic interpretations. Rogerian writing is filled with phrases such as "truly free," "actualize one's nature as an organ of awareness," and "move toward wholeness and integration."

Rogerian therapy is the most influential of the "phenomenological" approaches in which behavior stems from and is appropriate to, not objective reality, but the world as experienced and perceived by the individual. Other major figures in phenomenological therapy are "humanists"

* For a brief but thorough description of Rogerian therapy and other types, see C. H. Patterson, *Theories of Counseling and Psychotherapy* (New York, Harper & Row, 1966).

Abraham Maslow and Erich Fromm, existentialist Rollo May, and Gestalt therapist Fritz Perls. Of these, Fromm, May, and Perls influenced the lay public directly through their writings. Although they appeared as a welcome relief from the Freudians' interpretations and assumptions of a human nature driven by sexual and aggressive instincts, the phenomenological therapies remain insight therapies, and, as much as psychoanalysis itself, are based on theories which are recalcitrant to scientific investigation.

In his presidential address to the British Psychological Society in 1973, Professor Max Hamilton of the Department of Psychiatry, University of Leeds, complained that when clinical psychologists took up the practice of psychotherapy, they threw "away their one great asset: scientific method." The change did not foster scientific advances, of course, but it did bring money into their pockets—particularly to those in private practice. Hamilton said:

> The retreat from Science has become clearer in recent years with the development of Existentialist and so-called Humanistic psychiatry and psychology. Based on these systems, new methods of therapy have been developed and proclaimed with religious fervour, and when outsiders like myself ask for proof of their efficiency, we are not given evidence. Instead we are faced with a complete rejection of science and with claims that proof and experiment are irrelevant. Nothing equals the Messianic delusions of these saviours of humanity, except the almost identical claims of the psychoanalysts, made at the beginning of this century. *Plus ça change, plus c'est la même chose.*[1]

Given the subjectivity of Rogerian therapy, it is ironic that Rogers himself has been a major participant in attempts to evaluate psychotherapy scientifically. In 1939 he fought and won a lonely battle with psychiatry for the right to practice psychotherapy. He did not forget his scientific training and, in 1956, was given an award for scientific contribution to psychology. In 1974 he said of this: "It was a vivid proof that psychologists were not only embarrassed by me, but were to some extent proud of me. It had a greater personal meaning than all the honors which have followed."[8]

But Rogers is unique. Among phenomenological psychologists, it has been mainly Rogers himself, and a few of his followers, who have tried to keep scientific inquiry alive in psychotherapy.

INTERACTIONAL PSYCHOTHERAPY: AN EXAMPLE OF A SYSTEM

It is often noted that scientific theories are not discarded simply for being invalid. Being false is not sufficient for rejection; replacement occurs only when a more satisfying theory comes along. This may explain the endurance of psychoanalysis and its psychodynamic offshoots. Freud's true genius was his ability to appeal to the public and the profession with just the right type and number of uncommon terms and rituals of practice. It has become fashionable among therapists to claim independence from the strictures of "orthodox Freudianism," but any deviations are often trivial. The couch is eschewed, the therapist talks, even directively, he gives advice, encourages changes, holds that a "will to power," a "striving toward self-actualization," the formation of an "idealized self-image," not repression of aggressive and sexual instincts, is the core of human psychic functioning. Therapy proceeds, according to the claims, in a manner which meets the needs of the individual patient; many techniques may be utilized. But the modifications and innovations in theory and in guidelines for practice have not really changed individual interview psychotherapy greatly. The contribution made by the personality of the therapist, qualities of behavior possessed before training and retained despite it, makes the potential for harm or for help unpredictable through mere knowledge of a therapist's orientation.

University of Massachusetts psychologist Sheldon Cashdan, in *Interactional Psychology: Stages and Strategies in Behavioral Change*, attempts to "depict the ways in which the therapist uses himself as a therapeutic tool—as a professional who allows himself to be temporarily used for the benefit of others."[9] Cashdan notes that while psychotherapies may differ, the interpersonal relationship is, as Franz Alexander noted, central to the therapeutic process.

For Cashdan, therapy takes place in five distinguishable stages, each of which "involves certain therapist techniques as well as some sort of incremental change on the part of the client."[10] In the first stage, "hooking," the therapist becomes a "warm," "caring," "significant" figure for the patient. The patient-therapist relationship created during this stage fills "a motivational void": it provides "the client with a motive for remaining in therapy later," when "the going gets rough," and anxiety or other complaints may have disappeared:

> Faced with disquieting insights and painful confrontations, there often arises a temptation to bolt which, if acted upon, could lead to premature termination. . . . The client remains in treatment not because of great psychological pain, not because of esoteric notions involving personal growth, but because [she] has become very invested in the therapist.[11]

The main therapist strategies for accomplishing hooking are "advising" and "emotional coupling," in which the client is convinced that the therapist understands and sympathizes with her. In emotional coupling,

> The therapist takes what is essentially a factual report, extracts what appears to be the emotional reaction associated with it, and mirrors it for the client.
>
> Application of the emotional coupling rule leads to a variety of statements that take the form of:
> "It makes you *happy* when you talk about _____."
> "You seem *upset* whenever the subject of _____ comes up."
> "You're really *annoyed* at _____."
> "_____ makes you *embarrassed*."
> Such comments function to persuade the client that the therapist is capable of appreciating what [she] really is experiencing.[12]

It is a relatively simple matter to "guess right." Most statements reflect some feeling, and there are usually nonverbal indicants such as rapid breathing, blushing, weeping, or tone of voice which are giveaways to identifying the right feeling. Furthermore, many feelings are mixed; they contain emotional dualities: for example, hate implies love; dominance, submission; coldness, warmth; and so on.

The therapist is on fairly safe ground if he alludes to the presence of one whenever the other is being overemphasized.

This is demonstrated in the following excerpt in which a recently divorced young woman bitterly describes her ex-husband:

> Cl: He used to . . . drink . . .
> (long pause)
> Th: . . . and . . .
> Cl: . . . the bum beat me . . .
> Th: . . . and . . .
> Cl: . . . he really didn't care about the family . . .
> Th: . . . and you wish you had him back.
> The client immediately began sobbing.[13]

Advising might be somewhat more tricky:

> Since the primary concern is to hook the client, the therapist must be careful not to offer advice that is likely to result in failure or in other ways compromise his position as a "significant" figure.[14]

The therapist is in little danger when his "advice" merely supports a decision already made.

> The knack involves offering suggestions only when they have a high probability of success to make sure that an "out" is available should they fail. The "out" entails subtly placing the responsibility for whatever action is taken squarely in the client's lap. Thus, such advice as:
> "Why don't you try to be a little more outspoken with your mother?"
> should be more properly phrased:
> "It seems to me that you *would like* to be a little more outspoken with your mother."[15]

Through the use of the second statement, the therapist escapes blame if the suggestion turned out to be a poor one. Generally, the "rule" of advising during the hooking stage means making comments in the forms:

"It seems to me that you want to. . . ."
"You might want to go ahead and act on *your* wish
to. . . ."
"If you decide that way, you *could* go ahead and. . . ."
By placing the locus of responsibility in the client, the
therapist avoids losing the client's confidence if the advice
fails.[16]

Cashdan is unusually open about therapist strategies, but one
suspects that his "rules" for hooking bear an uncomfortable
resemblance to codified principles of salesmanship. Acting to
induce a relationship while pretending spontaneous warmth
and genuineness is dishonesty practiced on persons who may
be particularly vulnerable to its effects.

Having established a need in the client for this particular
interpersonal relationship, the therapist is able to continue
through four succeeding stages. In the second, the therapist
(here, quite unlike the Freudian) leads "the client to the
present whenever [she] is mired in the past and into the
therapy room whenever [she] gravitates to events outside of
it."[17] The objective is to get the client to focus on the relationship between herself and the psychotherapist to establish
the "here and now." The therapist is advised to use direct
confrontation, in which the client's conditional statement is
transformed into a statement about the therapeutic relationship:

> Thus, when the client says:
> "I wonder what you'd think *if* I ever started crying in
> here?" The therapist replies:
> "I think you feel like crying in here."[18]

Cashdan concludes his discussion of this stage by saying:

> In sum, the goal in Stage Two is to transform vague and
> conditional versions of the dependency, sexuality, and
> martyr strategies into unambiguous declarations. . . .[19]

"Dependency strategies" on the client's part often involve
"tidbit-telling" in which "the client monotonously recapitu-
lates life's minor trials and tribulations." The therapist begins to feel "pestered, put upon, and annoyed, . . . the nat-

ural response for one who is on the receiving end of a dependency strategy."[20] "Sexual strategies" are identified by Cashdan by such behaviors as:

Detailed descriptions of promiscuous behavior
Hiking skirt or dress well up on thighs
Wearing suggestive clothing (low-cut or tight-fitting garments)
Unsolicited descriptions of deep versus clitoral orgasm
Repeated reference to restrictive sexual mores, etc.[21]

But, he continues, "perhaps the best subjective indication of its presence in the therapy is sexual arousal—on the part of the therapist."[22] Unfortunately, Cashdan gives no suggestions about how a therapist can differentiate between a sexual seduction strategy by the client and sexual arousal in the therapist that is not the result of a client strategy. In fact, he does not even attempt to make a distinction: "Explanations regarding transference and countertransference notwithstanding, most sexual strategists will have little difficulty arousing even the most 'adjusted' therapist. Sex, after all, is the sexual strategist's stock in trade."[23]

Dependency and sexuality are only two of the "maladaptive" strategies. The third is the "martyr" strategy in which the client says such things as:

"I'm suffering more than ever."

"If someone only knew what I'm going through."

"I went through hell last week."[24]

Such comments make Cashdan feel guilty but, again, he says, the therapist's subjective reaction "only validate[s] the fact that the therapist has been targeted." Just as feelings of annoyance and sexual arousal, respectively, function as subjective indications of targeting in the dependency and sexuality strategies, so guilt feelings fulfill this role in the martyr strategy.[25] Thus the therapist invariably "knows" how the client feels by reading his own emotional reactions!

The "maladaptive" strategies are permitted the client only temporarily. In Stage Three, they are stripped away by the therapist's refusal to relate to the client on the client's terms.

The therapist initiates Stage Three "by abandoning the role of target and attacking the client's strategies through silences, sarcasm, and other techniques designed to directly deny the client's exploitative demands."[26] The examples Cashdan gives of third stage "refutation" of client strategies by the therapist seems likely to elicit reactions of hurt and anger, and a feeling by the client that she has been insulted and abused. The young woman who wondered whether or not she should wear flat-heeled shoes was told, "Doesn't it strike you as kind of silly, our spending time discussing what kind of shoes you should wear?"[27] and, "I have the feeling you'd make up some problem for me if one didn't actually exist."[28] Another woman made the mistake of inviting the therapist to dinner. She was told, "I think there's more to you than just getting in your pants. . . . Let's not play games."[29] Small wonder that clients at this stage respond with "violent personal attacks marked by sobbing, shouting, and sometimes even depression."[30] Cashdan continues:

> Along the way, the therapist is subjected to accusations that take the form of:
> Cl: You treat me like an object!
> Cl: Who told you you could help anyone!
> Cl: You've only made things worse!
> Cl: You sadistic S. O. B.[31]

The same client behaviors (seeking advice, for example) which are encouraged in stage one are severely punished in stage three after client has been "hooked" into a need for the relationship with the therapist. Cashdan reports that the "interesting" phenomenon of "pseudotermination" often occurs at this point. The client assumes that therapy is finished:

> In their hurt and confusion, they mistake the annihilation of their strategy for the annihilation of the relationship.
> When this happens, it is necessary to affirm the relationship. The therapist does this by emphasizing his commitment to the client and the treatment process. . . .[32]

The therapist may say

> Th: I'll be here for our appointment next week.

or

> Th: I'm keeping this hour open for you.[33]

Cashdan says that this stage in the process is "also difficult for the therapist. Faced with a chagrined, frustrated and frightened individual, the therapist does not know from moment to moment whether the client will stay in treatment."[34] The importance of initial hooking procedures are here reaffirmed.

Finally, the client, or at least many clients, arrives at stage four; Adaptive Strategies, in which the client begins to gain insight into how her behavior affects others and prevents her from maintaining meaningful relationships. The client begins to tell very personal things, a process Cashdan calls "risky revealing," and the therapist interprets the client's "strategic maneuvers." He comments on her aggressiveness, her attempts at seduction, her tone of voice, or her facial expressions—always emphasizing the way he, the therapist, responds to them. In Cashdan's terms, he provides "transactional feedback" which may take the form of:

> Th: Do you know that you have a tendency to
> _____?[35]
>
> or
>
> Th: You really turn me off when you _____.[36]

Such responses are accepted and assimilated, although at an earlier stage of therapy they would not have been. The purpose of this is to clue the client in on how she appears to others.

Stage Five is, of course, "unhooking" or "termination," and Cashdan boasts that in "interpersonal therapy" it is easier than in some other types: "There are many therapists that drone on monotonously year after year simply because the therapist has become too much of a fixture in the client's life or because the therapist cannot let go."[37] After a few dead-end discussions and some lengthy silences, the client is expected to stop coming and she "usually does."

Although the terms used are different, and the interactional psychotherapist engages in specific and deliberate actions, Cashdan's description of the courses of therapy and his recommendations of therapist behaviors ("strategies") bear gross resemblance to descriptions by psychoanalytic writers.[38] Perhaps Cashdan has crassly explicated what other therapists talked of only over lunch or in the cloak rooms at conventions. He himself seems to believe that he has merely set down what is actually done. Meant as a textbook for therapists, to the patient it reads like an exposé.

GROUP THERAPY

Group psychotherapy . . . is the most vitally alive, currently most popular, and clinically most effective approach to civilized man's quest for self and community improvement.[39]

GEORGE R. BACH AND YETT M. BERNARD,
"Deserts and Oases"

The group therapy movement has grown to such phenomenal proportions, especially in the last two decades, that it must be discussed, however briefly.

Group therapy was initially controversial, and no wonder: psychoanalytic psychotherapy was essentially transference therapy; insight and hence therapeutic gain was directly attributed to this one-to-one relationship. Analytic patients were specifically requested not to discuss their fantasies, dreams, or inner thoughts with family members or friends lest they dilute the transference relationship. Although the idea of a therapy in groups may seem commonsensical—the group is more similar to everyday reality and allows for observing others, trying out new ways of interacting, and receiving a wider range of reactions to one's own behavior—it does not fit at all well with the original principles of individual psychotherapy. Yet, even as early as 1945, every school of psychotherapy was involved in group psychotherapy. Although there were a few systems that used group methods exclusively, group therapy did not arise as a separate system in itself. There were psychoanalytic groups as well as other types. This development is remarkable and inexplicable in theoretical terms. The explanation is economic.

Groups, which traditionally range in size from five or six to as many as ten or twelve, enable the patient to pay less money and the therapist to receive more money, all at the same time. In the face of this consideration, discussion was closed. Today little of the controversy can be found in current literature. Like General Motors and McDonald's hamburgers, group therapy is accepted, even by those for whom one might naively assume it could not logically be tolerated. As one group therapist said, "You can't argue with success."

Financial success, yes. What about scientific evidence of effectiveness? In many ways, the picture is like that of individual therapy—few studies, inadequate controls, disagreement over criteria—but worse. Psychotherapy research psychologists Richard L. Bednar and G. Frank Lawlis stated in their 1971 article "Empirical Research in Group Psychotherapy":

> Few areas in psychology are characterized by as diffuse experimentation as group psychotherapy. This may partly be the result of a practical interest in specific areas, but mainly it represents the elementary status of group psychotherapy as a scientific discipline. Most of the literature is not experimental in nature, but rather descriptive of therapists' experience or recommendations.[40]

Bednar and Lawlis found evidence of "deterioration effects," and concluded that group therapy is a "two-edged sword that can both help and hinder client adjustment."[41] It has also been suggested that in contrast to psychoanalytic expectations, when group therapy is helpful it is interpersonal reaction, not the therapist's verbalizations or expressed "insights" that produce the benefits.[42]

Group therapy was widely accepted as an adjunct to traditional psychotherapy in the 1950s, but it was clearly a second-runner to the real thing, individual psychoanalytic psychotherapy. The 1960s saw the steady development of what psychoanalyst Donald M. Kaplan has pejoratively termed "pop psychology."[43] Pop psychology is undeniably a group movement or, rather, a movement of groups, and innovator Carl Rogers is its most famed and respected exponent.

THE POP GROUP MOVEMENT

You *say* pass the salt, but I *hear* you say you feel
neglected.

An encounter group leader[44]

The most evident difference today seems to lie between
those therapists who believe that "real therapy" requires
insightful connection of present behavior with its origins in
early childhood (analysis of transference) and those who
believe that just as fundamental improvement takes place
in patients without examining life-history, as a consequence of the operation of group norms, and authentic interpersonal encounters in the "here and now."

GOODWIN WATSON, "Growing Edges in Groups"[45]

When the swing away from psychoanalytic insight-giving
group therapies to "here and now" encounter groups occurred in the late sixties, the idea of groups for the "therapy"
treatment of emotionally disturbed persons was largely abandoned in favor of the concept of groups for "growth."
Frederick H. Stoller, codeveloper of the marathon group,
describes the new clientele:

> They were members of a different kind of group, one of
> the new intense encounter groups whose goal was explora-
> tion rather than ours, and whose orientation was self-
> education rather than the amelioration of psychopathology.
> Many techniques of the new group are not dissimilar from
> traditional psychotherapy, but the assumption made about
> the members is that they are *not* sick. . . . Everyone can
> benefit from experimentation with new ways of behavior
> and new social arrangements, and the most effective
> groups are made up of "chronic undifferentiated peo-
> ple."[46]

Stoller describes the groups as both "explosive" and
"unpredictable." In a marthon, "dramatic, frightening, moving exchanges are likely to occur. Tears and threats are not

uncommon." According to another advocate writing in the underground press:

> The typical encounter group runs through three phases:
> these may interpenetrate but usually appear in this order:
> a) Coming into the body and into the here and now.
>   (Almost entirely nonverbal)
> b) Encounters with others.
>   (Partly verbal, partly nonverbal)
> c) Encounters with the self.
>   (More verbal, partly nonverbal)[47]

As described by British psychologist Rowan Bayne of the University of Aberdeen:

> Generally, encounter groups . . . emphasize an experience, or getting "turned-on" rather than change per se. Although the participants face a very ambiguous situation, there is some structure. They have agreed to stay together for a certain period, to exclude alcohol, not to make use of physical violence or tact, and that all events are confidential—it is important that people hold to these and think the others will too. Then there is a wide range of possible exercises, from jumping up and down bellowing (which is exhilarating and could be tried before and during all meetings) to more exotic ones. . . .[48]

Participants in encounter groups engage in such activities as: communicating by touch alone, humming, free associating, engaging in "games" or exercises, reacting to one another. William C. Schutz, psychologist, and author of *Joy: Expanding Human Awareness* describes some of his techniques:

> *Feeling Space.* All members of the group are asked to gather close together, either sitting on the floor (which is preferable) or sitting in chairs. They then are asked to close their eyes and stretching out their hands, "feel their space"—all the space in front of them, over their heads, behind their backs, below them—and then be aware of their contact with others as they overlap and begin to touch each other. This procedure is allowed to continue for about five minutes.[49]

> *Milling.* The leader of the group stands up, moves a few feet away from the group, and states, "I would like you to

get up, one at a time, and walk toward me and keep walking in any direction you want. Stop wherever you feel most comfortable. Don't try to figure out where you want to be. Just let your body lead you to where it wants to go. If you don't feel like settling, keep milling around. When others come near, you may feel like turning, moving away, moving toward them, or staying still. Do what you feel. We will just continue milling until everyone is located somewhere, or is constantly moving." The group leader follows his own instructions. When the group members have completed this task, they usually sit down and discuss the experience.[50]

Pushing. The two participants stand facing each other and clasp both hands, palm to palm, intertwining fingers. When they agree, they begin pushing each other, attempting to make the other give ground. They stop whenever they want to.[51]

Breaking out. The group forms a tight circle, interlocking arms. If the group is very large, members form two concentric circles. One person stands in the middle of the inner circle and must break out in any way [she] can, over, under, or bursting through. Members of the circle try their utmost to contain [her] and not let [her] out.[52]

In "Give and Take Affection," participants tell the member who is the momentary focus of attention whatever good feelings they have about the person. Or, in a nonverbal variant, the focal person stands with lips closed in the center of a circle while others express position feelings one at a time through "hugging, stroking, massaging, lifting, or whatever each person feels." Schutz cautions that "the effect may be powerful and that crying is not uncommon."[53] The methods "work," he says, because they help the participants "realize potential" and gain feelings of "renewal." Participants come to "accept, respect, and love" themselves more than they did.[54]

Aims of here and now "growth" groups are typically described as follows:

To get in touch with one's authentic feelings.

To communicate intimately with others.

To develop potential for new growth.

To find the real person beneath the social role.

To learn from the experience itself.

To enlarge consciousness by stepping outside normal routines.

Although distinctions can be made among various types of groups, as with psychotherapy trends have merged, and groups probably differ more as the result of the individual and personal characteristics of their leaders and participants than according to whether the group is called "therapy," "sensitivity," "psychodrama," or "encounter."

In the antiestablishment atmosphere of the 1960s, it is not surprising that encounter groups often were without "institutional backing" and led by untrained and nonprofessional leaders. Some groups used no real leader at all; others followed instructions played on a tape recorder. On the other hand, since the most avid participants were mental health professionals and other members of the Friends and Supporters of Psychiatry, it did not take ordinary practitioners long to step on the bandwagon. In November 1973, the American Academy of Psychotherapists titled its Annual Institute and Conference "New Realities in Psychotherapy: Ways of Extending Consciousness." Workshop leaders included Stanley Keleman, Senior West Coast trainer for Bioenergetic Institute, James S. Simkin, Gestalt trainer, Ralph Metzner, coworker of Timothy Leary and Richard Alpert during the initial exploration of L.S.D. effects at Harvard University, and Magda Proskauer, "breathing therapist" and former Jungian. The brochure announcing the conference stated:

> We are witnesses to and participants in an exciting new era of cultural transformation. We are moving beyond our traditional scientific conception of man [sic] to one that includes centering, becoming sensitive to subtle sources of energy and developing capacities which transcend ordinary perceptions of what we usually call waking consciousness.[55]

The human potential movement, as it has come to be called, has included the formation of many "workshops" in which training for professionals, introductory lectures for lay persons, and experiential groups are presented side by side. The newsletter of the Hartford Family Institute announces Family Sculpture Work Shops ("a delightfully refreshing way to gain energy-releasing self-knowledge and an ability to accept and use your whole self") and Training for Professionals ("designed for those academic professionals who want to 'stay alive' and add to their effectiveness"). The institute offers instruction in Gestalt Therapy, Transactional Analysis, Bioenergetics, and Transcendental Meditation.

The New Haven Center for Human Relations of New Haven, Connecticut, offers a similar menu. Its brochure for Fall 1973, for example, offers

> an eight-session course of personal exploration and discovery in community, using the insights of Transactional Analysis and Gestalt, verbal and nonverbal exercises, to gain insight into ourselves and as a way of making decisions about future directions for our lives. . . . [and] emphasis will be placed on acceptance and empowering of self in the face of doubts, uncertainty, and conflicts in which so many of us live. . . .[56]

Other titles listed by the New Haven group are "Weekend Workshop on Human Sexuality," "Psychodrama Workshop," and "Lessons in T'ai-Chi Ch'uan, an ancient form of classical dance which is a health exercise, a moving meditation, an art of self-defense."

Courses on similar topics can also be found in continuing education programs and in undergraduate college catalogs. If the plethora of terms is confusing, the reader is referred to catalogs which have been published to help novices find their way around.[57]

The response of traditional psychotherapists to all of this has been interesting. Most of the movement's leaders—Carl Rogers, Frederick Perls, Arthur Janov, Daniel Casriel, Eric Berne, to name a few—were credentialed and accepted members of the psychiatric and psychological professions.

But in the "do your own thing" atmosphere of the times, as well as in the very concept of self-actualization, it was hard for advocates to rationalize restricting the activities to those with Ph.D.'s, M.D.'s, or M.S.W.'s. Furthermore, the public demand for groups and workshops exceeded the supply of professionals in the movement.

Frank H. Boring, Chairperson of the Committee on Scientific and Professional Ethics and Conduct, issued a personal statement in which he used the term "Growth Group" (GG) to include encounter groups, psychodrama, human potential groups, and various workshops, as well as traditional group therapy, and noted the degree of disagreement over such groups among psychologists:

> The chief plaint, coming from one sector of the psychological "establishment," is over the large and rapid growth of unskilled practitioners whose economic motives are seen as outweighing and overriding their humanitarian purposes. . . . While some complain it is being passed off as education or entertainment when in truth it is therapy, others complain it is being passed off as therapy when at best it is entertainment and at worst it is mis-therapy or mal-practice.[58]

Boring lists the following objections made by others to GG:

"Blatant or subtle coercion" when individuals are encouraged to participate by persons in authority, the encouragement of "insincerity and dishonesty despite their avowed goals," "excessive openness" which may lead to "psychological trauma," and "negative effects" in the form of "suicide and precipitated psychosis."

> A less openly expressed objection is the resentment of economic competition. A number see GG as an affront to the dignity and proper public image of psychology as a profession with a major spin-off being to provide "singles" with a match-making atmosphere for securing bed partners. Finally, a significant number believe APA or state associations should *do* something about GG before Congress or state legislatures apply overly restrictive statutory measures.[59]

Although Boring views GG as clearly "therapeutic," the "Guidelines for Psychologists Conducting Growth Groups," which was approved by the Board of Directors of the American Psychological Association on February 15, 1973, recognized that groups may be used for "both educational and psychotherapeutic purposes."[60] The guidelines stressed advising participants in writing beforehand of the group's purposes, the techniques to be used, the relevant background of the leader, and any fees or other expenses that may be incurred. According to the guidelines, the use of growth groups for research or exploration is recognized, and such professional activity "must be protected and encouraged, the welfare of the participant is of paramount importance."

"Casualties" occurred with 9 percent of encounter participants, according to a study conducted at Stanford University by psychologist Irvin D. Yalom.[61] These were defined as having experienced "an enduring, significant, negative reaction." Persons with "low self-concept and unrealistically high expectations and anticipations of change" were most vulnerable. In locating individuals designated as casualties, peer evaluation was more useful than leader evaluation. The leaders ranged from "primarily analytic and interpretive," to very directive, stimulating, and dramatic. Some groups "were highly productive learning environments, some were innocuous, and others were generally destructive." The researchers comment:

> While not all groups are successful at people changing, they excel at creating instant, brief and intense interpersonal experiences. Strangers assemble, interact intensely, and then become strangers again. We saw many deep but temporary relationships form—true encounters. People want and need and can even learn from such experiences. This chance to learn something about oneself from the open reactions of others is real, important, and not often available in our society. But we find that such experiences are not the crucial ones that alter people permanently.[62]

The psychotherapy and human growth consumer is faced with a seemingly endless array of possibilities. In addition to those already mentioned are various forms of family therapy, marriage counseling, dance therapy, poetry therapy, art therapy, and many, many others.

NONPROFESSIONAL INDEPENDENTS

Psychotherapy has often been likened to religion and psychotherapists to medicine men.[63] Psychoanalysis practiced in the manner of Freud himself is called "orthodox." From the main branches of psychoanalysis and of the existential-humanist therapies have sprung many twigs or sections. Some of these merge with or resemble religions. Religion and psychotherapy are both ways of coming to terms with one's life, one's pain, and one's fears. Both depend for their effectiveness on the power and authority of their leaders. And both function as a force in society to allow oppressive conditions to persist whenever the causes of problems are projected to a metaphysical realm: to the equally unobservable supernatural on the one hand, or internal on the other. If a profession hides its secrets and mystifies its clients, how different is it from a priesthood?

Credentialed professionals in psychotherapy have lately explored virtually every type of cure imaginable. Some of the more extreme forms of therapy methods which utilized nudity, sex, or physical harm have sometimes elicited legal action against their perpetrators. But the harshest criticism from within the professions has not been inflicted on professionals who harm patients, but on nonprofessionals who attempt to operate autonomously. The "human potential" movement has produced many of these. Some reject association with therapy and emphasize exercises, breathing or meditation, thus tying themselves to ancient or Eastern religions. These groups attract Friends and Supporters of Psychiatry, those "patient types" who shop ceaselessly for the "cure" or the philosophy that will quell their soul's disquietude. Former political activists Jerry Rubin and Rennie Davis have turned their attention, respectively, to bioenergetics and deep meditation. Thousands of other participants in the psychedelic-hippie-political-protest movement have become participants in some aspect of the "growth" movement. In Severin Peterson's *A Catalog of the Way People Grow*, humanist, Gestalt, and psychoanalytic psychotherapies are listed beside astrology, Yoga, prayer, encounter groups, and transcendental meditation. I have spoken with persons who have tried as many as five different professional psychotherapists plus Yoga, encounter, and two or three other means to "growth experiences."

The growth movement, whatever else it may be, is also a business. Fortunes are being made. Weekend "workshops" can cost hundreds of dollars per person. Yet it may, in the end, turn out to be a helpful way to drain normal persons from psychiatry and to release them from the disease model. Psychiatry might be induced to return to the treatment of real illnesses, psychology to research and teaching, and social work to the community. Because political pressure for strict and severe licensing laws which will enable professionals to monopolize "growth" would retard progress in this direction, consumer alertness is needed. The development of alternatives to psychotherapy may in the end be one of the major forces for change within the psychotherapy professions. When people are able to take their business elsewhere, those who lose economically are always more inclined to take heed.

PARAPROFESSIONALS, SUBPROFESSIONALS

Guidance counselors, graduate students, nurses, and social service agency employees are some of the types of persons who have legitimately engaged in psychotherapy. They did so as part of training, in a research project, or under supervision as an aspect of their job, not in autonomous, private practice. Aides, parents of patients, college undergraduates, housewives, and convicts have exhibited "psychotherapeutic potency" in research studies.[64] General practitioners have been found to treat "psychologically ill" patients more successfully than psychiatrists, with reduced risk of damage resulting from confinement in a mental institution among the benefits to patients.[65] Although members of the major psychotherapy professions generally minimize or ignore the role of nonpsychiatric physicians and of members of the clergy, these professionals have been traditionally sought out for counsel with psychological problems, and they continue to treat thousands of persons who are not referred to psychotherapists and who would not consult a psychotherapist if a referral were made.[66]

The reaction of professional psychotherapists to these nonprofessionals or semiprofessionals has been mixed and at times heated. In one study, college students were found to be effective, but jealousy on the part of the hospital staff and a general power struggle between professionals and nonprofessionals developed.[67] The nonprofessional psychotherapist is threatening in two ways: directly, since he is treating persons who might otherwise go to professionals; and less directly but perhaps ultimately more severely, since he is undermining the mystique of the professional. The language of the professional defending his territory sometimes approaches the level of *Alice in Wonderland*. In one case, mentioned earlier, a psychoanalyst is explaining to a lay person why training in medicine is important for psychotherapists:

> Doctors feel that their long years of medical training, plus the very fact that they chose medicine as a vocation, have embued them with a desire to cure, to heal; whereas nonmedical analysts, because of their background in the behavioral sciences, have an intellectual approach which may underestimate the human need.[68]

One can just as easily contend that physicians, with their emphasis on pathology, physiology, and making money* may "underestimate the human need." There is no logic here, only brute competition.

Clinical psychologist Theodore H. Blau, writing in the journal *Professional Psychology* is direct in expressing concern about the encroachment of nonprofessional workers in his domain:

---

* A well-informed medical and science journalist, who wishes to remain anonymous here, estimates that one half to two-thirds of the medical doctors in the United States are millionaires.

Having practiced clinical psychology for over 15 years in the same city, I feel I have a special and jealously held place in my community. . . .

If large numbers of nonprofessional "helpers" are turned out in the next two years, how will these people be viewed by the professional psychologist in the community who has struggled to attain his status, his prestige, his affluence?[69]

Surprisingly Blau says that one problem that can be expected to prevent the nonprofessionals from supplying adequate service to the community is their university training. He forgets that the professional spends many more years than the nonprofessional off in training outside the community, and a major advantage of nonprofessionals is the possibility of recruiting community members who will bear greater cultural similarity to clients than professionals do. In another part of the article, Blau himself brings up this very point, but he implies that its relevance is limited to certain patients that mental health professionals have found "undesirable"—alcoholics, drug addicts, delinquents, and sexual deviants.*

The anxieties of professionals over the intrusion of new groups are also evident in statements of Ph.D. psychologists who opposed allowing M.A. psychologists full membership in the American Psychological Association. In the *APA Monitor* of July 1972, psychologist Robert Tyson wrote:

Permit me to submit a brief comment about the possibility of admitting M.A. holders to full membership:

Why not admit people with majors in psychology?

Why not admit any one who *deeply feels*, in his unique personality, that he is truly interested?

You have to draw the line somewhere. That far and no further.

What's in a name? Plenty. The name is "doctor," and to the people in this practical world a person who is entitled to the designation, "doctor," the connotation is immediate. Every psychiatrist and every neurologist is a "doctor." What are they, and our legislators, going to conclude (per-

---

* Whether or not these are helped by psychotherapy is open to public inspection, but they do have one thing in common: the goals of therapy in their cases are not vague.

haps without thinking too much) about a watered-down
population of an APA with an enormous mixture of people
called "Master"?

Let's quit deluding our professional selves. Hold the
line.[70]

In a similar straightforward view, Baltimore psychologist
Jerome Rubin says:

> The recent discussion over full membership privileges for
> master's level psychologists seems to be omitting the basic
> reason for professional exclusion. Licensing, certification,
> full status membership, half status, no status, all have a
> motivating factor. Behind the impressive statements about
> protecting society, high quality standards, and superior pa-
> tient treatment is the unspoken reason: economic protec-
> tion.
>
> Unfortunately economics lies at the basis for admission
> to professional practice in almost every field from plumb-
> ing to psychiatry. The quiet organized hand of profes-
> sional income protection limits admissions to American
> schools of medicine, dentistry, and law and controls licens-
> ing of many manual crafts. There are simply *too many*
> able people to meet the demand for services in health, ed-
> ucation, and construction. Opening the gates to ability
> would effectively flood the market and reduce incomes for
> the in-group.
>
> A recent example in my own state is a bill for Licensed
> Professional Carpet Installers. Who is this licensing really
> going to protect? Another in-state example: Anyone can
> practice psychology as long as he doesn't do it privately.
> Come now, who does this law really protect?
>
> To my respected colleagues at the Master's level, I can
> only say it is unfair but we do not live in a just world. Is it
> realistic to expect psychologists to be more generous in
> sharing the market than are physicians, dentists, and law-
> yers? Humanity has a long way to go.[71]

Although Tyson's and Rubin's statements summarize the
professional issues, they do not indicate the far-reaching importance of this question. Dozens of investigations have
found that professionals in training, paraprofessionals,

subprofessionals, or peers can be as effective as fully credentialed psychotherapists.[72] The demand for therapy is high; the use of nonprofessionals would enable it to be met and to reduce costs.

In 1961 the report of a five-year study undertaken by the Joint Commission on Mental Illness and Health urged psychologists to train teachers, attendants, public health nurses, and other lay persons.[73] Several studies found that less highly credentialed persons were actually more effective.[74] Others have urged that selection procedures partly replace training, since personality factors have been found to be important.[75] In one study therapists who displayed more empathy toward the client were those who performed less well in coursework and other measures of academic performance.[76] One psychologist has expressed the hope that in the future all practitioners would be nonprofessionals, because "doctors" are essentially self-selected, and they are difficult to weed out.[77] Much medical treatment is actually carried out by nurses, attendants, parents, and other nonphysicians, and it is suggested that psychotherapy should also be carried out by underlings. This arrangement has been very profitable for M.D.'s since nurses' or attendants' incomes may be as low as one-twentieth of the doctor's, but it may be more difficult to divide up psychotherapy tasks without destroying public confidence in the profession.

There is a final point to be made on the use of subprofessionals with respect to the possible harmfulness of psychotherapy. When harmfulness occurs, it appears to result largely from insensitivity and authoritarianism on the part of the therapist which leads him to induce guilt and low self-esteem through "hurtful interpretations." The more in awe of the therapist the client is, the greater is the capacity to inflict such harm. Not only do impressive credentials fail to protect the public, but they increase the dangers. Licensing and certification, if they are really to work for the public good, should not be based on irrelevant and possibly harm-inducing academic and training diplomas or degrees. But we have already seen that the purpose of licensing is not the protection but the exploitation of the public.

FEMINIST THERAPY

Throughout this book I have referred to the patient as "she" and to the therapist as "he," both to avoid use of the universal masculine and to remind the reader that most patients are women and the vast majority of therapists are men. In fact, of course, there are male patients and there are female therapists. As in other professions, the few female therapists have not scaled the heights of wealth or reputation sometimes reached by many males, but some of them have managed to make a living. Traditionally, patients, especially female patients, have preferred men as therapists. But times are a-changing, at least slightly, and more than ever before women have begun to seek out the services of other women.

Women Friends and Supporters of Psychiatry often want to be psychotherapists. They have themselves been through therapy, and they feel they can "do" it. Women who are feminists feel that they are needed as psychotherapists because otherwise women will be subjected to the antifemale prejudices rife in the profession. They have read the books and journals and they know how deeply rooted sexist thinking is in psychotherapy principles and practices. The term "feminist therapist" is used to describe therapists who are feminists, or who profess to use a feminist approach to psychotherapy. Some who call themselves "feminist therapists" are men. Because the majority of patients are women, and because women Friends and Supporters are lately reading some of the many recent books by feminists, it is "good business" for the psychotherapist to adapt something of a pro-women's liberation line. One should beware, however, of the possibility that a few slogans overlie intense prejudice, even hatred, of women and of feminism. Nathanial Ross, clinical professor of psychiatry at Downstate Medical Center in New York, was recently reported to have said:

> Anatomy and biology are powerful influences in life. A woman is really denying a part of her self if she doesn't want motherhood and marriage. Let's face it, men and women really are different; and I say *vive la différence*.[78]

I believe that such statements probably still reflect the majority viewpoint among therapists, particularly among male analysts. Even when public statements favor more feminist viewpoints, men like Ross dominate the writing and teaching of psychotherapy, and their influence is hard to shake.

Furthermore, "feminist therapist" involves an inherent contradiction. The feminist objective is to change societal institutions so that women may have opportunities equal to those of men in education, employment, participation in government, and so forth. When a woman is depressed or anxious, the feminist looks for a probable cause in the facts of her underemployment—almost every woman in this culture is not only underpaid, but wasted through underemployment in which her work does not utilize her abilities—the burdens of housework and child care, or some other aspect of the role she plays in society. Solutions to these problems are not to be found in individual pathologies, but in changing the behavior of persons in the woman's environment. A "therapist," by definition, either views the woman herself as the locus of the problem or sets out to help the woman *adjust* or *adapt* to her unfavorable situation.[79] The support of another person may in fact provide the strength needed to deal with, cope with, and try to change unsatisfactory external conditions. But the term "therapist" still seems inappropriate. "Consultant" or "counselor" would be better unless the feminist therapist feels she needs the mystique of the medical terminology. But if the feminist who wishes to engage in psychotherapy uses the trappings of psychodynamic therapy, is she not misleading her potential clients? If she interprets her client's behavior, may she not be engaging in oppressive and abusive actions? Is she, just because she is a female, able to overcome her training in psychological mythologies related to women?

At the 1973 national convention of the American Psychological Association, Jean Ferson of the Feminist Therapy Collective of Philadelphia discussed her conception of feminist therapy:

We at the collective have absorbed the idea—crucial to our peaceful revolution—that the personal is political. Therefore, we do not simply give up, moan that it is too great a

problem to tackle, fade back into the wallpaper—no, as Su
Negrin puts it, we "begin at start." We seize our di-
minished, confused selves and we work toward being autonomous, self-defining women. What we learn we share
with other women so that they, too, can learn to fight oppression in their everyday lives and from there, moving
outward, in the lives of those around them. We want to be
—and we see—women who say to their men and children: *I*
will tell you what a woman is. Be still, watch, learn something.[80]

Although they emphatically do not view their services as
"simple support," they are

skeptical about professionalism. Nevertheless, we are glad
to be beyond the charge of amateurism. We have skills
which cost a lot to acquire and which merit payment. We
can render unto Caesar with the best of them, and we ac-
knowledge the importance of that.[81]

As a speaker for the National Organization for Women, Dr.
Ferson had received many requests from women looking for
feminist therapists: "I knew the market was out there. We
all understood that women must help other women—men
couldn't help, even if they might want to—and it would be a
rare male who would even want to."[82]

One of the reasons why males are unable to help, Ferson
explains, is that the women in the collective themselves function as positive role models for their clients. Through their
autonomy as persons, and in setting up and maintaining the
collective, they set examples for their clients to follow.
Describing the process itself, Ferson says:

[The client] tells us what her primary problems are: we
don't tell her. She tells us what she's doing about them and
if and when she thinks she has made progress. We offer
validation, support, a mirror of her feelings which can add
insight of its own. . . . The line between helper and helpee
blurs and sometimes disappears altogether. And why not?
No one has a monopoly on strength or wisdom.[83]

Except for the word "therapy" itself, no illness-model term
appears in Ferson's paper. The women who come for help

are clients, not patients, and no reference is made to neurosis, defense mechanisms, or psychopathology. The Feminist Therapy Collective of Philadelphia is obviously trying to reconcile professionalism with their feminist philosophy.

Many National Organization for Women (NOW) chapters and other feminist groups have developed referral services. A woman who is wary of psychotherapy's typical sexism, but still feels that she wants some form of therapy, can contact the nearest women's center or NOW chapter and obtain the name of a feminist therapy group or of individuals who consider themselves to be feminist therapists. The definition of feminist therapist does not rule out psychodynamic interpretations or other forms of abuse, but it gives some protection against extreme sexism, and assists women therapists in finding clients.

Many women have found an alternative to psychotherapy in "consciousness-raising" groups. Although both the aims and methods of c-r are quite different from, if not the exact opposite of, those of group therapy, the results of c-r participation is sometimes very comparable to what the woman entering therapy hopes to achieve. In a c-r group, individuals speak one at a time, usually by simply going around the group in a circle. Each woman speaks from her own experience. Most groups find it helpful to provide a topic. For example:

How I Feel About How I Look
If I Were Eleven Years Old Today
My Relationships with Other Women
Clothes I Wear and Clothes I Prefer
Shyness
Where I Want to Be in Ten Years
How to Deal with Sexism in My Children

When groups called "consciousness-raising" were first begun several years ago, the sessions were aimed at "politicizing." After a period of group discussion, the participants, sometimes under the guidance of a leader, attempted to analyze the general principles that emerged during the discussion and to consider those in relation to specific political actions that would be appropriate to them. But such groups often found that members disagreed with each other on theory or tactics or both, with resulting dissension. Since the groups were aimed at inducing action, inevitable differences in levels of involvement or political sophistication were additional sources of frustration.

Other nonpolitical groups which also called themselves consciousness-raising groups were run very much along the lines of group therapy. They stressed stable membership, commitment, honesty, trust, etc., and encouraged interpretation of each other as well as direct confrontation on personal issues. These groups often floundered as members became too deeply involved with each others' lives. After a few months, or perhaps as long as two years, the groups broke up, sometimes with permanent ill feelings among some of the members. Such groups also tended to foster dependency of the members on the group, which meant that the group's termination was particularly painful.

Gradually, women came to realize that the best thing about a c-r group was the opportunity it provided to speak and to listen to other women seriously discussing some of the most important issues that confronted them. They also began to understand that respect for women was rare in this culture and to feel determined that c-r would be a place in which they could provide it for each other. And they ultimately recognized that respecting a woman meant respecting her vision of her life. Guidelines for c-r groups today usually lay greatest stress on allowing each participant to speak as freely and as honestly as she wishes without threat of interruption or challenge. Women discovered that simply being listened to was a new experience. They began to notice that husbands and men in social situations frequently do not listen to what women say, showing it by their rude interruptions. Women who had previously blamed themselves for not being more effective in social situations realized that other women faced the same problems; it was not their behavior that was at fault.

C-r sessions were no longer viewed as a place to "get things off our chests" (although sometimes that was nice, too), or as a place to organize for political action (there were other kinds of meetings for that), but as a kind of seminar in which society itself was analyzed from this new perspective of respecting women. For many women, the self-respect gained thereby was one of the most "therapeutic" events of their lives.

This society blames women for most of their problems. Nowhere is this more blatantly apparent than in the writings of many psychodynamic psychotherapists whose theories and attitudes infected the culture. In c-r groups this terrible burden of guilt is lifted. Before, even in discussions with other women, they had always to defend themselves from those who would find the women's own inner pathology at the root of any difficulty revealed. Originally, c-r referred to the "raising" of a specific political "consciousness." But the rigidity and remoteness of codified ideologies had little appeal for the masses of women who have flocked to c-r meetings. Most women today think of c-r as a process of increasing awareness of the implications of being female in a male-dominated world. This raised consciousness has led to many actions which are political in both traditional and personal senses of the word, but the c-r group itself is most effective as a place of learning.

"RADICAL THERAPY" AND "ANTIPSYCHIATRY"

Psychoanalysis and its offshoots are accustomed to criticism from the political Right. The Daughters of the American Revolution have taken public stands against all forms of psychology, and the Silent Majority probably wouldn't be found dead free-associating on an analytic couch. Recently an uncoordinated attack against certain aspects of psychiatry has come from other sources—outspoken psychiatrists and the political Left. Thomas Szasz, psychiatrist and Professor at the State University of New York at Buffalo, opposes involuntary incarceration in mental hospitals and the use of medical terminology:

> Psychiatrists are now ready to classify anyone and everyone as mentally sick, and anything and everything as psychiatric treatment.
>
> The result . . . is an apparently irrefutable justification of psychiatric force and fraud—a justification based on ostensibly wholly altruistic motives and considerations: the "true interests" of the insane, 130 years ago; the "therapeutic needs" of the mental patient, today. . . .
>
> In short, just as, for millennia, involuntary servitude has been accepted as a proper economic and social arrangement, so, for centuries, involuntary psychiatry has been accepted as a proper medical and therapeutic arrangement.[84]

Szasz raises a civil rights issue, one that has been taken more seriously in the decade since his book *The Myth of Mental Illness*[85] appeared. Szasz also opposes legal interference with a citizen's right to ingest addictive drugs or other substances. He is a thorn in the side of psychiatry who has been hailed by critics at both ends of the political spectrum, and ultimately tolerated by psychiatry itself.

British psychiatrist R. D. Laing's "radical" thesis is that schizophrenia is a form of experience comparable to the drug-induced psychedelic experience. Psychotic "symptoms" are not nonsensical, but intelligible "as expressions of a fragmented or split Self." Trained as a psychoanalyst, Laing has accepted Bateson's double-bind theory and sees schizophrenia as the result of family influences. The psychotic is the product of a pathological family, the "scapegoat." Laing espouses the view that psychotic behavior is essentially *deviant* behavior. As Jan B. Gordon puts it, he "suggest[s], therefore, that sanity or psychosis is tested by the degree of conjunction or disjunction between two persons where the one is sane by common consent."[86]

Another critic of some aspects of psychotherapy is psychiatrist Seymour L. Halleck. In his book *The Politics of Therapy* he asserts that psychotherapists are inevitably engaged in political activity, since their political views color their interactions with patients:

Every psychiatrist who has ever treated a patient has had some notion regarding the best kind of life for that individual, and every patient who has benefited from psychiatric therapy has incorporated some of [her] doctor's values. Furthermore, by the very nature of his practice, the psychiatrist has consistently taken positions on issues that have political implications, namely, issues that involve the distribution of power within social systems.[87]

He is not the first to note that focus on a patient's internal problems reduces the likelihood of creating pressure against external sources of difficulty, but he may be the most emphatic:

> There is no way in which the psychiatrist can deal with behavior that is partly generated by a social system without either strengthening or altering that system. Every encounter with a psychiatrist, therefore, has political implications.[88]

Like Szasz and Laing, Halleck would do away with the mental health movement slogan that mental illness is "a disease just like any other disease." Psychiatric patients play a role in society and in mental hospitals that is quite different from that of the physically ill patient. Although Halleck's tone is often strident, his recommendations tend to be tame, e.g., that psychiatrists get behind social reforms such as improvement of medical care and dissemination of birth control information. In a similar "mild" vein are his proposals for "self-reform" by individual psychiatrists. They include allowing "the patient to achieve greater awareness of [her] external environment," protecting patients from the therapist's political biases by spelling them out for the patient, making greater use of family therapy, clarifying political values and intentions in connection with group and community psychiatry, making more careful use of diagnostic labels, refraining from making public statements concerning the mental health of public figures, trying to improve conditions in mental hospitals, and conducting research that focuses on finding solutions to moral problems. He also suggests the training of therapists at subprofessional levels which "need not in any way diminish the status of professional healers; in fact, the

professional's new commitment to a teaching role should enhance his importance and usefulness to society."[89]

Neither Halleck nor Laing nor Szasz, for all their public
images as critics, poses a serious threat, if any threat at all, to
the institution of private psychodynamic psychotherapy practice.

Remnants of the Radical Left on both American coasts and
across the Atlantic in Britain, have promulgated the concept
of "radical therapy" through underground publications. The
"Radical Psychiatry Manifesto" reads in part:

> Psychiatry must return to its nonmedical origins since most
> psychiatric conditions are in no way the province of medi-
> cine. All persons competent in soul healing should be
> known as psychiatrists. . . . Extended individual psycho-
> therapy is an elitist, outmoded, as well as nonproductive
> form of psychiatric help. It concentrates on the talents of a
> few on a few. It silently colludes with the notion that peo-
> ple's difficulties have their sources within them while im-
> plying that everything is well with the world. It promotes
> oppression by shrouding its consequences with shame and
> secrecy. It further mystifies by attempting to pass as an
> ideal human relationship when it is, in fact, artificial in the
> extreme.[90]

More specific instructions on "how to be a radical therapist" are detailed by "activist" Rick Kunnes:

> Wear a political pin to work, put a political poster in your
> office. . . . women can challenge sexism by wearing
> slacks, men can challenge professionalism by refusing to
> wear a tie and always wearing jeans.[91]

Others include pamphleteering, "guerrilla theater," demanding "innovative services," and the political "education" of patients:

> When you do "therapy" always suggest various political
> settings to help "patients" deal with their alienation and
> oppression. Always attempt to help patients understand
> the political causes of their "symptoms." Suggest to your
> patients that they work with existing political organi-
> zations. . . .[92]

It is significant that the truly radical step of exposing psychotherapy's lack of scientific validation is not espoused by any of these critics. The reason is that many of the "radical therapy" and "antipsychiatry" proponents are also antiscientific. Their feet are planted firmly in a humanist-existential-nihilist position. Their criticism of established psychotherapy is mild compared with the virulence of their attack on scientific psychology. As Professor Max Hamilton of the Department of Psychiatry, University of Leeds, puts it: "The great leaders of this movement, Dr. Ronald Laing and Dr. Thomas Szasz, paint a picture, in broad strokes on an immense canvas, of the evils of psychiatry, but when I look closely at the details they look very different."[93] Hamilton mentions the use of innovative techniques like encounter groups to assist "industrial executives to increase the efficiency of their managerial function and domination," and the acceptability of private treatment. The "young radicals" mistake the dangerous by-products of technology for the results of scientific understanding. Hamilton says we can anticipate

a world in which we will soon be choked in our own filth. The little good that we see is overwhelmed by the evil, . . . everything we have done to achieve our desires has turned into its opposite. We have to learn to do things properly, to control our behaviour so that we can do what we want to do and achieve what we want to achieve, not their opposites. Scientific psychology is not an amusement and it is not a game. It is not a mere end in itself, a source of intellectual satisfaction. It is the science which will enable us to understand and control human behaviour. I use the word advisedly, yes—*control* human behaviour. A control based on understanding, a control that is self-control. One day we will move away from the darkness of our bestial origins, one day we will become truly human and reveal our true potentialities and we can be led to this only by science.[94]

Unfortunately, there are few persons among those read by the general public who espouse Hamilton's view. B. F. Skinner, who will be discussed in the final chapter of this book, is the major exception.

SELF-HELP

> People who realize that they are
> in trouble are increasingly turning
> to each other for assistance.
>
> LEONA TYLER, "Tyler Foresees New Era of Hope for
> Psychology"[95]

The entrepreneurs of the human potential movement are
not the only nonprofessionals in the therapy enterprise. In a
growing number of organizations, help is provided by peers.
The oldest, largest, and most successful of self-help groups,
Alcoholics Anonymous, was formed in 1935. Alcoholism and
later drug addiction, both among the most prevalent of
behavioral problems, have largely been treated by nonprofessionals. Since the days of Freud, it has been acknowledged
that psychotherapy rarely helped the alcoholic. Today, many
textbooks on psychology and counseling do not even discuss
the subject, and psychiatrists themselves refer patients to Alcoholics Anonymous. In 1973, President of the American
Psychological Association Leona Tyler noted that recently
not only alcoholics, but persons trying to lose weight, former
mental patients, and persons seeking self-fulfillment, have
banded together for mutual assistance. Psychotherapy
researchers have recommended that such "naturalistic
therapeutic agents" as Alcoholics Anonymous, Psychotics
Anonymous, and Weight Watchers be studied for what can
be learned from them and applied to professional practices.[96]

Few deny the effectiveness of "peer self-help psychotherapy groups" (PSHPG). Psychologist Nathan Hurvitz
published an enthusiastic report of his investigations:

> It is moving, thrilling and inspiring to participate in a
> meeting in which PSHPG members describe the help they
> have received from their fellowships. Many of these mem-
> bers had their problems for many years, some had been
> jailed, institutionalized, and some had gone to many differ-
> ent conventional therapists to whom they paid thousands of
> dollars for help they needed but did not receive while they
> suffered the terrible agonies of their afflictions.[97]

Hurvitz feels that the relative success of PSHPG raises serious questions as to the legitimacy of traditional psychotherapy practice and even about the value of some psychotherapy research. He deplores the "condescending and patronizing attitude of conventional psychotherapists to this movement" and finds it especially irritating when "psychodynamic concepts whose value as a guide to treatment is questionable" are used to "explain and belittle PSHPG." For example, Alcoholics Anonymous has been interpreted as being a mother substitute. Hurvitz finds that not only do PSHPGs function without using the methods of professionals, but that reliance on professional consultants obstructs their operation. Although some groups "seek the 'underlying causes' of the present problems which they regard as 'symptoms,' in accord with the 'medical model' . . . they are not concerned with 'symptom substitution' or with the emergence of greater problems if these causes are not discovered."[98] Hurvitz continues: "Psychotherapy does not require searching for and interpreting the unconscious and/or the developmental sources of present behavior; and if such a search is useful it can be conducted by untrained personnel. . . ."[99]

Peer self-help groups should be differentiated from the services of volunteers or low-paid subprofessionals who work under the supervision of professionals. In the latter instances, the person providing help is not autonomous, and, ultimately, any procedures which threaten the professional supervisor's status and income are likely to be excluded, regardless of their effectiveness.

BEHAVIOR THERAPY

We have noted that Freudian and client-centered procedures do not deal directly with the disturbing behavior. This is the crucial difference between these techniques and behavior therapy.

LEONARD KRASNER AND LEONARD ULLMAN, *Behavior Influence and Personality*[100]

For many years, behavioral psychology, now the major competitor of the psychodynamic theories and therapies, was confined to the universities. The public was enticed with the Freudian drama, and easily bored or offended with anything based on rat studies,* presented through statistics, or couched in the complicated language that only scientists seemed able to comprehend. "Behavior" was dull as compared with "repressed sexual material fighting to erupt into consciousness." But academic psychology has shed its former association with religion and philosophy; it has become the science of behavior, not the "study of the soul." Ultimately, the influence of laboratory research extended into certain forms of psychotherapeutic practice.

Although how-to books that deal in behavioral specifics date back at least to Dale Carnegie's enormously popular *How to Win Friends and Influence People,* there have been few behavioral books that described applications of scientifically demonstrated principles. The recent "transactional" books (*Games People Play* and *I'm OK, You're OK*) might appear superficially to belong in a behavioral category, but they are close to psychoanalysis in underlying assumptions. The Child, Adult, and Parent, the three ego states, are roughly analogous to Freud's Id, Ego, and Superego. More important, the transactional group leader uses interpretation of inferred inner events as a major technique. And they are not based on laboratory experiments.

Public demand for behavioral methods has not been stimulated by best sellers. To the small degree that a demand exists, it has been the result of scientific reports comparing behavior and insight methods that were presented in the journals and at scientific meetings. Such reports reach members of the psychiatric and psychotherapy professions

---

* Aside from a humaneness issue (which for me personally is a big issue), I find no fault with rat experiments. Criticism of them by "humanists" who claim "you can't generalize" are just plain wrong. Rats are not behaviorally identical to humans—but there are important (and useful) similarities. The "animal" nature of human beings or the "human" nature of rats is not changed through protest. We cannot learn all about people from rats or any other infra human species, but we have already learned a great deal.

and persons in the related fields of medicine, sociology, and other biological and behavioral sciences. At least until very recently, information about behavior methods has reached the general public, including the Friends and Supporters of Psychotherapy, largely through college courses. This may happen indirectly, as in the case of a woman who came for help with the behavior problems of her eleven-year-old child. An older daughter, a college senior, had said, "Don't take her to a Freudian. Find a behaviorist."

The term "behavior therapy" had three independent origins in the 1950s, all related to the application of principles and procedures developed in or suggested by experimental investigation of the learning principles. However, few principles are truly "established," and now clinicians have come to use the term "behavior therapy" loosely to describe virtually any procedure that focuses on or relates to what a person does in "real" life, even when this is only "imagined" during a therapy session.

Hans Eysenck, one of the independent originators of the term behavior therapy, made the following comparisons between it and Freudian psychotherapy:[101]

Behavior therapy is based on "properly formulated theory leading to testable deductions," while Freudian theory is inconsistent.

Behavior therapy views "symptoms" as "evidence of faulty learning" to be treated directly, while Freudian theory views them as "the visible upshot of unconscious causes."

Behavior therapy is not concerned about past history; "interpretation, even if not completely subjective and erroneous, is largely irrelevant."

Personal relations such as "transference" are not necessary, although some degree of relationship between patient and therapist might be useful.

The behaviorist* goes directly after "symptoms," often

---

* Strictly speaking "behaviorist" is not really the correct term. Behaviorism refers to a method of psychological inquiry. However, it has already found some use in popular literature, and other ex-

considering that the undesirable behaviors are the actual problem and not "symptoms" at all. This contrasts with the approach of the psychodynamicist to whom symptoms are red herrings, distracting the treatment process from its true goals. It would appear therefore that Freudian therapists, Rogerian therapists, and other psychodynamic therapists who view the source of difficulty as lying within the individual would be unable, on principle, to utilize a behavioral approach. But just as psychotherapists incorporated group therapy without troubling unduly over principles, many today claim to use in their eclecticism behavioral techniques "whenever they are appropriate." For example, psychoanalyst Ivan Wentworth-Rohr finds "behavior techniques . . . an adjunct treatment method in psychoanalytic psychotherapy" especially for symptoms acquired after the crucial childhood period. It also happens that patients in psychoanalytic treatment are referred by their analysts to behaviorally oriented practitioners to clear up annoying "symptoms."[102]

With the notable exception of Joseph Wolpe and a few others, the major researchers and proponents of behavioral approaches in psychiatry have tended to be psychologists. Recently, however, organized psychiatry has shown increased interest in behavior methods. In July 1973, the American Psychiatric Association Task Force on Behavior Therapy issued a very favorable report.[103]

Some of the behavioral techniques that have come to be standard tricks in the behavior therapist's bag are, briefly:

Operant conditioning. In this application of research findings, the essential notion is a new set of 3 Rs: Reinforced responses recur. In other words, behaviors which have rewarding consequences acquire increased probability of reoccurrence. Responsibility for behavior belongs mainly to reward (reinforcement) systems in the environment.

Further discussion of operant methods and their applications to societal institutions will be presented later.

---

pressions seem more awkward. Other terms which have been suggested include "behavioral engineer," "change agent," "behavior analyst," "behavior modifier," but no one of them has taken hold as yet.

Systematic desensitization. Joseph Wolpe of the Department of Psychiatry at Temple University is both the originator and most outspoken proponent of this method. It is used mainly for reducing incapacitating anxiety surrounding specific objects or situations (e.g., phobias). The patient first constructs a list of fear-producing situations arranged in a "hierarchy" from the most to least frightening and is also instructed in deep relaxation methods. When both the hierarchy and the relaxation learning are complete, the therapist presents items from the list in a step-by-step procedure beginning with the least anxiety-producing items and gradually working up to the most feared items. The patient is asked to imagine the anxiety-producing situation as vividly as possible while remaining in the relaxed state.[104]

In a case study reported in *The Psychoanalytic Review*,[105] a patient with a fear of conducting a sales interview constructed the following hierarchy (from least to most anxiety-producing):

1. Thinking of making a call next week.
2. Thinking of making a phone call to a secretary.
3. Having name of potential buyer.
4. Thinking of going to the interview.
5. Enter cab to go to interview.
6. In cab on way to interview.
7. Cab stops at building.
8. Leave cab.
9. Enter building.
10. Walk to elevator.
11. Enter elevator.
12. Elevator ascending.
13. Leave elevator.
14. Walk down hall.
15. At door of office.
16. Speak to secretary.
17. Enter office.
18. See interviewer.

The results of studies in which systematic desensitization was evaluated have been "overwhelmingly" positive:

For the first time in the history of psychological treatments, a specific therapeutic package reliably produced measurable benefits for clients across a broad range of distressing problems in which anxiety was of fundamental importance. "Relapse" and "symptom substitution" were notably lacking. . . .[106]

However, some researchers have found even better results with other behavioral techniques,[107] and others have found relaxation is unnecessary to achieve the results.[108]

Aversion techniques. An alcoholic is given a drug which induces feelings of nausea if alcohol is consumed.[109] Homosexual males were presented with photographs of female and male nudes and given electric shocks if they did not rapidly depress the switch to turn off male pictures.[110] A severely schizophrenic girl was given electric shocks whenever she engaged in the self-mutilative act of head beating.[111] A nine-month-old infant with persistent vomiting was given electric shocks at the start of vomiting and at intervals during vomiting.[112] The patient is instructed to imagine the unpleasant consequences of her behavior whenever she is tempted to engage in it.[113] A boy who had engaged in frequent temper tantrums in the hospital ward was immediately removed and placed in his room for at least ten minutes.[114] A boy who exhibited obstreperous behavior in the classroom was sent home for the remainder of the day at the first behavior that exceeded clearly defined limits.[115]

Aversive techniques* are undoubtedly the most controversial major area of behavior therapy from both a theoretical and ethical point of view. They are often viewed with horror, especially if they involve electric shock. Although they are sometimes linked in the public mind with operant conditioning, B. F. Skinner of Harvard University, originator of that concept, has neither investigated nor recommended them. On the contrary, one of Skinner's major objectives is to reduce or eliminate the strong tendency in this culture to rely on such methods. He feels they do not produce lasting positive results and they entail many undesirable side effects.[116]

---

* That most time-honored of "folk methods," spanking, falls squarely into the aversive category.

In the situations listed above, however, it must be noted that the clinicians and researchers involved in them felt they had been successful. The nine-month-old child, for example, had suffered severe weight loss; no organic basis for the vomiting had been found, and many other methods had been tried. Six months later, she had gained weight, was responsive to people, and was generally healthy and normal. In a number of research studies, aversive methods have been found to produce better results than other techniques.[117] That punishment sometimes seems "to work" and that there may be situations for which no other method has yet been found is not sufficient reason, however, to advocate their general use or to abandon the search for effective nonaversive methods.

Contrary to popular opinion, aversive methods are not used by many behavior therapists and are used by a variety of insight and "humanist" therapists. Anxiety induction is a common tactic for "motivating" the patient to remain in psychodynamic interview treatment. A number of encounter group approaches use assaultive techniques involving severe criticism of each other by members of the group. Psychoanalysts have theorized that electric shock therapy has positive effects because it acts like a severe punishment, thereby relieving guilt feelings.

Modeling. "Modeling" refers essentially to teaching through providing a basis of imitation. An early therapeutic use was reported in 1924: children who were initially afraid of rabbits would touch and play with them after seeing other children do so.[118] Nursery school children who played by themselves all the time became more social after seeing a film in which other children engaged in active social interactions.[119] Adult schizophrenics began to talk more about their feelings in group therapy when two more talkative patients were added to the group.[120]

Implosive therapy. In implosive therapy, a person with a phobia is subjected repeatedly to situations that evoke the most extreme reactions:

A person afraid of a snake would be requested to view [herself] picking up and handling a snake. . . . [She]

would be instructed to feel how slimy the snake was . . .
[and] to experience the snake crawling over [her] body
and biting and ripping [her] flesh.[121]

This is actually another form of aversive therapy, and it is almost exactly the opposite of systematic desensitization.
Implosive therapy is also said to be successful. Furthermore,
it "appeals to psychoanalytic interpretations and clinical intui-
tions."[122]

These examples indicate some of the variety of techniques
of those who call themselves behavior therapists. They are
not equally well supported by research, but generally have
some basis in scientific experiments. When the goals and procedures of behavior therapists are clear, the client is provided with some degree of protection against the abuses of
insight psychotherapy. And it is less demeaning to be treated
for a bad habit or annoying fear than for a vague and mysti-
fying "neurosis" that only the doctor can see. For one thing,
and a very important thing it is, the patient can indicate
what the goals of treatment are and she can tell whether they
have been accomplished.

At least she can in theory. Behavior therapy is not immune
from the corruption inherent in professionalism. The use of
the term behavior "therapy" shows that practitioners are
ready to retain the advantage of association with the image
of the all-prestigious medical doctor despite pious acknowl-
edgment of the inappropriateness of medical terminology
within the behavior therapy journals. I have heard psychologists and psychiatrists who call themselves behavior therapists take pride in an eclectism which includes psychodynamic counseling for certain patients. When professional
behavior is unstandardized and allowed to range freely
across a broad spectrum of possibilities, there exists a clear
and present danger that the specific procedure adopted for a
particular individual client may tend toward what she will
find acceptable rather than what her "condition" requires.

Psychodynamic ideology and procedures proliferated
widely in this culture despite growing scientific evidence of
ineffectiveness and even harmfulness. This is because professionalism thrives on public acceptance of and faith in the au-

thority of the professional and the absence of accountability. For centuries, the status of the medical profession was ineffectiveness and harmfulness cloaked by mystique. The public desperately wanted to believe in medical treatment because it gave hope to the doomed. Today, despite scientific advances which enable medical doctors to provide real assistance, organized medicine is still riddled with the evils of professionalism that permit continued economic exploitation of the public.[123] Association with the medical image by psychotherapists, including behavior therapists, increases their ability to exploit in the same way.

6
Women and the
Psychotherapy Professions

IMAGES OF WOMEN IN THE PATRIARCHY

This culture defines female and male roles as polar opposites in many ways. Women are believed to be more emotional, intuitive, erratic, less intelligent, less persistent, and weaker. The stereotyped differences place women in a subservient position. There are only two reactions that a woman can logically have to this cultural assertion of her inferiority: she can accept it or she can reject it. To reject it is to be feminist.

Some women seek ways of avoiding the problem. The most typical is to maintain that although women may be inferior, it is only in certain ways; what they really are is *unlike* men. Men do some things well, but women do other things well. Each role is important. Man has his place and his functions, woman has hers. But woman's place turns out to be the very inferiority we began with, and this line of thinking implies acceptance of women's inferior status. Flagrant discrimination against women in employment, in education, and in social conditions tend to be unrecognized or rationalized: "Women don't work as well; they have less economic responsibility; they deserve less." When it comes to her own situation, the woman who accepts the cultural designations blames herself for her troubles. When she is not accepted into graduate school, when she does not receive that promotion, when her remarks at a cocktail party carry less weight than those of males, she assumes her own performance is at fault and vows to try harder next time. Perhaps she gets angry about the specific situation and the particular individuals involved in it. If she is not employed outside the home, and not assertive in social situations, she runs less risk of failure. A homebody is protected from some of the abuses her more ambitious sister suffers, although the woman who confines herself to purely domestic pursuits faces a more difficult time in later life when her "nest" empties.

For women of talent and ambition, for those who are doers, who may have excelled in childhood and been encouraged, and for those who, even in today's patriarchal world, have gained some awareness of their potential for contributing to their culture, identification with the traditional passivity of woman's cultural role is impossible. Although through labor, determination, and a considerable amount of luck, a woman can meet with some success, no matter how great her achievements, no woman in this society has ever accomplished what a male of her ability, drive, and circumstances could have achieved. The most renowned of female achievers are but a shadow of what they might have been had they not had to engage in additional struggle due to the discrimination and prejudice they suffered. It is, furthermore, a mistake to believe that this is no longer true, or that it is less true today than in the past. In her article "The Declining Status of Women: Popular Myths and the Failure of Functionalist Thought," Dean D. Knudsen reports that between the years 1940 and 1964 women "suffered a loss in status" as measured by occupation, income, and education.[1]

Early adult years, even the teens, are usually the most productive years in the lives of mathematicians and physical scientists. But Marie Curie, who won two Nobel Prizes for sci ence, spent those years as a governess earning money to pay for her brother's education. During the years of collaborative effort with her scientist husband, Pierre, she alone cooked and cleaned their living quarters and was responsible for child care. Later, despite international recognition of her scientific achievements, she was denied a faculty position at the University of Paris because of her sex. In fact, women achievers, with the notable exception of Curie and a very few others, have almost all been writers. Even so, it is doubtful whether George Sand or the Brontë sisters would have been as successful had they not initially used men's names.

Even for the most accomplished of women, the sex role she is obliged to assume is a liability when it comes to contributing to the larger society. We might well wonder how women of ability and achievement reconcile the culturally defined inferiority of women with their own ambitions and attainments. Some few attribute their problems realistically to unwarranted discrimination against them. But, as Marilyn Salzman-Webb has pointed out, such a feminist and self-confident view is a difficult one to maintain. In her article "Woman as Secretary, Sexpot, Spender, Sow, Civic Actor, Sickie," Salzman-Webb lists some of the roles for which women in this society have been trained. "Feminist" is not among them.

Most "successful" women view themselves as different from and superior to other women. But their goals for themselves are usually unattainable, and therein lies their tragedy. Their colleagues and their superiors react with feelings of jealousy and superiority toward them.[2] Simone de Beauvoir claims not to have experienced any direct discrimination within her circle of French intellectuals, but she was surprised and hurt at the response of writer and friend Albert Camus and others to her feminist book *The Second Sex*. Their reactions showed that they had always felt themselves to be superior, and they were angered by a woman's saying the things she had said in her book.[3]

Talented women seldom rise to the top of their profession or realize their full potential, no matter how great their ability or how prominent they become. Furthermore, they are induced to try for superhuman achievement, to add to the success they may achieve in the outside world the ability to maintain the most attractive home, best beloved husband, best behaved children, most perfect "figure," and gourmet cuisine. The TV career girl-housewife is a sex object who cheerfully makes the best coffee for her husband in an immaculate kitchen where breakfast is served with real china and fresh flowers. When the woman who tries to fulfill this ideal meets setbacks, her guilt over her failure often sends her to a psychotherapist to discover and correct what is wrong with her.

Because the culture demands impossible and contradictory behaviors from women, they experience a culturally induced dissatisfaction with themselves and their lives. This dissatisfaction is more acute in women, whether domestic or abroad in the world, who have an urge to accomplish that has met obstacles both in themselves and imposed on them by others. As Simone de Beauvoir said: "It is perfectly natural for a . . . woman to feel indignant at the limitations imposed by her sex. The real question is not why she should reject them: the problem is rather to understand why she accepts them."[4] Involvement of women in psychotherapy, which promises to alleviate their pain, cure their defects, and help them realize their potential for happiness, has led, directly and indirectly, to acceptance of these conditions.

Throughout most of this book, I use male pronouns to refer to psychotherapists. This is not because all psychotherapists are male (as many as 25 percent are female)* but because the kinds of psychotherapy with which I am concerned are very male-dominated and misogynist enterprises. Women whose problems emanate from the sex discrimination and prejudices of the society they live in are additionally damaged by psychotherapists who find the roots of the difficulties in the women's own behaviors, attitudes, and feelings. The principle of individual causation is the very corner-

* This may be an overestimation. In "Sex and Salary," Judith N. Cates reported that "in 1970, the doctorate work force in psychology consisted of 86 percent men and 14 percent women." The percentage of women psychiatrists is even lower. On the other hand, women among M.A. level psychologists and social workers are a higher percentage.

stone on which the edifice of individual psychodynamic insight therapy has been erected. Both in principle and in practice, such therapy ignores the role of the societal environment.

Higher rates of women in psychotherapy are often interpreted as evidence that women are genetically prone to psychic disturbance. This view, which began in antiquity, supports the stereotype that women are more emotional and less rational than men. Although classified as a neurosis for the first time by Cullen in 1769, the term "hysteria," which first appeared in the Hippocratic writings, referred to an "affliction of the uterus." In the nineteenth century, thousands of oophorectomies (and clitoridectomies) were performed on innocent but "hysterical" women, according to W. F. Knoff in "A History of the Concept of Neurosis with a Memoir of William Cullen." Even recent writers have called it a female disease.[5]

The sexes differ in the kind of mental illness they are likely to suffer from: there are more male alcoholics, more women with depressions, more males (and lower-income persons) with "personality disorders," more middle-income women with phobias, and more women than men sent into therapy by their spouses as a condition of a divorce settlement. But societies also differ in how pathology is defined; the same behavior may be viewed as pathological in one sex and nonpathological, even desirable, in the other.

Sociologists Walter R. Gove of Vanderbilt University and Jeannette F. Tudor of Central Michigan University explored the relationship between adult sex roles and mental illness in an article published in the *American Journal of Sociology* in 1973.[6] They confined their study to persons with conditions of no known organic origin, the "psychoneuroses" and "functional psychoses." Gove and Tudor indicate many reasons why women might be expected to suffer from emotional strain: their sources of gratification are more limited (men have job and home, women only home); household duties are frustratingly demanding yet relatively unappreciated, largely repetitive, and invisible except when neglected; opportunities for women outside the home are restricted, making it exceedingly rare for a woman to find employment commensurate with her talents and educational background; and working outside the home tends not to appreciably reduce her household responsibilities. Several recent studies indicate that women "have a more negative image of themselves" and are more likely to become depressed. From the results of community surveys, first admissions to mental hospitals, psychiatric care in outpatient clinics, private outpatient psychiatric care, and the prevalence of mental illness in the general practice of physicians, Gove and Tudor conclude that:

> All the data on mental illness (as we have defined it) indicate that more women than men are mentally ill. It is especially important to note that this finding is not dependent on who is doing the selection. For example, if we look at admissions to mental hospitals, where the societal response would appear to be of prime importance, women have higher rates; if we look at treatment by general physicians, where self-selection would appear to be of prime importance, women have higher rates; and if we look at community surveys, where the attempt is to eliminate selection processes, women have higher rates.[7]

The fact that these differences between the sexes are among *married* persons—single men are slightly more likely than single women to be mentally ill—supports Gove and Tudor's contention that it is the social system, not inherent tendencies toward emotional disturbance, that produces the high incidence of mental illness among women.

All forms of depression are more frequent in women than in men, a finding that has led to varying, and contradictory attempts at explanation. It is said that women have more time to complain, lead more unfulfilling lives due to their inferior opportunities for rewarding employment, have more "unruly" physiological natures, and so on. Fieve has suggested that some depressions are carried by a defective gene in the X chromosome. Given the prejudice against women by members of the psychiatric and psychological professions, scientific understanding may be retarded until that condition itself is changed.

That attitudes prejudicial to women prevail among psychotherapists themselves is well documented. Some of the most revealing indications that sex-role stereotypes influence clinical judgments of mental illness can be found in an article published in 1970 in the *Journal of Consulting and Clinical Psychology* by psychologist Inge K. Broverman and her associates. Their investigations illuminated the existence of a double standard of mental health. Actively functioning clinicians were asked to select attributes that defined as "healthy, mature, socially competent" an adult (sex unspecified), a woman, and a man. It was found that:

> The clinicians' concepts of a healthy, mature man do not differ significantly from their concepts of a healthy adult. However, the clinicians' concepts of a mature, healthy woman do differ significantly from their adult health concepts. Clinicians are significantly less likely to attribute traits which characterize healthy adults to a woman than they are likely to attribute these traits to a healthy man.[8]

Broverman and her associates consider this bias to result from an "adjustment" concept of mental health:

> Thus, for a woman to be healthy, from an adjustment viewpoint, she must adjust to and accept the behavioral norms for her sex, even though these behaviors are generally less socially desirable and considered to be less healthy for the generalized competent mature adult.
> By way of analogy, one could argue that a black person who conformed to the "pre-civil rights" southern Negro stereotype, that is, a docile, unambitious, childlike, etc. person, was well adjusted to his environment and, therefore, a mature and healthy adult.[9]

The clinicians defined healthy as being independent, skilled, dominant, direct, adventurous, self-confident, ambitious, and not easily influenced. For a woman to behave in this fashion is to risk having her femininity questioned. The acceptance of the sex-role stereotypes by psychotherapy clinicians affects the culture through both their influence on individuals who come to them for treatment and their function as consultants to governmental and private institutions and agencies of various kinds.

While male patients are also adversely affected by abuses of psychotherapy, this is not equal in degree or manner to the way women are affected. A female patient with a male therapist differs from a male patient with a male therapist in at least two ways: (1) Women are treated differently outside the therapy sessions in a myriad of ways that psychology and psychiatry have never studied, and (2) the specific training that psychotherapists receive puts the woman patient at a disadvantage. The male patient is a member of the respected upper caste and a potential buddy for his male therapist. In *The Making of a Psychiatrist,* David S. Viscott illustrates this attitude when he describes a female patient with whom it "would be wrong" to discuss details about his personal life because it might encourage "erotic transference." But he felt it was quite reasonable to reveal himself by sharing an interest in sports with a male patient.[10]

Another difference between female and male patients is that a large proportion of the female patients, most of those who are married, are not paying for their own treatment. Husbands, sometimes former husbands, when therapy costs are included in divorce settlements, or the insurance companies which cover their husbands' medical insurance pay the bills. Ultimately, the values of the financing agent tend to be served by any enterprise. In the case of husband's or husbands' employers, it is reasonable to assume that the value of the woman is related to whatever activities on her part keep her husband functioning on his job. Such activities are more likely to include homemaking and child rearing, less likely to include her independent employment.

It has frequently been observed that mental illness is essentially defined in terms of adequate performance relative to standards that may differ in various cultures, subcultures, and periods of history. There is, in other words, some arbitrariness about who is mentally ill. As psychologist Merton S. Krause noted, "the values that generically define disease are ultimately cultural or social rather than medical or other professional ones."[11] And standards are not necessarily the same for poor and wealthy, or for female and male. Among the reasons which have been advanced to explain the higher proportion of women in private psychotherapy is that it is more socially acceptable for women to admit to being depressed, because women are "normally" more neurotic anyway. Theodore R. Sarbin and James C. Mancuso, in "Failures of a Moral Enterprise: Attitudes of the Public Toward Mental Illness," say that when "a male's behavior reflects depression, it is regarded as more disruptive (and thus the man is more strongly rejected) than is the same behavior in a female."

A number of studies and surveys indicate that psychotherapists prefer female patients,[12] and it has been observed that female patients are more likely to feel "warmth" for the therapist.[13] The preference by female patients, especially unmarried female patients, for male therapists is also well known.[14] In *The Second Sex,* Simone de Beauvoir observes that it is the masculine world which is admired by women, even after marriage: "man . . . remains the truth of the universe, the supreme authority, the marvelous master, eye, prey, pleasure, adventure, salvation; he still incarnates transcendence, he is the answer to every question."[15] A woman turns to a man when she looks for a guiding hand in her life. Beauvoir notes that "there are two categories of men especially destined by profession to become confidants and mentors: priests and doctors."[16] Most of Freud's famous cases were female, and the concept of the female rather than the male as private therapy patient is so prevalent that authors occasionally use the female pronoun when referring to patients in general. And yet, beginning with Freud, who complained that he did not understand women or know what "they want," psychotherapists have perpetuated extremely damaging images of women within the profession and to society at large.

Naomi Weisstein, in one of the most popular of recent protests against the male psychologist's "construction of the female," notes that the views of such renowned psychotherapists as Erik Erikson, Bruno Bettelheim, and Joseph Rheingold

reflect, in a surprisingly transparent way, the cultural consensus. They not only assert that a woman is defined by her ability to attract men, they see no alternative definitions. They think that the definition of a woman in terms of a man is the way it should be; and they back it up with psychosexual incantation and biological ritual curses. A woman has an identity if she is attractive enough to obtain a man, and thus, a home; for this will allow her to set about her life's task of "joyful altruism and nurturance."[17]

The basic argument of Weisstein's paper is that psychology has nothing of importance to say about women because the "central assumption for most psychologists of human personality has been that human behavior rests on an individual and inner dynamic, perhaps fixed in infancy, perhaps fixed by genitalia, perhaps simply arranged in a rather immovable cognitive network." While evidence is mounting that what a person does and how a person feels will be determined by the expectations and behavior of people in the environment, psychotherapists, clinical psychologists, and psychiatrists remain entrenched in biased and misogynist viewpoints. Weisstein, a scientific psychologist as well as a feminist, indicts the psychoanalytic tradition for not considering it "necessary to have evidence in support of their theories"[18] and for looking for "inner traits when they should have been looking for social context."[19] She describes an experience as a Harvard graduate student in which her seminar class was asked to identify the sex of the writers of two sets of responses, one by females, the other by males, to the Thematic Apperception Test (TAT) pictures, a standard clinical test in which the client invents a story in response to a set of photographs. Although the group had been studying sex differences intensively for six weeks before they made their judgments, the stories were correctly identified by only four students out of twenty; sixteen students judged that the stories written by men were written by women, and the stories written by women were written by men—a result that would have occurred by chance only four times in a thousand.[20]

The study of women is rarely included as one of the topics that comprise the field of psychology. Of thirty-five introductory textbooks in social psychology published between 1940 and 1970, only one contained a full chapter on women.[21] The average number of pages devoted to women was 5.4, a figure bloated by that one book and one chapter (thirty-six pages). Eleven books had between two and seventeen pages containing references to such woman-related topics as "sex roles," "sex identification," "role behavior," "sexual behavior," and "penis envy"; ten of the textbooks had no reference at all to these topics. Furthermore, the omission of topics concerning women is a recent and continuing phenomenon. The book with a full chapter was published in 1966; all other books with more than six pages on women-related topics were published before 1964. A well-known social psychologist listed twenty-five types of victims of prejudice, without including women.[22]

When women appear in social psychology textbooks, their roles of child rearer and homemaker are unquestionably accepted as universals. Also unquestioned is the child's need for sex identification, as shown in this typical statement: "Children who are denied the opportunity to clearly identify female and masculine standards are likely to suffer confusion of sex identification all their lives."[23]

The failure of social psychology to deal with women is a reflection of the Freudian influence. The psychoanalytic orientation, which has dominated clinical psychology, psychiatry, and social work for decades, is one in which women are viewed as biological, intellectual, social, and moral inferiors of men. Many women with just grievances against the social order considered themselves, and were considered to be, psychologically ill and received "treatment" at the hands of practitioners who interpreted their difficulties as the outcome of internal pathology rather than as a reaction to oppressive social forces.*

Recently, the feminist writer Kate Millett has taken Freud to task for his views on women and their "universally experienced" envy of the male phallus. Millett reminds us that

* The resistance of psychoanalysts to attributing the cause of pathology to cultural forces has roots in European history. The turn-of-the-century movement for Jewish integration led to understressing differences. Furthermore, the many psychoanalysts forced to emigrate during the Nazi era, including Freud himself, who spent his last years in England, would have had nontransferable skills if differences between groups of patients and the societies in which they were reared were emphasized (see Gorer, "Psychoanalysis in the World," in *Psychoanalysis Observed*).

the three most distinguishing traits of female personality were, in Freud's view, passivity, masochism, and narcissism. Even here, one can see a certain merit in the Freudian paradigm taken as pure *description*. The position of women. . . . is such that they are expected to be passive, to suffer, and to be sexual objects; . . . This is not however what Freud had in mind. . . . He believed that the elaborate culture construction we call "femininity" was largely organic. . . .[24]

Unlike academic psychologists, therapists have not ignored women. In the writings of psychotherapists, especially psychoanalysts, outright hostility toward women is a recurrent theme. Entire books have been written which attempt to validate misogynist views. Millett attributes the failure of early twentieth-century feminists in part to a "counterrevolution," of which Freud was the spiritual leader who sanctified male supremacy in terms of inevitable biology and closed the door on exploring cultural forces contributing to female oppression.[25] With renewed scientific and ideological support provided by Freudian psychiatry, patriarchal concepts were strengthened.

For a time, sexual "emancipation," which Freud did not himself support but which the emphasis on sexuality in psychoanalytic theory was used to rationalize, clouded the issue. In the thirties and forties, the sophisticated male's ideal was a woman with a diaphragm who had been "analyzed." The obvious implication was that she would then be a sexual playmate without fear of pregnancy, because "repression" of sexuality had become, in popular Freudianism, a contribution to mental illness.

It also began to be assumed, by therapists and by the public alike, that the "mature woman" was one who flattered the male with vaginal orgasms. Freud was emphatic in his declaration that clitoral pleasure was infantile and, ultimately, something to be ashamed of, that only the pleasure given by the male through vaginal penetration was "healthy," "mature," and proper. At puberty, the normal girl transfers the site of sexual sensations from the clitoris to the vagina. Alix Shulman notes: "A woman who fails to [do that] is . . . regressive, infantile, neurotic, hysteric, and frigid. . . . A woman is frigid according to many of Freud's followers even today, if she does not have vaginal orgasms. . . ."[26] Clinical refutation came from the research of Virginia Johnson and William E. Masters when direct observation revealed that the orgasm of intercourse is physiologically the same as orgasm achieved through clitoral stimulation.[27] The woman's orgasm is a total sexual response, a response found by the sex researchers to be more reliably reached by clitoral stimulation than through intercourse. Yet generations of women were so convinced that vaginal orgasm was essential to their image, if not to their physiological functioning, that the practice of orgasm-simulation became widespread. If she did not experience orgasm, the woman was compelled to fake it. If she didn't, Shulman observes, "she must submit to being called frigid or infantile by professional name-calling psychologists, doctors, and all who listen to them, and she must risk the displeasure and reprisal of her mate."[28]

In 1970, at the Annual Meetings of the American Psychological Association, a symposium on "frigidity" was presented by a panel of male psychologists. At the time, for most of the two hundred or so people in the audience there was nothing questionable about either the topic or the choice of speakers, but it is doubtful that such a panel will ever be formed again. Feminist psychologist Jo-Ann Evans Gardner, organizer of the Association for Women in Psychology, made it clear that the era of female passivity in these matters had ended. Before the panel had even begun, she challenged its legitimacy from the floor, and before the session was finished, two hundred people had learned that women would no longer sit back and listen quietly to men discussing what they could not know anything about. Although she began her challenge alone, Dr. Gardner was joined by other female members of the audience as the session progressed. The most unanswerable point made by the women was that the panelists, all males, defined sexual adequacy of women in terms of male pleasure, and that this was both oppressive and fallacious.

"Women do not tell men honestly how we feel," the women said. "We lie. We have become expert at pretending to experience sexual excitement and orgasm to appease men."

PSYCHOTHERAPY IS A MALE ENTERPRISE

Like sociology, English literature, and biology, academic and professional fields in which there are at least a substantial minority of female aspirants, psychology shows the usual pyramid pattern in which the proportion of women steadily diminishes as one climbs upward in the hierarchy of professional status, employment, rank, and income.[29] At the college level approximately half of the psychology students are female; the percentage is less at the graduate level; and only about 20 to 25 percent of members of the American Psychological Association are women. In 1973 the *APA Monitor* ("Survey Paints Picture of Psychology Manpower,")[30] reported that about 75 percent of all psychologists—not just psychotherapists—are male, but the figure for doctoral psychologists is higher. Most of my examples are from psychology. But since 89 percent of psychiatrists are male as compared with only 76 percent of psychologists, so my emphasis on psychology underestimates the severity of the problem of inadequate female representation among psychotherapy professionals. Although the percentage of women in social work is high, very few women social workers are conducting autonomous private therapy practices, and the leadership in psychotherapy is clearly among psychologists and psychiatrists.

From another report published in the *APA Monitor* in 1974, we learn that "service providers" (those who spend some proportion of their time in providing direct services in the practice and application of psychology, mostly psychotherapists) totaled 62.5 percent of 27,530 APA members questioned. Of these, 76 percent were male. Of psychotherapists with a doctoral degree, 81.7 percent were male; at the master's degree level, the percentage of men dropped to 63.1 percent. The 9,680 men who were doctoral-level service providers reported an annual median income of $24,000 with 10 percent reporting $36,000 or more; women Ph.D.'s reported a median income of $17,250 with the highest 10 percent reporting only $26,000 or more, $10,000 a year less than the males. For males with master's degrees, the median income was $17,400 (higher than for female doctorates), for women with master's degrees it was $14,000. Most psychologists are employed in institutions—only 27.4 percent of all respondents indicated part-time fee-for-service practice—but for those who "occasionally hang out a shingle," incomes were higher: $25,130 for men; $19,027 for women, with the highest 10 percent cutoff at $42,667 for men, $30,639 for women—a difference of over $12,000.[31]

A survey of the APA Directory reported in 1970 found lower proportions of women in all higher-ranking positions and statuses. Of relatively well-known women psychologists, only 35 percent held the academic rank of professor, compared with 87 percent of comparably well-known men. Distribution of women among various subdivisions of psychology follow two principles: there are more women in fields more closely associated with traditional conceptions of women's role in society, and there are fewer women in the higher-paying fields. Women were only 3 percent of engineering psychologists, 6 percent of industrial and personnel psychologists, and 11 percent of physiological psychologists, compared with 42 percent of developmental (child) psychologists, 40 percent of school psychologists, 24 percent of clinical psychologists, and 23 percent of educational psychologists.[32]

Associate APA members are graduate students and persons with two years of graduate study in psychology who are employed as psychologists. Members are those with a doctoral degree in psychology and those who became members under a "grandfather clause" which permitted nondoctorates who were already members of the organization when the rule requiring the doctorate went into effect to retain their memberships. Fellows are persons nominated by divisions of the Association and voted on by the Council of Representatives of the Association. In addition to a Ph.D. in psychology, Fellows must have five years' experience following the doctorate, be a member of the Association for at least a year, a member of the Nominating Division, and "present evidence of unusual and outstanding performance in the field of psychology." The percentage of male Associates was 71.3 percent; of Members 81.9 percent; of Fellows 85.6 percent. Again, the pyramid. At the 1970 APA Convention symposium, 89.9 percent of participants were male. Excluding the sessions that were formed that year by feminist psychologists in order to explore women's problems and to increase the contribution of women to the convention, the proportion of men symposia participants was 93 percent. Comparing the 1968 and 1970 editions of the Biographical Directories, the proportion of female Members decreased in three of six divisions examined, and proportion of female Fellows decreased in nine of the divisions examined.

In January 1974, the *American Psychologist* published a list of persons who had served as oral examiners or field observers of 1972–1973 candidates for the American Board of Professional Psychology diplomas. Of the almost two hundred names, 17.6 percent were of women. Women were elected to the office of APA president in 1972 (Anne Anastasi) and 1973 (Leona E. Tyler) after feminist psychologists became active in the Association, but the persons who held that position for the *fifty* years prior to 1972 were all males. Nor should this recent "tokenism" which permits a few visible members of a discriminated-against group to attain high level positions obscure the fact that the American Psychological Association governing body is still predominantly male.

The percentage of women on all faculties of colleges and universities has been falling in recent years, and it is lower today than it was a hundred years ago. The percentage of women graduate students is less now than it was in 1930. Of forty-six past presidents of the American Orthopsychiatric Association, only two were women.

Editorial boards of professional journals have been said to be among the most powerful direct influences on the profession, since the decisions of these persons largely determine the content of professional literature, and having articles accepted for publication has a great deal to do with professional advancement in academic and research institutions. Women have been consistently absent from these boards.[33] The journal *Behavior Therapy* on the cover of its January 1973 issue listed thirty-two editors; only one was a woman.

Of twenty-eight listed in the Summer 1973 issue of the *Journal of Contemporary Psychotherapy,* two were women. The examples given well represent the proportion of women editors of the major psychiatric and psychological journals.

June 1973 saw the publication of "the first general psychology handbook in two decades . . . the most substantial collaboration of outstanding minds in the history of psychology . . . [surveying] the most recent developments and directions in experimental psychology."[34] The six coeditors were all male. Only 6.7 percent of its forty-five chapters were authored or coauthored by women; only one chapter of twenty-eight singly authored chapters was by a woman. The only chapter in which three persons coauthored, the chapter on developmental psychology, was by women. In a husband and wife collaboration, a wife was the junior author. These were the five women out of a total of sixty authors. They were not even spread out among the topics but concentrated in "women's" areas, the topics related to children.

Women are discriminated against along every step of the way. Whatever women accomplish is more critically evaluated. Although the most determined and competent may pass through the doors at the lower levels, the criteria grow ever more stringent and subjective at the top levels. Most people, if they think of any psychologists or psychiatrists at all, will find that only men come to mind. If asked to name the most influential living female psychologists, even relatively sophisticated persons will draw a blank, with the possible exception of Anna Freud. When I made this point in one of my female psychology undergraduate courses, I saw a lot of puzzled faces—only one student had heard of Anna Freud!

The general attitude toward women was probably well expressed by a professor of psychology at Bryn Mawr College. When asked to explain and, if possible, justify the decreasing proportion of female faculty members at schools with predominantly female enrollment, he said, "In order to get quality, we have to hire men." Quality, which exists in women as well as in men, is not perceived as such in female applicants for faculty positions.

The commercial magazine *Psychology Today* has become very influential as a public relations organ for the behavioral sciences. In its first two years of publishing, it used proportionately fewer women even than the professional journals. About 6.5 percent of its articles had women senior authors. Of seven articles with women coauthors, the woman's husband was senior author of four. A feature of the magazine is an interview with a well-known person. Of thirty-four such interviews, three included women. Not one, however, included a woman psychologist discussing her theories or her research. A book of articles collected from the magazine reduced the female representation still further. Of sixty-nine articles, one was solely authored by a woman, and four others were written by wives writing as junior author under their husband's senior authorship. Twenty-two articles in which women were involved either as senior or junior authors were on topics generally regarded as "female domain"; sixteen of these were about child development, motherhood, female sexuality, or family life. On the other hand, the majority of the total number of articles in these areas were *not* written by women. Men wrote over 60 percent of articles on women, sex, and sex roles, and over 70 percent of those on children. Three of the six articles directly related to motherhood were written by men.

There are many wife-husband teams in psychology. Possibly half of the twenty best-known women psychologists are members of such teams. Many doors are opened to such women that would otherwise be closed. Most women of high professional potential are stifled in an atmosphere of oppressive responsibilities in the office and at home. Stimulation from colleagues is often lacking. If a woman is on a college campus, it is likely to be at an institution considered inferior, one that lacks the opportunity for intellectual cross-fertilization. Marriage to a successful psychologist removes some of these barriers. While she may not have (probably never has) equal rank or pay to that of her husband, she has the opportunity to interact informally with him and his colleagues. Martha S. White, in "Psychological and Social Barriers to Women in Science,"[35] says that because of moving from one location to another to follow her husband's schools and jobs, having babies, and simply because of discrimination itself, women are likely to miss an important aspect of professional training in which the young professional learns about many aspects of institutions, journals, professional meetings, methods of obtaining source materials, and finding grant applications. These things are not taught formally, but are learned in the course of associations that women are typically excluded from. Furthermore, White says that young women are less likely to become a "protégé" of an older professional, and therefore less likely to be introduced to colleagues or sponsored for jobs. In many ways, having a husband in the field helps to overcome these barriers.

One of the more flagrant displays of the male chauvinist attitude in the field of psychotherapy, although by no means an unusual one, can be found in the book *Changing Frontiers in the Science of Psychotherapy* by Allen E. Bergin and Hans S. Strupp. The authors, both leaders in the fields of psychotherapy and psychotherapy research, embarked on a government-financed round of interviews in which they explored the feasibility of collaborative research in psychotherapy. How they selected their consultants is not described, but in a field in which women do exist, and where estimates of "service recipients" are generally estimated at about 80 percent female, not one of their more than forty consultants was a woman! Probably, Bergin and Strupp set out their criteria for selecting consultants more or less informally, in terms of who they knew and who was known in the field, subjective evaluation of the probable value of the interview to the project, and so forth. Somehow, no woman fitted the criteria.

In concluding this brief and entirely inadequate glimpse into the world of the barriers faced by women professionals, I want to assure the reader that my selections represent the problems accurately. Most of them were taken from the field of psychology, which is known to be more open to women than is psychiatry. While social work used to be a "woman's field," men have recently begun to conduct a wholesale invasion, especially of the more prestigious and lucrative positions and of private practice. Women may be the patients, but few of them are therapists, and fewer still are in positions of leadership and influence in the training institutions or among published spokespersons.

PSYCHIATRY WRITES ABOUT WOMEN

In a psychology not pinned down to objective assessments and dominated by patriarchal concepts, it is not surprising that patriarchy-serving, woman-derogating themes should emerge. One of the most common and most virulent is the concept of the "castrating woman." Wishing unconsciously to physically desex males, in fact she evidences her "pathology" largely in verbal and other interpersonal behaviors. "Castrating" is anything a woman does which suggests or can be interpreted as undermining the dominant status of a male. It is, for example, "castrating" for a woman to excel over a man in any activity generally regarded as the male domain, or in any game or sport in which women and men are in competition. (It is devastating to the male ego when a woman consistently excels at chess, science, or tennis.) Used loosely, as the term so often is, it refers to anything a woman does which is not in the best interests of a man. Psychologist Matina Horner's findings that women often show a tendency to avoid succeeding[36] may reflect their attempt to avoid the label castrating. Fortunately, one hears that term less often these days, but it has by no means died out among psychotherapists.* I have even heard the term used to describe a patient whose "castrating" actions toward her analyst consisted in not improving in therapy. This idea, expressed during an interview with a practicing psychotherapist, does not seem at all remarkable in the context of psychotherapy writings about women. It fulfills the definition of castrating as *anything* done by a woman (in this case, the patient) which adversely affects the situation of a man (the therapist).

Historically, the demeaning of women is an integral part of psychotherapy theory. To Sigmund Freud, woman was or-

---

* Bergin and Strupp, in *Changing Frontiers*, use the term "castrating female syndrome" as an example of a common "homogeneous problem" in setting out questions and topics for their interviews with male consultants (p. 173).

ganically inferior. According to psychotherapy historian Gregory Zilboorg, the expression "anatomy is destiny" was first expressed by one of the most misogynistic of men, Napoleon Bonaparte,[37] but it so well expressed Freud's position that most people believe him to have originated it. Zilboorg writes that "the superiority of man, both implied and asserted in psychoanalytic theory, [was] treated with postulative conviction."[38] Furthermore, he states:

> psychoanalysis failed to shed much light on man's [i.e., men's] fundamental hostility toward women, and failed to give in substance any more satisfactory answer than that this is a man's world, the woman has a hard time in it, and that this is her fate. More than that, psychoanalysis seemed to lend some support to the traditional attitude of modern civilization by pointing to the woman's organic, psychological, and cultural inadequacy.[39]

The "angry woman syndrome," presented in 1971 by psychiatrist Nathan Rickles, is all too representative of much of the psychiatric writing about women. Rickles claims to have observed the symptoms of this "condition" during his thirty-five years of experience with psychotherapeutic treatment:

> The patients, all women, usually over 40, present a striking similarity in background, marital adjustment, proneness to excesses in alcohol and drugs, suicidal threats, and characteristically extreme bursts of uncontrollable temper. Sex enjoyment is enhanced after displaying their anger and demeaning their consorts.[40]

Rickles's own feelings appear to be exposed by the very terms he uses to further describe these patients:

> They take fiendish delight in deriding their husbands by such epithets as "mother-lovers" or "sister-lovers" or "daughter-lovers." They ridicule shared intimacies or confidences with baleful disregard for decency. They are extremely possessive and jealous women.[41]

According to Rickles, these women tend to be married to "uniquely passive" men who are "willing sufferers." The women themselves are "physically attractive and appealing to men" and are "surprisingly" successful in their careers.

Most of them come from homes in which their own mother is dominant in the family, sexually promiscuous, and a user of alcohol.

The tendency to locate the origin of pathology in a patient's "dominating mother" is one of the most pervasive themes in the psychotherapy literature. It suggests, among other things, that therapists are very sensitive to deviations from culturally designated sex roles. This willingness to see pathology in women is accompanied by resistance to finding the man at fault. Emphasis on the female influence in analyzing the roots of psychopathology has led to overlooking of even highly deviant behavior such as child molestation, desertion of the family, and actual physical assault by males. Rickles's description of the fathers of his "angry women" is typical of the leniency afforded males in psychoanalytic writing:

> The fathers were usually ineffectual men who, while striving to show some affection for their daughters, were so intimidated by the mothers as to remain almost neutral in their display.[42]

It must be underscored that Rickles's "syndrome" is not presented as the product of objective research, but in a loose and subjective case-study method. Descriptive comments are not supported by quantitative or behavioral evidence, and pejorative interpretations and terminology are not inhibited, as in the following:

> Any threat was overreacted to by spewing out vituperation and by taking alcohol and drugs. . . .[43]

> She rules the home with an iron fist and when crossed uses her temper outbursts as a means of constantly getting her own way.[44]

> This is one of the deplorable tactics of these women—nothing is sacred to them in their fits of anger and their need to humiliate their lover.[45]

Although the women "seemingly adjust well" and appear on the surface to be poised and well organized, Rickles maintains that their "growing egos" were "shattered" by the treatment they received from *their mothers*, treatment so devastating that they developed a "morbid, negative approach to life."[46]

Unquestionably, something was bothering Rickles's patients; they had, after all, sought treatment. But in the cases he describes in detail, they refused to submit to treatment. This may be an indication of their strength, frustrating though it was to the therapist. Unfortunately for women patients, the values of the society and those of psychotherapists often coincide, especially those regarding sex roles. Rickles's syndrome is likely to be seen as mental illness rather than the result of women of ability being frustrated by an unresponsive world.

Difficulties surrounding pregnancy and childbirth have been simplistically and cruelly interpreted by psychotherapists, particularly psychoanalysts, as a reflection of the woman's unconscious wishes. Complicated childbirth indicates rejection of the female role and the literal attempt to retain a symbol of masculinity; the baby represents the woman's longed-for penis. One of Rickles's patients reported that at the time of the birth of her child, while she was in labor, her husband had taken her sister out to dinner. For Rickles, it was an example of "these patients' phenomenal recall of past events" which, "regardless of their import, is magnified a thousand times over."[47] It is in fact perfectly normal for such an event to be remembered, since the circumstances surrounding childbirth are often recalled vividly. Rickles has no grounds for implying that recall of events at the time of parturition is in any way pathological, or even unusual.

According to some members of the medical profession, women have a "protective amnesia" concerning their labor and delivery experiences. I have found little evidence of this in over thirty interviews with women who described their childbirth experiences, even in some cases in which the amnesiac, scopalomine, had been administered.

Psychotherapists apply their interpretations of unconscious design on the mother's part to the childbirth experience so readily that not even an uncomplicated delivery is safe from attack. Florence Rush, writer and former social worker, who describes her younger years as ones in which she was a committed and conscientious Friend of Psychiatry, writes in her article "Who's Afraid of Margaret Ribble?" of her strong wish to be a mother and her interest and willingness to explore, discover, and remove any obstacles that might stand in her way. For this reason, she became a psychiatric patient. She had an uncomplicated pregnancy and a rapid and easy delivery of her child. Rush was interested in breast feeding her infant, primarily because her psychoanalytic orientation led her to the view that nursing was psychologically desirable for the child. Against her wishes, the nurses insisted on bottle feeding the infant. Her therapist, however, had a different view of it:

> I wonder if the unusually fast delivery was not, in fact, the somatic rejection of your child. You avoided a reasonable labor and in great haste discharged your son from your body. The panic around breast feeding was the result of guilt and to overcome this panic, you tried to obsessively control the child through food. Your deep rejection and hostility broke through when you forced the nurse not to feed the hungry baby.[48]

To call Rush's concern "panic" and "an attempt to obsessively control," revealed grave misunderstanding on the psychiatrist's part of the reality of her situation.

John H. Houck, Medical Director of the Institute of Living in Hartford, Connecticut, described the "intractable female patient" in an article in the *American Journal of Psychiatry*. As with Rickles's "angry woman," the "intractable female patient" syndrome does not fit into standard psychiatric classifications and, of course, is found only in women. Initial symptoms are depression and anxiety. According to Houck, the patient's mother dominated the family. The father was either absent or a passive personality.[49] The diagnoses of "intractable" patients range across psychoneurotic and psychotic categories. She is usually intelligent and a Friend and Supporter of Psychotherapy.[50] But, Houck warns, she is actually "a cold person, easily angered and unable to relate comfortably either to women or to men.[51] She tries to control the treatment situation, which then becomes stalemated and ultimately frustrating despite initial promise. She enjoys being hospitalized for the relief it provides from the everyday responsibilities of wife, mother, or daughter. Houck feels that therapy should be relatively brief and reality oriented. Her attention should be directed to her home and family responsibilities.[52] No further hospital admissions should be permitted, because of the relief they provide her from the normal obligations appropriate to the psychiatric conception of the female role.

The "castrating woman," the "angry woman," and the "intractable woman"—none of whom is usually or necessarily considered seriously mentally ill, and all of whom are troublesome with respect to fulfilling the normal, passive, feminine role—may in fact represent the emotional reactions of the psychotherapists to their patients' misbehavior. These women succeed, they assert themselves in their career aspirations, and they attempt to escape household chores. It seems obvious that they are reacting to the impossible conditions imposed on capable women in this society, but the hostility of their male therapists and the general commitment of psychiatry to locating pathology within the patient inhibit a true comprehension of the situation. Houck recognizes some relevance of the woman's external conditions when he recommends that the therapist's concern must often extend to social environmental change, but this turns out to be an attempt, through "aggressive" therapy, to turn her husband from his "passivity and diffidence" to a "posture of strength and resolution—especially towards his wife."[53] Thus, the environmental changes Houck favors are ones which would further entrap her. Houck is, in essence, asking the husband to keep the "intractable" woman in line, an approach that is entirely appropriate to patriarchal traditions.

Although much space in the psychiatric literature has been devoted to "dominant" women and "passive" men, the far more common and severe damage caused by the aggressiveness of men has been virtually overlooked. Rape is attributed to the seductiveness of the victim. Even child abuse is seen as primarily the woman's problem. Violence against wives is almost totally ignored.

Psychiatrist Melitta Schmideberg notes that "numerous social workers up and down the country are involved almost every day with wife-beating cases."[54] Schmideberg finds it "strange that for so long the community, the courts, the police and social workers lacked concern for persons in such need."[55] She suggests that the neglect of the "battered wife" is a survival from the days when a man "owned" his wife:

> Traditionally, the man was master in his own house. In old times, he sat in judgment of his children, servants and wife, and had not only the right, but the duty to chastise them if they deserved it. . . . Things have slowly changed, certainly, but to what degree?[56]

It is not that modern psychiatry condones wife-beating, but that the assaultive husband "suffers" from a condition not amenable to psychiatric treatment, the so-called untreatable personality disorders.

Another vision of the psychological approach to women who strive to transcend societal limitations in some way can be found in *Letters from Jenny*, by the influential psychologist, Gordon Allport. Jenny's story epitomized the struggle of a bright, creative, and energetic woman alone in a world which opened few doors to her. Lacking wealth and formal education, she was forced throughout her life to work at unskilled and semiskilled jobs in which her gifts found no outlet. Incapable, in her day, of articulating the base of her frustrations in the eternal underemployment to which she was doomed, she lavished her attention and ambitions on her only child, her son. Unfortunately, he rebelled against her plans for him, and many years were spent in estrangement prior to his death as a young man. After presenting Jenny's correspondence during the last ten years of her life with a young couple who had been friends of her son, Allport attempts to analyze Jenny from three different psychological viewpoints: the "existential," the "depth approach," and the "structural dynamic." In none of these, however, was there any attempt to view Jenny's situation in terms beyond those of personal causation. No notice whatever was accorded the waste of Jenny's intellectual potential, through absolute lack of opportunity. She followed the only life pattern open to her, the rearing, education, and encouragement of her child. She herself never realized that in another world she might have spent her days in scholarly, artistic, or scientific pursuits of her own, or been accorded a place in society as other than a mother sacrificing herself vainly for her offspring. Allport seemed not to have had any understanding of the glaring problems imposed on this woman from without or to have thought that her reactions were the inevitable result of external pressure. Jenny's heroic adaptation to her unbelievably oppressive and lonely existence, the dignity of her pride, and her resourcefulness under adversity attract the reader, but neither Jenny herself nor Allport were able to look beyond her personality for the source of her pain.

In contrast to Jenny, Dorothea Dix, nineteenth-century social reformer, made a mark on the pages of history through her own efforts and despite the obstacles encountered because of her sex. She was a crusading Massachusetts school teacher who in 1841 investigated the neglect and brutality prevalent in asylums, almshouses and jails. She continued her work with indefatigable energy for forty years, influenced the building of over thirty state-supported hospitals, reformed the asylum systems of Scotland and Canada and established firmly the modern principle of public responsibility for the mentally ill.[57] Because of Dix's work, public legislation was enacted to provide humane care for inmates of mental institutions.

According to a psychoanalytic interpretation of Dorothea Dix by psychiatrist William A. Browne, however, mental illness lay beneath the surface of her personality and dictated her activities.[58] She identified unconsciously with her "weak, frail, nervous, intemperate, and mentally unstable"[59] father. That he was an itinerant traveling preacher was the basis of her crusades. According to Browne, she also identified with her physician grandfather, "the paradigm of doctors, who devoted his life to caring for others, and who became idol and ideal."[60] Browne stressed her lifelong urge to emulate this male figure, who had in fact died when she was a child of seven. In contrast, Dorothea's mother, an invalid, was "constantly tired, unhappy, and sick."[61] Later, Dix lived with a severe and unyielding grandmother. Although she developed a deep and lasting friendship with a somewhat older woman, Ann Heath, "more than a woman confidante was needed to compensate for maternal deprivation and to sustain her for a lifetime of serving others."[62]

Comparing Dix to other female reformers, St. Teresa of Avila, Florence Nightingale, and Jane Addams, Browne found that a stimulus to the life work of these women came from the death and sacrifice of men: mental prisoners for Dix, an image depicting Christ's Passion for St. Teresa, and a bull (ancient symbol of spring and male sacrifice) for Addams. Their reformist activities were "reaction formation"; the motives were not what they seemed to be: "In these women the unconscious hostility (internal evil) was projected as an external evil upon which their reforms could focus. . . . The impetus for this process was hostility toward men. . . ."[63]

Because of the prejudice and discrimination inflicted on them, the achievements of these women required assistance from influential men. It is not surprising, therefore, that none was a "rabble-rouser" or concerned with women's rights"; they worked "through existing political channels and power structures."[64] And they all suffered from depressions. Browne attributes this to their basic pathology. It might also be interpreted as due to the frustration one endures when attainment of one's life goals is in the hands of others. (One of Dorothea Dix's depressions was precipitated by President Pierce's veto of a bill for federal aid to the insane while she, a woman, was forced to remain in the background.)[65]

Browne labels the aims and achievements of these remarkable women as "masculine strivings," which were not fully expressed until the time of the menopause, with its "retributive loss of femininity, and the concurrent dampening of sexual conflicts. . . ."[66] The unarguable accomplishments of these women are thus due to the development of unfemale characteristics and the availability of a positive ideal male to emulate. Although the agents in these unusual cases were women, the ultimate stimulus to action in Browne's interpretation, was entirely masculine. Thus Browne dismisses female accomplishment. It has been subverted to male accomplishment via female neurosis. The value of these women as human beings was also lost somewhere along the way.

In his case history of a male patient, Reuben Fine, Director of the New York Center for Psychoanalytic Training, shows the usual tendency to locate the source of the son's difficulties in the mother's "domination." Jim, the patient, originally visited Fine for vocational guidance, unaware that Fine was a psychoanalyst. He was persuaded that his problem was emotional, not vocational, and was persuaded to remain for a full psychoanalysis.

Although 37 years old, without a job and without a girl, he felt he had no problems. He wanted the analyst to tell him what could be gained by deep analysis. To this the analyst replied that an intellectual discussion would be of little avail, but that in such cases it was customary to have a trial period of two months, at the end of which time Jim would have a better idea of what the analytic experience was. This he finally accepted.[67]

Background information revealed that up until age twenty-nine, Jim had had no heterosexual experiences, and one brief homosexual experience at age twenty-seven. He had worked at various low-level jobs, attended college irregularly, and later went for a time to a seminary school which he also abandoned. When inducted into the army, he showed resentment by refusal to cooperate and by failing to carry out tasks assigned to him. Court-martial was followed by an acute reaction in which he spent months in an army hospital weeping. After that he spent time drinking and gambling, and had his first heterosexual experience, with prostitutes.

Jim's aimlessness and conflicts were traced to the "lifelong battle with his mother"; "he had very vivid memories . . . of her dominating ways." During his childhood after an unsuccessful period on a farm because "his father had no talent for farming," the family purchased a small candy store:

[This] prospered because, Jim said, the mother took over. She had sole charge of the cash register. Once the father had gone to the register to pay some bill, which turned out to be not due. Ever since, the mother had redoubled her vigilance, because if left in the father's hands the business would go to rack and ruin. The father was deprived of the right to handle money.[68]

It is not clear from the account whether the idea that the father was deprived of his rights was Jim's or the therapist's. Fine continues:

> In the household the mother also bossed the father completely. She even prepared his food down to the last slice of bread and butter, and [Jim's] father was obliged to eat it. Several times—once even during therapy—the father had simply thrown his plate out *in toto*, in protest against being spoon-fed. The protest did not last.[69]

Further criticism of the mother centered on her "overconcern" for the welfare of her daughters, one of whom was retarded. "Extreme vigilance was practiced by the mother to see to it that the daughters did not stray from the path of righteousness."[70] During analysis, for which Jim came eventually to "see the need," he turned his resentment of his mother onto the therapist. His "vehement denial of sexual desire" was interpreted as a "transference of feelings called out by mother."

An alternative view, in contrast to Fine's interpretation, is that Jim's mother had developed a set of survival tactics designed to salvage the family's financial situation, protect her damaged child's safety, and monitor her very inadequate husband's eating habits out of concern for his health. Her dual crime, however, was her combined "domination" and "overprotection," terms which in the psychoanalytic lexicon can cover the entire range of possible maternal behaviors. The specific behaviors of the mother cited by Fine in presentation of Jim's case record would not have been seen as neurosis-inducing or problematic had they originated from Jim's father.

A woman's lack of credibility before the psychotherapy establishment is undoubtedly greatest when she appears in the role of the mother of a son. A woman who brought her boy for psychiatric care was described by psychiatrists Saul I. Harrison and Donald J. Carek in their *Guide to Psychotherapy* as "a provocative, aggressive woman whose superficial independence scantily covered an insatiable dependence. . . ."[71] In a report by the same authors of a fourteen-year-old boy who had been hospitalized for various serious reasons "the examiners had been especially impressed with the sadomasochistic nature of his relationship with his mother."[72]

Although mothers are often said to place their children in a can't-win (or double-bind) situation, it is in fact the mothers themselves who cannot win in the psychological and psychiatric literature. Like the Jew seen by the anti-Semite as stupid for failing and crafty for succeeding, the mother is indicted for overprotectiveness, rigidity, excessive affection, tyranny, coldness, and seductiveness. She is damned if she does and damned if she doesn't. A mother who is affectionate toward her child is "overprotective"; otherwise, she is "cold" and "rejecting." If she disagrees with her husband on aspects of child rearing and asserts her view, the family is in danger of becoming that classic of a pathology-inducing constellation, a castrating mother who forces the father to weakness and submission.

In *The Art of Loving*, psychologist Erich Fromm asserts that the neurosis-producing family "structure" is one in which there is a loving but overindulgent or domineering mother, and a weak and uninterested father. Note that to be a psychopathology-inducer, the woman must meet either of two opposite and therefore all-encompassing criteria. If she tried to avoid both through passivity or escape, she would still be "rejecting." The father, on the other hand, must be both "weak" and "uninterested" to be considered pathogenic. If he is one but not the other, he is spared. Thus not a great deal is asked of father, but the impossible is demanded of mothers. Fromm continues:

> In this case [the male neurotic] may remain fixed at an early mother attachment, and develop into a person who is dependent on mother, feels helpless, has the strivings characteristic of the receptive person, that is, to receive, to be protected, to be taken care of, and who has a lack of fatherly qualities—discipline, independence, an ability to master life by himself.[73]

To Fromm, the "development from mother-centered to father-centered attachment, and then their eventual synthesis," forms the basis for mental health and maturity. The failure of this development is the "basic cause of neurosis." The child (Fromm's orientation is clearly to the male child) fares no better if the mother is not overindulgent and domineering, but is instead "cold, unresponsive, and domineering," since this might produce a "one-sidedly father-oriented" person, which is also undesirable. Perhaps Fromm did not realize that the term "domineering" occurred in both of his supposedly contrasting types of pathogenic mothers. It clearly underscores the extreme undesirability of this "unfeminine" behavior. Unfortunately, the specific actions by which a woman comes to be characterized as domineering are not delineated.

Another description of a pathology-inducing family constellation comes from an article published in the *American Journal of Psychiatry*:

> The outstanding common feature is the wife's exclusion of the passive and masochistic husband from leadership and decision making. She derogates him in word and deed and is emotionally cold and distant to him. Her attention is focused on her narcissistic needs for completion and admiration. These wives are extremely castrating and their husbands are vulnerable. The husband withdraws from the relationship in an effort to preserve some integrity when defeated in the struggle and may find solace in alcohol. . . .[74]

When the father asserts his "male dominance to a pathological degree," it is a reaction to his "feminine strivings." If his wife is inadequate, he may experience "exasperated frustration," a condition with which the authors clearly sympathize. (She drives him to drink.)

There are two points to be made: first, to the psychotherapists, it is pathological when individuals, females or males, step outside the culturally approved behaviors for their sex, and these criteria are based on rigid and patriarchal concepts.* Second, even when pathology or inadequacy

* Although a therapist himself, George Weinberg in his book *Society and the Healthy Homosexual*, notes that the conclusions of psychoanalysts, "especially those about homosexuals, are merely restatements of the Judeo-Christian code" (p. 22). The majority of psychotherapists of all schools have viewed homosexuality as

in the male is admitted, a woman's behavior (wife or mother) is viewed as the major contributing circumstance, even when the man is recognized to be more emotionally disturbed. In their case studies, and presumably in their thinking as well, psychotherapists describe women in highly derogative and pejorative terms, while men command their sympathies.

Psychologist Jonathan Kellerman of the University of Southern California recently surveyed the psychological literature concerning attribution of parental blame for children's psychological disturbances and found that it was usually the mother who was held responsible for psychopathology in the child. Kellerman asserted that "this represents a traditional notion, espoused by those who are clinically active in dealing with psychological disorder,"[75] that is, psychotherapists. He cited an investigation from which it was concluded that "deficient mothering was related to hostility, resentfulness, rebellious delinquent acts, sexual problems, depression, and anxiety. Deficient fathering was seen as much less clearly related to well-defined clinical clusters of symptoms."[76]

WOMEN PROFESSIONALS ADOPT THE MALE VIEW

In view of the prejudice and discrimination toward women, it is remarkable when women attain even moderate levels of real achievement. Those who do often appear to "opt out" of their own sex role. They do not identify with it. Women are "the other" in Simone de Beauvoir's sense, just as they are in the eyes of men. It is possible for such women to write as outsiders about "women" and what is "the trouble with women." Derogation of women in psychological and

---

an illness and their task as to cure it. Recent changes in this attitude reflect the fact that psychotherapy responds to public opinion. As Weinberg said, "At one time public opinion was appalled at masturbation. Technically, it was against the law and topflight psychologists and medical doctors believed it was both depraved and harmful. Now that the public has won its right to masturbate without guilt, psychologists grant them that right" (p. 33).

psychiatric literature is not confined to male writers. Melanie Klein, Helene Deutsch, Maria Bonaparte, and Mary Chadwick are some of the women writers who have helped in the production of antifemale psychiatric literature.[77] There have been psychotherapists, including psychoanalysts, who have gone against the tide and emphasized cultural factors in female psychology,[78] but by far the majority, even down to the present day and even among women psychologists and psychiatrists, have accepted the stereotyped conceptions of their professional heritage.*

Psychologist Judith Bardwick of the University of Michigan has in her writings to date repeated many of the conceptions that have proven so damaging to women patients. Although Bardwick expresses disagreement with certain psychoanalytic assumptions, she agrees with Freud in emphasizing biology and deemphasizing culture as determinants of sex-role behavior.[79] Social psychologist Nancy Henley described Bardwick's overall outlook as "androcentric and heterosexist," geared to "women's adaptation," not to changes in male behavior.[80] Bardwick's belief that biological factors influence sex-role behavior is not necessarily a problem; genetically-determined attributes may possibly underlie quantitative differences in aggressive behavior between the two sexes. But Bardwick makes pronouncements about what is "normal" and "abnormal." She appears to assume that the contribution of biology to sex-role behavior is largely known, and that it is woman's destiny to play out that biological role. "Normal" for Bardwick bears a remarkable resemblance to the familiar patriarchal customs of Western society. (But,

---

* It was not an easy decision for me to include these comments on women who have joined the male majority in disservice to our sex. Male domination over women is largely maintained through what Florynce Kennedy calls the "D & C" (divide and conquer) mechanism in which women are so antagonistic toward each other that it is impossible to work together effectively. I therefore had qualms about criticizing women writers, even if my criticism was of their lack of feminism. I decided in the end to include the remarks because I felt that protest against the attitudes reflected in these works was important, and because disagreement is not disrespect.

Bardwick may herself be in a process of reorientation toward a more woman-identified viewpoint.)

Another woman who has taken up cudgels against the feminist outcry is Corinne Hutt, an experimental psychologist at the University of Reading in England. In the editor's foreword to her book *Males and Females*, one learns that it is a "scholarly work" which stays "very close to the evidence" by a person of "rigorous training" who is able to "take a steadfastly scientific approach." (We also learn that Dr. Hutt is a wife and mother.)[81] The major thrust of the book is essentially the same as Bardwick's, but lacks Bardwick's frequent admissions that her assertions are hunches, guesses, or based on intuition. Hutt speaks as an authority when she makes her case for the biological bases of psychological sex differences:

> The evidence strongly suggests that at the outset males and females are "wired-up" differently. Social factors thus operate on already well-differentiated organisms— predisposed towards masculinity or femininity.[82]

While the sexes undoubtedly differ in certain psychological propensities, considerable evidence suggests that "femininity" and "masculinity" are largely the result of cultural influences. However, Hutt concludes:

> The fact that males predominate in the intellectual and creative echelons seems to have a basis other than masculine privilege. . . .[83]

Substances (androgens) which stimulate the development of masculine characteristics in the developing fetus provide

> a common neurochemical basis for aggression, drive, and attention.

> In sharp contrast to these predispositions of the male are the altruism, the regard for intimacy and personal relationships, and the protective nurturance of the female.[84]

Hutt's unequivocal viewpoint is that "woman's primary role is that of motherhood."[85] Like Bardwick, Hutt considers woman's cultural role to be the biologically based norm:

It would be a pity indeed if women sought to make this less a man's world by repudiating their femininity and by striving for masculine goals. It seems that few women can or wish to compete in the competitive, assertive spheres of the male.[86]

And that role, for Hutt, is very traditional:

Nurturance, whether in the wider educational sense or in the narrower domestic sense, is and will remain women's forte.[87]

IS IT CHANGING?

Although there are those who will want to argue that attitudes toward women by members of the psychotherapy professions have changed, unfortunately, changes seem few, small, late, and more apparent than real. There is evidence that the misogyny of the literature is indeed carried over into practice. It seems very unlikely that revisions in attitudes toward women will come about rapidly.

Despite the fact that most patients are women, much of the theory is still male oriented. For example, Freud's Electra Complex (female counterpart of the male Oedipal Complex) is largely unknown outside of the profession, and it was added on to psychoanalytic theory as something of an afterthought. The frequent use of male terms, e.g., "man," "mankind," rather than terms which more fully connote reference to members of both sexes, e.g., "person," "people," in psychiatric writings provide further evidence of the male bias. Sigmund Freud, for example, wrote "The Sexual Life of Man"; Walter Bromberg wrote *The Mind of Man: A History of Psychotherapy and Psychoanalysis;* Fred Spaner entitled an article on Rogerian concepts of a functioning person, "What a Man Should Be"; Fromm contended that the fundamental kind of love is "brotherly"; and, in 1974, Albert Bandura entitled his Presidential Address to the American Psychological Association "Behavior Therapy and the Models of Man"!

On the other hand, one cannot ignore the many books on women which are being written, some from a feminist perspective. Among new books, especially those by women, these seem to constitute the majority. In *Psychoanalysis and Women*, for example, psychoanalyst Jean Baker Miller provides a collection of essays by eminent psychoanalysts who were critical of Freud's phallocentric viewpoint. They present images of woman more consistent with those of feminists today, although some of them were written decades ago.

Psychiatrist Charlotte Wolff in *Love Between Women* gives a view of female homosexuality in which she considers the lesbian not an emotionally ill person, but a woman "unquestionably in the avant garde of the fight for equality of the sexes, and for the psychical liberation of women."[88] She characterizes them primarily as women not in bondage to males. The admiration which she came to feel for the lesbian in her study is revealed when she compares meetings of the lesbian organization with ordinary women's meetings:

The effect produced by a group of women alone is different from that of a group of men alone. Women by themselves appear to be incomplete, as if a limb were missing. They do not come into their proper place and function without the male.[89]

Wolff reports that she never felt this at lesbian meetings. She was impressed by the attention and concentration the women showed during the discussions.

Many of the essays in the book *Women in Therapy*, edited by Violet Franks and Vasanti Burtle, are less pro-women or pro-women's liberation than the data and the times demand, although the very publication of a book of that title now is indicative of a felt need for some reexamination of the relationship between women and psychotherapy. Some of the authors are so pro-interpretative therapy (for example, Albert Ellis)[90] that their egalitarian protests are less impressive than their wholesale tendency to derogate all "patients," women included. In contrast, Barbara Kirsch discusses consciousness-raising groups as an alternative to psychotherapy.[91] Although her conception of the consciousness-raising group is closer to that of group therapy in its aims and procedures than the consciousness-raising groups described in the last chapter, she clearly places blame on the culture and on the roles women are forced to assume and looks to the development of a culture in which all people would be encouraged to develop their unique abilities.[92]

Finally, there is *Female and Male: Dimensions of Human Sexuality* by Elaine C. Pierson and William V. D'Antonio. In the first chapter, "Female and Male: *He* Created Them," the authors discuss some of the myths and traditions that have contributed to the conception of female inferiority. About psychoanalysis, they say:

> The mistaken diagnosis of "penis envy" in older females has always been associated with any evidence of success or ambition beyond home or family. It may seem unbelievable, but its greatest effect during the thirties, forties, and fifties was the limitation it put on bright, capable women. . . .[93]

I think we must conclude that change is coming, but crucial questions remain: How long it will be before words translate to action, and how many more women will suffer in the interim?

7
Alternatives to Psychodynamic Insight Therapy

THE ALTERNATIVE DEPENDS ON THE FUNCTION SERVED BY THERAPY

An astrologer on a radio program was asked, "Do you really believe?" She said, "Look around. This could not be all there is." In accepting the ideology of psychodynamic interpretation, Friends and Supporters of Psychotherapy believe that a therapist can penetrate the mystery of the marvelous and important things that go on in the psyche. Like religion, psychotherapy answers affirmatively that there is more to life than our mundane conscious experience. Furthermore, if troubles arise through our own badness, whether called sin or neurosis, they can be self-erased, so we are powerful. Just as people placed themselves under the treatment of physicians during the bloodletting era when physicians had no power other than their patients' faith in them, hope for relief from emotional stress brings patients to the psychotherapist's office. As long as there are those who seek it, there will be others selling hope that the dreaded promise of mortality can be avoided, that there exists Another Reality. To those for whom psychotherapy functions to provide a kind of internal supernatural, there exists a plethora of available substitutes that similarly promise "something else."

The human situation is highly variable. Some of us have power, some are hungry, some are educated. Some of us have secretaries, some of us spend forty hours a week typing other people's words. Condition in life is a poor reflection of inherent ability. Prejudice, discrimination, inherited wealth, and acquired power determine our opportunities. Psychotherapy helps perpetuate these forces when it encourages the victim of discrimination to look within herself for a cure. The patient will never find an explanation for her failure to obtain the promotion and raise in pay she deserves by examining her sexual fantasies. Fixation on her inner life will, however, divert her attention away from the prejudice based on her sex that prevents achievement of her goals. Feminism, by which I mean the assumption that women are not inferior to men in their potential for contribution to the society in all ways and at all levels, and feminist activism, the effort to produce a society which accepts the feminist assumption, can change women's oppressive situation.

Psychotherapy has been patriarchy's tool. The woman overburdened by domestic responsibilities and prevented from utilizing her creative capacity through employment sought relief on the analyst's couch and learned to accept her "feminine role." For example, *Psychotherapy: The Private and Very Personal Viewpoints of Doctor and Patient* is a recent book in which a psychotherapist and a former patient collaborate to present a fictionalized version of what they regard as a successful, if not ideal, case of psychotherapy. The bright and talented female heroine was economically dependent on a dull, coarse, and unloving husband for whom she was required to provide sexual and domestic functions, and an ill-paying job as a clerical servant to men no brighter than herself. None of this was given consideration. Therapy instead emphasized her potential for sexual attractiveness. The distraction of psychotherapy, which was described as like a love affair (although no overt sexual acts were reported), could carry that woman beyond her years of greatest capacity. Afterwards she would fall with a thud to the grim reality of the waste her life had been.[1]

Why people enter therapy may have little to do with why they stay. Transient interpersonal difficulties, marital and family crises, and the anxiety and depression that accompany such problems bring most patients to private psychotherapy. The ability of the therapist to convince them that they suffer from a pathological condition which requires continued treatment and their subsequent "addiction" causes about one patient in four to remain in therapy for an extended period of time. If noninterpretive, nonaddictive consultation were available, it would provide an alternative for those who simply feel they need to talk to someone about something they prefer not to discuss with friends or relatives.

OPERANT BEHAVIOR PRINCIPLES

There is need for consultants whose approach is not psychodynamic, who look to the external environment, to the social context, and to behavior for explanations and solutions. Some of the problems that bring people to psychotherapy could be handled effectively by application of principles that emerged from laboratory investigations. Psychoanalysts probe the patient's inner life to exorcise conflicts and complexes originating in the family dramas of early childhood, and phenomenological therapists emphasize feelings in the "here and now."* The behaviorist looks to the environment. The environmental response to one's actions, especially the re-

---

* The phrase "get in touch with your feelings" drones throughout the phenomenological litany with maddening insistence. One speaker used it fourteen times in as many minutes. It is a curious phrase because it flouts scientific examination. The phrase implies that one has feelings ones does not feel! It also expresses the value that feelings are good, and that it is good to get them out, to express them. An excellent counteraction to this position was given by James Laidlow of York University, Ontario, in "Is 'Real Self' a Useful Topic for First-Year Psychology Courses?" To the behaviorist, feelings, whatever their experiential significance, are reactions, not causes.

sponse mediated through other persons, contains the key to explaining and influencing behavior. Events that follow behavior affect the likelihood of that behavior's recurrence. The term "operant" behavior is used because subsequent actions depend on how previous behaviors "operate" in the environment.[2] Actions followed by positive events are strengthened (reinforced) so that they are more likely to occur in the future. Much of the terminology originated with B. F. Skinner. His and his coworkers' systematic exploration of the principle of reinforcement, using various species including the human species, demonstrated unequivocally the extent to which manipulation of the payoffs in the reacting environment influences behavior. While grandmother, Dale Carnegie, salesmen, and Machiavellian princes may be said to have successfully utilized and approximated expression of this behavioral principle, they did not articulate its generality or recognize its profound strength. Not even Edward L. Thorndike, the psychologist whose "law of effect" was an immediate precursor of the reinforcement principle, recognized the ubiquity of the mechanism. Thorndike assumed that reinforcement and punishment have equal and opposite effects, an idea not borne out by the research evidence and still a matter of controversy among scientific psychologists.

In a world divided into situations one prefers to avoid, one hopes to enjoy, and about which one is neutral, behavior is gradually molded, at least in part, by the consequences of one's actions. Stated thus, the reinforcement principle appears adaptive, obvious, and rational, but laboratory exploration of the phenomenon and, indeed, everyday observation itself indicates otherwise.

Operant researchers have found that situations which produce unpredictable reinforcement, even if that reinforcement is infrequent, can have strange and irrational effects once the person has somehow been induced to engage in the behavior. For example, there are similarities between psychotherapy and gambling. Both are costly and persistent. The term "addiction" has been applied to both. Professional gamblers entice their victims by providing them with false "wins" at the outset. We have seen that psychotherapists use similar tactics: much attention in the psychotherapy literature is given to the problem of how to handle the first few interviews so as not to lose the patient. If a given act produces positive results erratically; as when one repeatedly draws a five-card poker hand but rarely and unpredictably finds four aces in it, quantities of behavior may be generated at little cost to the gambling house and with considerable loss to the player. Other behaviors fall in the class of those which produce immediate pleasure and later harm. Society labels these "sins" or "indulgences" and has sought to reduce them through moral exhortation and threat of punishment. In fact, there are many behaviors which are undesirable to those who emit them and to others but which have resisted treatment of any kind thus far.

Analysis of behavior in terms of its consequences (if-the-organism-does-this, the-environment-does-that contingencies[3]) produces great respect for the minutiae of everyday life. The little girl who has a temper tantrum every time her mother talks on the telephone is better understood and dealt with through study of the specific and immediate consequences of her actions than by consideration of the inner feelings of child or mother. When baby begins fussing, mother typically and "naturally" reaches for a candy, gives baby the toy or object she reaches toward, takes her up on her lap, or does whatever results in immediate, if temporary, peace, so that the voice in the telephone receiver can be heard. Thus the disruptive behavior is reinforced. Although the mother may on some occasions become so fed up that she terminates her conversation prematurely in order to administer punishment to the child, this tactic is insufficient to eliminate the reinforced tantrums. Many parents have puzzled over the peculiar behavior their children exhibit when they are trying to carry on a telephone conversation. Psychodynamic theorists have offered explanations in terms of what the telephone symbolizes,* but few parents realize that they themselves produce the behavior. Once they learn how

---

* One psychoanalyst viewed the telephone as a phallic symbol and the act of telephoning as similar to intercourse. The child's temper tantrum, he explained, was the result of panic at having to witness the mother in the act of "vicarious sexual intercourse" or "masturbation" during which the child was rejected.

the problem behavior is reinforced, it is not so difficult a matter to change it.

Recognition of the influence of the immediate environment on behavior can lead to change in classroom conditions that inadvertently maintain poor learning behavior at school. Because disruptive behavior attracts attention, and attention itself may be reinforcing, schoolteachers, like the mother at the telephone, frequently strengthen the very behaviors they would like to abolish. School psychologists who operate from a psychodynamic orientation often do more harm than good through their diagnoses and evaluations, because of the stigma of association with psychologists, and because such evaluations do not tend to lead to changes in the conditions that produce the problems. Psychodynamic principles attribute undesirable school behaviors to conditions in the home rather than to events that take place in the classroom. This damages the relationship between home and school while focusing away from effective solutions. School psychologists and "counselors" could very appropriately be used to analyze the reinforcement contingencies in the children's everyday situation and to help those who deal with them to alter the responding environment so that educational goals could be achieved. Such successful uses of nonpsychodynamic psychologists and psychology programs in the schools has already occurred.[4] They show what can be done when psychodynamic diagnoses and therapies are cast aside and behavior is dealt with directly and without stigmatization.

The use of positive reinforcement contingencies is often "unnatural" and requires systematic planning. A parent is likely to enjoy a moment of relaxation when baby is being "good" and begins to respond only when the peace is disturbed by baby's undesired behaviors. The burglar is reinforced by the loot obtained; most burglaries go unpunished. Crime is not always reduced by increasing the severity of an unlikely punishment. The opposite occurs if juries and judges become more hesitant in the case of a capital offense. This phenomenon prevails in the case of much university and college examination cheating. When the penalties are severe, instructors refrain from accusing students except in rare, obvious instances, thus allowing much cheating to go unpunished. In such a case, milder punishments of increased likelihood would result in fewer instances of the offense.

OPERANT METHODS APPLIED IN INDIVIDUAL SITUATIONS

Although we undoubtedly have much more to learn about dealing with behavior problems, what we know already is severely underutilized. It is argued that the types of specific problems with which behavior approaches seem most successful are not those of which the voluntary patient in private individual psychotherapy complains. The most common reasons given for entering psychotherapy are depression, anxiety, and marriage or family problems; the behavioral approach is geared to specific behaviors or reactions, such as lack of assertiveness in interpersonal situations, phobias, or undesirable "habits."

Behavior consultants have found that attacking seemingly minor behavioral difficulties in a situation affects a person's "feelings." Most of us are familiar with the concept of the "vicious cycle" in which interpersonal relationships spiral downward as recrimination is piled upon recrimination, and a seemingly endless pattern of anger and distrust develops. Behaviorists have found that attention to specific details can initiate upward spirals in which one good thing leads to another and relationships improve. Although the patient consults the psychiatrist or other psychotherapist because of feelings, it does not follow that lengthy and sustained attention to these feelings and examination of the "inner" life are needed to change them. Quite often, the emotional pain is traceable to behavioral events. When those are altered, feelings change too.

A thirty-five-year-old woman consulted me for help with the behavior of her six-year-old son, Paul, who was refusing to attend school and who committed severely destructive acts at home such as breaking dinnerware, spilling milk deliberately on the living room carpet, and so forth. Ms. R. indicated at the outset that while she hoped that Paul's behavior could be modified, she knew that nothing behavioral could do anything about the severe depressions from which she was a chronic sufferer. Together, she and I devised and set into motion an "intervention plan" for Paul. In essence, the plan assisted Ms. R. in seeking out, and reinforcing, Paul's positive behavior. Reinforcement of the "good" things Paul did increased their occurrence, and his previous destructive behavior gradually receded. Within a few weeks, the situation had greatly changed, and Paul had even begun to attend school without complaint. Ms. R. was also surprised and delighted to find that her depression had disappeared.

Changing Paul's behavior had had positive ramifications within the family that Ms. R. had not anticipated. Her depression had been a reaction both to feelings of frustration and hopelessness about her ability to manage Paul and to her husband's increasing neglect of the family. Mr. R. was rarely home in the evening, and Ms. R. had begun to suspect that he was involved with another woman. The truth was that Mr. R. found reasons to stay out in the evening in order to avoid the trauma of trying to deal with his son. Once, when Paul tore up some of Mr. R.'s business papers, Mr. R. had become so enraged that he hit the child very hard, although not as hard as he wanted to at the moment of his anger. Mr. R. subsequently feared what he might do to the child if a similar incident occurred. He had begun to actively dislike Paul because Paul's presence produced conflicts and fear in him. As Paul's behavior changed through the effectiveness of the behavioral intervention plan, an upward spiral of happy events occurred. Mr. R. was no longer afraid to be at home, and Ms. R. lost her jealous suspicions. Her feelings changed. The chain reactions within the family affecting all interpersonal relations had reversed direction.

Nor is the R. case unusual. In my experience, such chains of positive consequences result whenever a behavioral intervention is successful. While strictly behavioral approaches may appear limited in their effects to the specific behavioral goals to which they are directed, the actual effects tend to be more widespread. Many individuals and families are in trouble in readily correctable ways, and it is a tragedy that so many people are unaware that help is potentially available. Therapies, whether individual or family, that attempt to utilize a cathartic approach may in fact increase the interpersonal difficulties and therefore the unpleasant feelings.

The idea that people go about with anguish and rage that is "bottled up" and must be "let out" was presented formally within psychology back in 1939 with the publication of John C. Dollard's monograph written in collaboration with four colleagues, each of whom eventually became a psychologist of considerable reputation.[5] The monograph was entitled *Frustration and Aggression.* Its thesis, which was quite close to certain early Freudian ideas, was that every frustration necessarily led to aggression. Allowing the aggression to "come out," preferably in socially nondestructive ways, was the logical treatment. For decades, the frustration-aggression hypothesis reigned supreme as both explanation and therapy, despite the fact that Freud himself had given up pure catharsis as a treatment decades earlier. But it is an attractive idea, simple in conceptualization, and with obvious implications for action. It was responsible for the punching bag in the basement and hammering toys for toddlers, and is still the basis of contemporary scream-and-hit therapies.

Scientific research has not borne out the frustration-aggression theory. True, in some situations a painful stimulus produces an immediate lashing out at the environment or at persons or objects in it. This occurs both in animals and in human beings. But such behavior is now understood to be a kind of reflex, and there is no evidence that aggression will appear later if for some reason this reflex does not occur.

Recent findings indicate that, like other behaviors, aggression can be learned. If aggressive acts are reinforced, they are more likely to persist. Like other behaviors, they follow the "Three Rs" of operant behavior: reinforced responses recur. Egging ten-year-old Johnny on at the punching bag is likely to increase, not decrease, the probability of his directing similar blows at schoolmates. The football player, other things equal, is more likely to get into a fist fight at the local saloon. Many institutions have adopted the cathartic viewpoint. When, if ever, the public comes to understand that aggression is both contagious and reinforceable, competitive sports will be removed from school athletic programs, and violence in movies and television will be X-rated.

The use of operant methods in individual situations is far more subtle, complicated, and difficult than asking the client to cry like a baby, scream in rage, punch a pillow, or say whatever comes to mind. Perhaps the main advantage of the operant method is its success, which, I think, is advantage enough.

CONTROVERSY

At the time of this writing, something of a public outcry has been raised against the use of "behavior modification." Among the specific objections which have been leveled are: the behavioral approach is a dehumanizing one in which people are "manipulated", it is simplistic; it denies the human experience and human consciousness; its determinism implies a mechanical universe.

In contrast, phenomenological approaches supposedly exalt human experience and appreciate unconscious motivation; they "highlight the essential humanity of man [sic]";[6] they view human beings as goal-directed, free to make decisions about the direction of their lives and free to achieve self-fulfillment and joy. Humanist Carl Rogers puts it as follows:

> If the extreme behaviorist position is true then everything any individual does is essentially meaningless, since he [sic] is but an atom caught in a seamless chain of cause and effect. On the other hand, if the thoroughgoing humanistic position is true, then choice enters in, and this individual subjective choice has some influence on the cause and effect chain. . . .[7]

Rogers, as he puts it, "loses control" by asserting the existence of choice rather than accepting scientific evidence of the influence of environmental events on behavior. However philosophically untidy or unaesthetic it may be, behavior is modified by its consequences. To fail to utilize operant method and analyze society in operant terms simply in order to preserve an illusion of "free choice" is to behave like the proverbial ostrich. The effects of reinforcement on behavior do not go away because influential psychologists refuse to admit they are there.

Aside from the philosophic-religious dissatisfaction that the operant approach seems to induce in some persons, there are two other types of criticism. One is a confusion between operant methods and such forms of "behavior modification" as aversion therapy, drug therapy, and psychosurgery.* In a letter to *Science*, B. F. Skinner observed that while those procedures may "'modify behavior,' . . . so do religious rituals, military and police operations, advertising, state lotteries, piece-rate wages, protective tariffs, traffic signs, and wage and price controls."[8] Skinner would retain the use of the term "behavior modification" as restricted to operant methods and emphatically excluding drugs, surgery, and aversive techniques.

The other criticism can, crudely, be stated as follows: "Operant procedures are effective. They can change behavior. Dictators try to control people's behavior. If an evil dictator got control of these powerful operant methods, people would be unfree and controlled for evil purposes. Horrors! Let us oppose the use of operant methods. Otherwise we will become mere puppets forced to behave at the whim of those who pull the reinforcement strings." In fact, this is what is actually happening. The reinforcement power of large industries serves their interests through political campaign financing in which voting behavior is influenced. While operant methods can of course be misused, the best way to prevent their misuse is to be aware of their existence. If operant principles were taught in grade school, Congress would probably have been forced to pass campaign-financing legislation long ago.

The conflict may gain in intensity over the next decades because it is part of a major cultural change. Ultimately, it will be necessary to reject methods of moral absolutism in which problems of cultural ideology are resolved through reference to basic tenets as supplied in some form by religions. Human survival will depend on the adoption of pragmatic, nonabsolute decisions arrived at through the assumption of collective responsibility. It is easier to follow a guidebook.

---

* Some of the "confusion" has been engendered deliberately by persons philosophically offended by operant principles and applications.

Making such decisions involves uncertainty if not vertigo as one painstakingly travels step by factual step. But now that we are developing effective techniques of behavior influence and management, decisions must be made concerning how and when behavioral technologies will be used, and toward what aims.

THE SOCIAL ENVIRONMENT

Some have recognized that pleasure in life comes through actions to which the environment gives response. Yet for vast segments of the population—unattended children, incarcerated persons of all types, welfare recipients, the aged, the poor, and women—the environment reacts sluggishly if at all. Many years ago it was discovered that infants who received only custodial care in orphanages became seriously ill. Many of them developed the emaciation and wasting medically termed "marasmus" and died. At the time it was thought that lack of loving care was responsible, and, in a way, it was. Parents who love their children interact with them. When baby smiles, mommy and daddy smile back; when baby cries, they try to find out what may be wrong. The infant in the institution was cared for according to a schedule that had little to do with what the infant did.

But infants are not the only ones affected: Lack of control over one's environment is what makes modern poverty tragic; it is also here that we find an explanation for the mystery of "unmotivated" vandalism and crime. In a generally unreactive environment, the individual may use heroic means to produce a response, to do something with consequence. For the most part, individuals caught in a web of custodial care quietly "lose their minds," which is to say that they lose their impulse to action. Their behavior diminishes and becomes stereotyped. In a sense, they undergo a partial death.[9]

In this perspective, youthful vandals whose world gives no response have found a way of impinging themselves on their environment that will not allow it to remain silent. Rats in a noncontingent environment suffered physical signs of distress although they were amply supplied with food and water.

The rats in the control group which pressed levers to get those necessities for themselves were not distressed.[10]

Analyzing psychotherapy from an operant viewpoint, the therapy session in which the psychotherapist focuses entirely on the patient may constitute a more responding environment even with its "analytic silences" than a home in which the husband is engrossed in a baseball game on television and the children do not come in for dinner when called. The therapist's intermittently raised eyebrows, his occasional sigh, especially when interpreted by the patient as a response to her words, can be a more rewarding situation than her everyday life. Furthermore, the reinforcing responses of the psychotherapist are likely to be selective. Confirmation of a therapist's theory concerning the symbolic meaning of a dream, for example, might come about when a murmured uh-hmm, or a catch of breath, reinforces the patient's tendency to elaborate further on the subject of which she was speaking.

A given environment may respond in diverse ways at the same time. Consequence "dissonance" refers to reinforcement contingencies which conflict with one another so that either the same behavior is both punished and reinforced, or two incompatible behaviors are both reinforced. It also exists when a behavior which would destroy the person's chance at a large, but delayed, reinforcer is given immediate reinforcement. Examples of consequence dissonance conditions include:

Welfare systems that punish recipients for working by reducing payments so greatly that total income is less than if the person were not employed.

Fee-for-service private medical practice in which the physician is reinforced for providing many "services" rather than curing the patient.

Grading systems in educational institutions which put student and teacher in adversary roles vis-à-vis one another, so that instead of asking for needed help, the students in such systems try to hide their ignorance.

Employee evaluation systems that operate in a zero-sum manner in which individuals gain equally from causing another's performance to be devalued or their own to be valued more highly.

At the international level, a system whose purported common goals include a reduction in nuclear testing and stockpiling, but which accorded India extra power and prestige when she detonated a nuclear bomb.

A political system under which good government results if citizens study the issues and vote out of conscience and their own best interests, but which makes studying the issues so difficult that it is easier for citizens to decide how to vote on the basis of TV commercials and magazine articles paid for by powerful special-interest groups.

The response of the environment is "dissonant" in these situations: ostensible goals do not dictate the actual reinforcement contingencies that exist in the situation. ("Token economies" represent an attempt to deliberately produce a microcosm without consequence dissonance.)

An important application of operant principles is the analysis and modification of existing institutions so that such problems are reduced. Changes in penal codes, welfare systems, tax regulations, the method of financing medical care, and political campaign financing, for example, could reduce injustice and corruption.[11] Analysis of such institutions according to operant behavioral principles means giving major consideration to what behaviors are actually being strengthened as the result of a given regulation of policy.[12] To decrease use of automobiles on overcrowded urban highways during rush hours, individuals who have no passengers in their cars might be taxed by having to pay double tolls. Alternatively, rewards such as allowing them to go through free at the toll booths might be given to automobiles with several persons in them. Which plan is preferable should be decided not only on gains or losses of toll money and amount of traffic reduction but also on less obvious effects. Rewarding those who choose to round up a car pool may bring about more pleasant affective reactions than punishing those who drive alone.*

Feelings are affected by the reinforcement contingencies to which one is subject. Punishment contingencies and consequence dissonance produce conflict and unpleasant emotional reactions. Positive reinforcement brings good feelings. An alternative to psychotherapy is a more responsive and positively reinforcing environment. In general, there are fewer reinforcements available for women and for members of minority groups than for white males. Employment opportunities are opportunities for positive reinforcement. Prejudice and discrimination produce environmental nonresponsiveness or punitive response. The victim of sexist, racist or ageist prejudice may be ignored or punished for behaviors that would be rewarded if emitted by more culturally favored persons.

Sexism, racism, ageism, and other prejudices occur when an individual is viewed through the narrow tube of expectation rather than through the wide-angle lens of reality. The victim of prejudice strikes out in futility against the oppressors' biased perceptions. This is precisely the situation in which the object of psychodynamic diagnosis and interpretation is imprisoned.

Behaviorist methods do not ensure that the individual using them is without prejudice or that those prejudices have no effect on the persons they deal with. But when goals and procedures are specified, the behaviorist's client, unlike the insight therapy patient, can at least decide whether the procedures are effective. Structuring the social environment to contain more opportunities for positive reinforcement and fewer aversive contingencies will further reduce the inclination toward individual psychotherapy.

* Several states currently take advantage of the fact that intermittent reinforcement can produce behavior of great persistence. They increase the behavior of standing on line at designated booths to turn some of one's personal money over to the state in return for a valueless piece of paper. The individual feels free to gamble or not to gamble. But analysis of all the behaviors produced by lotteries and off-track betting might reveal that the system drains resources from many who can ill afford the losses. Voting on a gambling referendum might be quite different if the issues were presented in terms of behavior principles.

Afternote

Maybe many psychotherapy patients have been helped by their therapists. But some have not been helped. And some have surely been harmed. The profession provides the consumer with no assurance of protection. Neither therapy techniques, the goals of treatment, nor the outcomes of past treatments are described in the objective terms that such assurance requires. Some psychotherapy professionals have given up the attempt to put their procedures on a scientific basis; perhaps their immediate concern is protecting their economic interests. This book has been written for the consumer—not only for the patient, but for all of us who ultimately have been paying the bills for the psychodynamic psychotherapy enterprise.

Obviously, there is no simple answer to the problem of what will or what should replace psychodynamic psychotherapy. In the meantime, I predict that all of the following will be used: self-help programs; consultants selected for their abilities in supportive consultation (rather than because of academically acquired but irrelevant credentials); greater and more judicious use of psychoactive drugs; behavioral approaches; diet; health regimes; singles clubs; old-style and new-style religions; astrology; medical, including surgical, intervention; love affairs; and friends. I do not endorse these substitutes particularly; some of them frighten me. I merely predict that many of the private, voluntary, nonpsychotic female patients on whom this book is primarily focused will, should they turn away from psychodynamic psychotherapy, seek out one or more of these many other sources.

And one other. Some of the women whose failures in life sent them into psychotherapy, where their guilt and feeling of inadequacy was increased instead of muted, will embrace the feminist message and struggle to change society so that women's opportunities for positive reinforcement expand and expand. That I do endorse!

Notes

I. THE PSYCHODYNAMIC PSYCHOTHERAPY EXPERIENCE

Psychotherapy

1. Perry London, *Behavior Control* (New York: Harper & Row, 1969), p. 46.
2. For example, in *The Psychotherapy Relationship* (New York: Macmillan, 1961), William V. Snyder defines the relationship in terms of reciprocal emotional "attitudes" held by the persons involved.

Freud

3. See Theodore Millon, *Modern Psychopathology* (Philadelphia: W. B. Saunders, 1969), p. 19.
4. Carl Grove and John Radford, "Dear Colleague: A Replication," *Bulletin of the British Psychological Society*, Vol. 26 (1973), pp. 129-130.

5. Melitta Schmideberg, "A Contribution to the History of the Psycho-Analytic Movement in Britain," *The British Journal of Psychiatry*, Vol. 118, No. 542 (January 1971), p. 67.

6. Joseph D. Matarazzo, "Psychotherapeutic Processes," in P. R. Farnsworth and Q. McNemar, eds., *Annual Review of Psychology*, Vol. 16 (Palo Alto, California: Annual Reviews, 1965), p. 217.

7. John Leo, "Psychoanalysis Reaches a Crossroad," *New York Times* (August 4, 1968).

8. Melitta Schmideberg, "Sociolegal Consequences of Psychiatric Diagnoses in U.S.A. and Britain," *International Journal of Offender Therapy*, Vol. 14, No. 3 (1972), pp. 171–172.

The Image of the Therapist

9. Leonard Krasner, "The Therapist As a Social Reinforcer: Man or Machine," paper presented at the annual meetings of the American Psychological Association, Philadelphia (1963).

10. James F. T. Bugental, "The Person Who Is the Psychotherapist," in Alvin R. Mahrer and Leonard Pearson, eds., *Creative Developments in Psychotherapy*, Vol. I (Cleveland: Press of Case Western Reserve University, 1971), p. 292.

11. Ibid.

12. Herbert Goldenberg, *Contemporary Clinical Psychology* (Monterey, California: Brooks/Cole, 1973), p. 192.

13. Lawrence S. Kubie, "The Destructive Potential of Humor in Psychotherapy," *American Journal of Psychiatry*, Vol. 127, No. 7 (January 1971), p. 864.

14. Allen E. Bergin and Hans S. Strupp, *Changing Frontiers in the Science of Psychotherapy* (Chicago: Aldine-Atherton, 1972), p. 274.

15. Ibid., p. 274.

16. David S. Viscott, *The Making of a Psychiatrist* (New York: Fawcett, 1973), p. 137.

Aims of Psychotherapy

17. Ernest Kramer, *A Beginning Manual for Psychotherapists* (New York: Grune & Stratton, 1970), p. 11.

What Brings Patients to Psychotherapy?

18. Jerome D. Frank, *Persuasion and Healing* (Baltimore: Johns Hopkins University Press, 1961), p. 6.

19. Ibid.

20. Schmideberg, "A Contribution to the History of the Psycho-Analytic Movement in Britain," p. 67.

21. Dorothy Tennov, "Women Evaluate and Describe Their Psychotherapy Outside the Clinical Setting," paper prepared for presentation at the annual meetings of the Society for Psychotherapy Research, Denver, Colorado (June 1974).

22. Gerhart Saenger, "Patterns of Change Among 'Treated' and 'Untreated' Patients Seen in Psychiatric Community Mental Health Clinics," *Journal of Nervous and Mental Diseases*, Vol. 150, No. 1 (1970), p. 43; and Saul I. Harrison and Donald J. Carek, *A Guide to Psychotherapy* (Boston: Little, Brown, 1966), pp. 47–48.

23. Jerome D. Frank, *Persuasion and Healing*, p. 137.

24. Anthony Storr, "The Concept of Cure," in Charles Rycroft, ed., *Psychoanalysis Observed* (New York: Coward, McCann, & Geoghegan, 1967), p. 60.

25. A. B. Hollingshead and F. C. Redlich, *Social Class and Mental Illness: A Community Study* (New York: John Wiley, 1958).

26. Thomas J. Scheff, "Users and Nonusers of a Student Psychiatric Clinic," *Journal of Health and Human Behavior*, Vol. 7 (1966).

27. E. H. Fischer and J. L. Turner, "Factors in Attitudes Toward Seeking Professional Help," *Proceedings of the 77th Annual Convention of the American Psychological Association*, Vol. 4 (1969).

28. Nora Budzilek, "Women and Psychotherapy," unpublished (1973).

29. Charles Kadushin, *Why People Go to Psychiatrists* (New York: Atherton Press, 1969), p. 81.

30. Ibid., pp. 201–202.
31. Pauline Bart, "Social Structure and Vocabularies of Discomfort: What Happened to Female Hysteria?" *Journal of Health and Social Behavior*, Vol. 9 (September 1968), p. 189.
32. Ibid., p. 192.
33. Hans S. Strupp, "Psychotherapy," *Annual Review of Psychology*, Vol. 13 (1962), pp. 470–471.
34. Saenger, op. cit.
35. Jim Mintz, "What is 'Success' in Psychotherapy?" *Journal of Abnormal Psychology*, Vol. 80 (1972), p. 14.
36. Arthur K. Shapiro, "Placebo Effects in Medicine, Psychotherapy and Psychoanalysis," in Allen E. Bergin and Sol L. Garfield, eds., *Handbook of Psychotherapy and Behavior Change: Empirical Analysis* (New York: John Wiley, 1971), p. 460.
37. Ibid., p. 460.

Symptoms

38. Hans S. Strupp, M. S. Wallach, and M. Wogan, "The Psychotherapy Experience in Retrospect: A Questionnaire Survey of Former Patients and Their Therapists," *Psychological Monographs*, Vol. 78 (1964).
39. Melitta Schmideberg, "Principles of Psychotherapy," *Comprehensive Psychiatry*, Vol. 1 (June 1960), p. 192.
40. Storr, op. cit., p. 59.
41. Ibid., p. 60.
42. Leonard P. Ullman and Leonard Krasner, *Case Studies in Behavior Modification* (New York: Holt, Rinehart and Winston, 1965), pp. 13–15; and Arthur K. Shapiro and Elaine Shapiro, "Clinical Dangers of Psychological Theorizing," *The Psychiatric Quarterly*, Vol. 45 (1971).
43. Schmideberg, "Principles of Psychotherapy."

The Image of Psychotherapy

44. Frank, *Persuasion and Healing*, p. 115.
45. Nathan Hurvitz, "Psychotherapy as a Means of Social Control," *Journal of Consulting and Clinical Psychology*, Vol. 40 (1973), p. 233.

46. Shapiro, "Placebo Effects in Medicine, Psychotherapy and Psychoanalysis," p. 460.

47. Geoffrey Gorer, "Psychoanalysis in the World," in Charles Rycroft, ed., *Psychoanalysis Observed* (New York: Coward-McCann), p. 29.

48. Arthur K. Shapiro, "The Curative Waters and Warm Poultices of Psychotherapy," *Psychosomatics,* Vol. 7 (February 1966), p. 23.

49. Martin Shepard and Marjorie Lee, *Games Analysts Play* (New York: Berkeley Medallion, 1972), pp. 97–107.

50. Howard B. Roback, Alfred Webersinn, and Harry Guion, "Effects of the Psychotherapeutic Experience on Emerging Psychotherapists," *Mental Hygiene,* Vol. 55 (April 1971), p. 228.

51. Ibid., p. 229.

52. Ibid., p. 229.

The Initial Interview

53. Harrison and Carek, op. cit., p. 98.

54. Ibid., p. 98.

55. Ibid., p. 97.

56. Bergin and Strupp, op. cit., p. 244.

57. Shapiro, "Placebo Effects in Medicine, Psychotherapy and Psychoanalysis," p. 440.

58. From direct interviews with former patients; Tennov, "Women Evaluate and Describe Their Psychotherapy Outside the Clinical Setting."

59. Melitta Schmideberg, "Psychotherapy with Failures of Psychoanalysis," *British Journal of Psychiatry,* Vol. 116 (1970), p. 195.

Ground Rules

60. Perry London, *The Modes and Morals of Psychotherapy* (New York: Holt, Rinehart and Winston, 1964), p. 46.

Transference

61. Harrison and Carek, op. cit., p. 174.

62. Ibid., p. 175.

63. Goldenberg, op. cit., p. 229.
64. London, *Behavior Control*, p. 52, and Richard D. Chessick, *How Psychotherapy Heals* (New York: Science House, 1969), p. 26.
65. Harrison and Carek, op. cit., p. 174.
66. Schmideberg, "Psychotherapy with Failures of Psychoanalysis," and Chessick, op. cit., p. 26.
67. Arnold A. Rogow, *The Psychiatrists* (New York: Dell, 1970), p. 87.
68. Herman Feifel and Janet Eells, "Patients and Therapists Assess the Same Psychotherapy," *Journal of Consulting Psychology*, Vol. 27 (1963).
69. Chessick, op. cit., p. 50.
70. Ibid., p. 50.
71. Harrison and Carek, op. cit., p. 226.
72. Snyder, op. cit., p. 361.
73. Bergin and Strupp, op. cit., p. 370.

Countertransference

74. Douglas Orr, "Transference and Countertransference: A Historical Survey," *Journal of the American Psychoanalytic Association*, Vol. 2 (1954).
75. Shapiro, "Placebo Effects in Medicine, Psychotherapy and Psychoanalysis," p. 453.
76. Snyder, op. cit., p. 358.
77. Chessick, op. cit., p. 87.
78. Harrison and Carek, op. cit., p. 88.
79. Chessick, op. cit., p. 88.
80. Rollo May, "Contributions of Existential Philosophy," in Alvin R. Mahrer and Leonard Pearson, eds., *Creative Developments in Psychotherapy* (Cleveland: The Press of Case Western Reserve University, 1971), p. 149.
81. Phyllis Chesler, *Women and Madness* (New York: Doubleday, 1972).
82. Chessick, op. cit., p. 84.
83. Salvatore V. Didato, "Therapy Failure: Pride and/or Prejudice of the Therapist?" *Mental Hygiene*, Vol. 55 (1971).

Interpretation

84. Harry K. Wells, *The Failure of Psychoanalysis: From Freud to Fromm* (New York: International, 1963), p. 121.

85. See Storr, op. cit., p. 75.

86. Nathan G. Hale, Jr., *Freud and the Americans: The Beginnings of Psychoanalysis in the United States, 1876–1917* (New York: Oxford University Press, 1971), p. 456.

87. Viscott, op. cit., p. 133.

88. Ibid., p. 133.

89. Chessick, op. cit., p. 56.

90. Donald R. Stieper and Daniel N. Wiener, *Dimensions of Psychotherapy* (Chicago: Aldine-Atherton, 1965), p. 6; and Storr, op. cit., p. 73.

91. J. Sandler, C. Dare, and A. Holden, "Basic Psychoanalytic Concepts: X. Interpretations and Other Interventions," *British Journal of Psychiatry*, Vol. 11 (1971).

92. Robert H. Dolliver, "Concerning the Potential Parallels Between Psychotherapy and Brainwashing," *Psychotherapy: Theory, Research and Practice*, Vol. 8 (1971), p. 171.

93. Chessick, op. cit., p. 61.

94. Viscott, op. cit., p. 124.

95. Ibid., p. 124.

96. Feifel and Eells, op. cit., p. 317.

97. Donald W. Light, Jr., "Psychiatry and Suicide: The Management of a Mistake," *American Journal of Sociology*, Vol. 7 (1972), p. 828.

98. Rose Zeligs, "Do Therapists Play God?" *Mental Hygiene*, Vol. 54 (1970), p. 161.

99. Schmideberg, "Psychotherapy with Failures of Psychoanalysis," p. 197.

100. Florence Rush, "Notes From a Social Worker," *The Radical Therapist*, Vol. 2, No. 2 (September 1971).

101. Ibid.

102. Ibid.

103. Jay Haley, *Strategies of Psychotherapy* (New York: Grune & Stratton, 1972), p. 79.

104. Edwin Holt, *The Freudian Wish and Its Place in Ethics* (New York: B. W. Huebsch, 1915) as cited in Nathan G. Hale, Jr., *Freud and the Americans: The Beginnings of Psychoanalysis in the United States, 1876–1917* (New York: Oxford University Press, 1971), p. 429.
105. Chessick, op. cit., p. 74.
106. Ibid., p. 44.

The Interpretation of Resistance

107. Sigmund Freud, *A General Introduction to Psychoanalysis* (New York: Simon & Schuster, 1969), p. 253.
108. Millon, op. cit., p. 637.
109. Raymond Corsini, *Current Psychotherapies* (Itasca, Illinois: F. E. Peacock, 1973), p. 20.
110. Robert W. Hagebak and George V. C. Parker, "Therapist Directiveness, Client Dominance, and Therapy Resistance," *Journal of Consulting and Clinical Psychology*, Vol. 33 (1969), p. 536.
111. Isaak M. Marks, "Empiricism is Accepted," in Allen E. Bergin and Hans H. Strupp, eds., *Changing Frontiers in the Science of Psychotherapy* (New York: Aldine-Atherton, 1972), pp. 133–134.
112. Schmideberg, "Psychotherapy with Failures of Psychoanalysis," p. 198.
113. Viscott, op. cit., p. 289.
114. Ibid.
115. Ibid.
116. Morton M. Hunt and Rena Corman, with Louis R. Ormont, *The Talking Cure* (New York: Harper & Row, 1964), p. 124: "The patient must be in enough pain to go on."
117. R. Brockbank, "On the Analyst's Silence in Psychoanalysis: A Synthesis of Intrapsychic Content and Interpersonal Manifestations," *International Journal of Psycho-Analysis*, Vol. 51 (1970).
118. Strupp, Wallach, and Wogan, op. cit.; and Dorothy Tennov, "Psychotherapy, Women, and the Women's Movement," paper presented at the annual meetings of the

Society for Psychotherapy Research, Philadelphia (June 1973).

The Responsibility Belongs to the Patient

119. Millon, op. cit., p. 258.
120. Donald M. Kaplan, "Comments on the Screening Function of a 'Technical Effect,' With Reference to a Depression and Jealousy," *International Journal of Psycho-Analysis,* Vol. 51 (1970), p. 489.

Dependency of the Patient on Therapy and the Therapist

121. Dolliver, op. cit.; Frank, *Persuasion and Healing;* and Robert R. Holt, "Forcible Indoctrination and Personality Change," in P. Worchel and D. Byrne, eds., *Personality Change* (New York: John Wiley, 1964).
122. Robert Lifton, *Thought Reform and the Psychology of Totalism* (New York: W. W. Norton, 1961).
123. London, *Behavior Control,* p. 51.
124. Frank, *Persuasion and Healing,* p. 156.
125. Albert Bandura, "Psychotherapy as a Learning Process," *Psychological Bulletin,* Vol. 58 (1961), p. 143.
126. Kubie, op. cit., p. 864.
127. Schmideberg, "Psychotherapy with Failures of Psychoanalysis," pp. 196–197.
128. Schmideberg, "Principles of Psychotherapy."
129. Schmideberg, "Psychotherapy with Failures of Psychoanalysis," pp. 195–196.

Psychotherapists Interpret One Another

130. Schmideberg, "A Contribution to the History of the Psycho-Analytic Movement in Britain," p. 64.
131. Ibid., p. 64.
132. Ibid., p. 65.
133. Ibid., p. 63.
134. Ibid., p. 64.
135. Martin Shepard and Marjorie Lee, *Games Analysts Play* (New York: Berkley, 1972), pp. 132–133.
136. Viscott, op. cit., p. 106.

137. Hale, op. cit., p. 374.
138. William McGuire, ed., and Ralph Manheim and R. F. C. Hull, trans., *The Freud/Jung Letters: The Correspondence Between Sigmund Freud and C. J. Jung* (Princeton: Princeton University Press, 1974), letter 264F, 13 July 1911, Karlsbad.
139. Ibid., letter 270F, 1 September 1911, Klobenstein.
140. Ibid., letter 286F, 3 November 1911, Vienna.
141. Ibid., letter 290F, 31 December 1911, Vienna.
142. Ibid., letter 340F, 5 March 1912, Vienna.
143. Ibid., letter 323J, 11 November 1912, Küsnach-Zürich.
144. Ibid., letter 320J, 3 December 1912, Küsnach-Zürich.

Stigma

145. Theodore R. Sarbin, "On the Futility of the Proposition that Some People Be Labeled 'Mentally Ill'," *Journal of Consulting Psychology*, Vol. 31 (1967), p. 448.
146. Ibid., p. 451.
147. Theodore R. Sarbin and James C. Mancuso, "Failure of a Moral Enterprise: Attitudes of the Public Toward Mental Illness," *Journal of Consulting and Clinical Psychology*, Vol. 35 (1970).
148. Shirley Star, "The Public's Ideas About Mental Illness," paper presented to the annual meeting of the National Association for Mental Health, Indianapolis, Indiana (November 5, 1955), as cited in Paul V. Lemkau and Guido M. Crocett, "An Urban Population's Opinion and Knowledge About Mental Illness," *American Journal of Psychiatry*, Vol. 118, 1962, p. 692.
149. See Sarbin and Mancuso, op. cit.
150. Schmideberg, "Sociolegal Consequences of Psychiatric Diagnoses in U.S.A. and Britain," p. 167.
151. Robert L. Taylor and E. Fuller Torrey, "Mental Health Coverage Under a National Health Insurance Plan," pamphlet (Rockville, Md.: National Institutes of Mental Health, 1973).
152. William J. Curran, Eugene M. Laska, Honora Kaplan, and Rheta Bank, "Protection of Privacy and Confidentiality," *Science*, Vol. 182 (November 1973).

153. From "Interview: David Bakan," in Bergin and Strupp, op. cit., p. 382.
154. Schmideberg, "Sociolegal Consequences of Psychiatric Diagnoses in U.S.A. and Britain," p. 160.
155. Richard B. Stuart, *Trick or Treatment: How and When Psychotherapy Fails* (Champaign, Illinois: Research Press, 1970), p. 104.
156. A. Farina, C. H. Holland, and K. Ring, "The Role of Stigma and Set in Interpersonal Interaction," *Journal of Abnormal Psychology*, Vol. 71 (1966).
157. Stuart, op. cit.
158. A. Farina, D. Gliha, L. A. Boudreau, J. G. Allen, and M. Sherman, "Mental Illness and the Impact of Believing Others Know About It," *Journal of Abnormal Psychology*, Vol. 77 (1971).
159. Farina, Holland, and Ring, op. cit.
160. Hunt, Corman, and Ormont, op. cit.
161. Stanley L. Brodsky, "Shared Results and Open Files With the Client," *Professional Psychologist*, Vol. 4 (1972).
162. Juris G. Draguns and Leslie Phillips, *Psychiatric Classification and Diagnosis: An Overview and Critique* (New Jersey: General Learning Press, 1971).

Diagnosis

163. Kenneth B. Little, "Problems in the Validation of Projective Techniques," *Journal of Projective Techniques*, Vol. 23 (1959), p. 287, as cited in Richard B. Stuart, *Trick or Treatment: How and When Psychotherapy Fails* (Champaign, Illinois: Research Press, 1970), p. 90.
164. Goldenberg, op. cit., p. 173.
165. Ibid., p. 173.
166. Stuart, op. cit., p. 91.
167. Viscott, op. cit., p. 278.
168. Viki Holland, "The Tyranny of Grimping," *Human Behavior* (October 1973), p. 33.
169. Anthony F. Donofrio, "Child Psychotherapy—Help or Hindrance?" *Mental Hygiene* (1970), p. 511.

170. Ibid., p. 511.

Psychotherapy as Social Control

171. Michael Glenn and Richard Kunnes, *Repression or Revolution? Therapy in the United States Today* (New York: Harper & Row, 1973), p. 1.
172. Hurvitz, "Psychotherapy as a Means of Social Control," p. 233.
173. Ibid.
174. Ibid.
175. Ibid., p. 235.
176. See Kate Millett, *Sexual Politics* (New York: Doubleday, 1970), ch. 4.
177. D. Pivnicki, "The Beginnings of Psychotherapy," *Journal of the History of Behavioral Science*, Vol. 5 (1969), p. 246.
178. Seymour L. Halleck, *The Politics of Therapy* (New York: Science House, 1971).
179. C. M. Lowe, *Value Orientations in Counseling and Psychotherapy* (San Francisco: Chandler, 1970).
180. George W. Albee, "The Uncertain Future of Clinical Psychology," *American Psychologist*, Vol. 25, No. 12 (1970), pp. 1072–1073.

II. PSYCHOTHERAPY AND SCIENTIFIC RESEARCH

The Nature of Scientific Research

1. During a debate among feminists and socialists tape-recorded by the author in London (October 1971).

Experimentation

2. Many have complained that reliable but inconsequential effects are often given more attention theoretically than effects of greater magnitude. For example, see David Bakan, *On Method: Toward a Reconstruction of Psychological Investigation* (San Francisco: Jossey-Bass,

1967), and Raymond Cochrane and John Duffy, "Psychology and Scientific Method," *Bulletin of the British Psychological Society*, Vol. 27 (1974).

Controlled Research

3. Robert R. Holt, *Methods of Research in Clinical Psychology* (Morristown, New Jersey: A University Programs Modular Study, General Learning Press, 1973), p. 25.

The Scientific Status of Psychoanalytic Theory

4. Theodore Millon, *Modern Psychopathology*, p. 637.
5. Naomi Weisstein, "Psychology Constructs the Female, or the Fantasy Life of the Male Psychologist," in Michele Hoffnung Garskof, *Roles Women Play: Readings Toward Women's Liberation* (Belmont, California: Brooks/Cole, 1971), p. 72.
6. Raymond E. Fancher and Robert F. Strahan, "Galvanic Skin Response and the Secondary Revision of Dreams: A Partial Disconfirmation of Freud's Dream Theory," *Journal of Abnormal Psychology* (1971); and D. Foulkes and A. Rechtschaffer, "Presleep Determinations of Dream Content: Effects of Two Films," *Perceptual and Motor Skills*, Vol. 19 (1964).
7. Charles L. Sheridan, *Fundamentals of Experimental Psychology* (New York: Holt, Rinehart and Winston, 1971), p. 28.
8. Weisstein, op. cit., p. 74.

Resistance to Research by Psychotherapists

9. Richard L. Bednar and Jeffrey G. Shapiro, "Professional Research Commitment: A Symptom or a Syndrome," *Journal of Consulting and Clinical Psychology*, Vol. 34 (1970), p. 28.
10. Neal Miller in Allen E. Bergin and Hans S. Strupp, *Changing Frontiers in the Science of Psychotherapy*, p. 350; Freud skipped the proof part; science consists of both.

11. Schmideberg, "Psychotherapy with Failures of Psycho-analysis," p. 198.
12. Strupp, Wallach, and Wogan, "The Psychotherapy Experience in Retrospect. . . ."
13. David G. Martin, *Introduction to Psychotherapy* (Belmont, California: Brooks/Cole, 1971), p. 21.
14. William V. Snyder, *The Psychotherapy Relationship*, p. 49.
15. Bednar and Shapiro, op. cit.
16. H. S. Stream and A. Blatt, "Long or Short Term Therapy: Some Selected Issues," *Journal of Contemporary Psychology*, Vol. 2 (1969), p. 117.
17. From a report of an interview with Neal E. Miller, Bergin and Strupp, op. cit., p. 343.
18. Referring to research by E. B. Brody, ibid., pp. 118–119.
19. Millon, op. cit., p. 578.
20. Schmideberg, "A Contribution to the History of the Psycho-Analytic Movement in Britain," p. 65.
21. Albee, "The Uncertain Future of Clinical Psychology," pp. 1074–1075.
22. Ibid., p. 1075.

Does Psychotherapy Help?

23. Storr, "The Concept of Cure," p. 59.
24. See Perry London, *The Modes and Morals of Psychotherapy*. This book views therapy as an incipient "secular priesthood."
25. Hans J. Eysenck, "The Effects of Psychotherapy: An Evaluation," *Journal of Consulting Psychology*, Vol. 16 (1952), pp. 319–324.
26. Allen E. Bergin, "The Evaluation of Therapeutic Outcomes," in Allen E. Bergin and Sol L. Garfield, eds., *Handbook of Psychotherapy and Behavior Change: An Empirical Analysis* (New York: John Wiley, 1971), p. 217.
27. Ibid., p. 228.
28. Alexander W. Astin, "The Functional Autonomy of Psychotherapy," in Arnold P. Goldstein and Sanford J.

Dean, eds., *The Investigation of Psychotherapy: Commentaries and Readings* (New York: John Wiley, 1966), p. 62.

29. Ibid., p. 63.

30. Millon, op. cit., p. 619.

31. I. D. Yalom, *The Theory and Practice of Group Psychotherapy* (New York: Basic Books, 1970), p. 386.

32. Storr, op. cit., p. 62.

33. Donofrio, "Child Psychotherapy—Help or Hindrance?" p. 510.

34. E. Levitt cited in Donofrio, op. cit., p. 511.

35. Harold E. R. Wallace and Marion B. H. Whyte, "Natural History of Psychoneuroses," *British Medical Journal*, Vol. 1 (January 17, 1959).

36. Storr, op. cit., p. 59.

37. Hurvitz, "Psychotherapy as a Means of Social Control," p. 232.

Recovery Without Treatment

38. Eysenck, "The Effects of Psychotherapy: An Evaluation."

39. Bergin, "The Evaluation of Therapeutic Outcomes," p. 241.

40. Ibid., pp. 244–245.

41. John O. Noll, "Needed—A Bill of Rights for Clients," *Professional Psychology*, Vol. 5, No. 1 (1974); Noll points out that the use of such nonprofessionals will also eliminate problems of prejudice against psychiatric patients.

42. Goldenberg, *Contemporary Clinical Psychology*, p. 216.

43. Frank Barron and Timothy F. Leary, "Changes in Psychoneurotic Patients With and Without Psychotherapy," *Journal of Consulting Psychology*, Vol. 19 (1955), p. 245.

44. Jerome D. Frank, "Common Features Account for Effectiveness," in Allen E. Bergin and Hans S. Strupp, *Changing Frontiers in the Science of Psychotherapy* (Chicago: Aldine-Atherton, 1972), p. 109.

Criteria for Improvement

45. Bergin, op. cit., pp. 304f.
46. Lester Luborsky, Arthur Auerback, Michael Chandler, Jacob Cohen, and Henry M. Bachrach, "Factors Influencing the Outcome of Psychotherapy: A Review of Quantitative Research," *Psychological Bulletin*, Vol. 75 (1971), pp. 157–158.
47. Jim Mintz, op. cit.
48. Bergin, op. cit.
49. Storr, op. cit., p. 84.
50. Hunt, Corman, and Ormont, *The Talking Cure*.
51. Jurgen Ruesch, *Therapeutic Community* (New York: W. W. Norton, 1961).
52. Kenneth Mark Colby, "Researchers Are Weeded Out," *International Journal of Psychiatry*, Vol. 7 (March 1969), p. 117.
53. Steven Lee Weiss, "Perceived Effectiveness of Psychotherapy," *Journal of Consulting and Clinical Psychology*, Vol. 39 (1972), p. 156.
54. Bergin, op. cit., p. 228, and G. L. Paul, "Strategy of Outcome Research in Psychotherapy," *Journal of Consulting Psychology*, Vol. 31, 1967.
55. Following Merton S. Krause's usage, the patient is the one who receives treatment; the client is the one who pays for it. They may or may not be the same; see Merton S. Krause, "Construct Validity for the Evaluation of Therapy Outcomes," *Journal of Abnormal Psychology*, Vol. 74 (1969), p. 525.
56. Hunt, Corman, and Ormont, op. cit., p. 153.
57. Julian Rotter, "Psychotherapy," *Annual Review of Psychology*, Vol. 11 (1960).
58. Joseph Wolpe, "Psychotherapeutic Efficacy and Objective Research," in Allen E. Bergin and Hans S. Strupp, eds., *Changing Frontiers in the Science of Psychotherapy Research* (Chicago: Aldine-Atherton, 1972), p. 143.
59. From "Comments by A. Hussain Tuma," in Bergin and Strupp, op. cit., p. 207.

Deterioration in Psychotherapy

60. Joseph D. Matarazzo, "Some Psychotherapists Make Patients Worse!" *International Journal of Psychiatry*, Vol. 3, No. 3 (1967).
61. Bergin, op. cit.
62. Ibid., p. 248.
63. Ibid., p. 250.
64. Charles B. Truax, "Effective Ingredients in Psychotherapy," *Journal of Counseling Psychology*, Vol. 10 (1963).
65. Stuart, *Trick or Treatment: How and When Psychotherapy Fails*, p. 58.
66. Goldenberg, op. cit., p. 217.
67. Schmideberg, "Principles of Psychotherapy."
68. Schmideberg, "Psychotherapy with Failures of Psychoanalysis."
69. Ibid., p. 199.
70. Ibid., p. 195.
71. Ibid., p. 197.
72. Ibid.

Suicide

73. Rogow, *The Psychiatrists*, p. 86.
74. Michael Rotov, "Death by Suicide in the Hospital: An Analysis of 20 Therapeutic Failures," *American Journal of Psychotherapy*, Vol. 25 (April 1970), pp. 76.
75. Merton J. Kahne, "Suicide Among Patients in Mental Hospitals: A Study of the Psychiatrists Who Conducted Their Therapy," *Psychiatry*, Vol. 31 (1968), pp. 32–33.
76. Ibid., pp. 32–33.
77. Ibid., p. 34.
78. Ibid., p. 32.
79. Erwin Strengel, *Suicide and Attempted Suicide* (Baltimore: Penguin Books, 1965).
80. Allan A. Stone, "Suicide Precipitated by Psychotherapy: A Clinical Contribution," *American Journal of Psychotherapy*, Vol. 25 (1971), p. 19.
81. Ibid., p. 19.
82. Light, *Psychiatry and Suicide: The Management of a Mistake*, p. 823.

83. Ibid., p. 824.

84. Ibid., p. 825.

85. Ibid., p. 825.

86. Ibid., p. 827.

87. Ibid., pp. 835–836.

88. Stone, op. cit., p. 23.

89. Kahne, "Suicide Among Patients in Mental Hospitals: A Study of the Psychiatrists Who Conducted Their Therapy," p. 68; Kahne's data disclosed more patient suicides for therapists who were foreign born and foreign trained.

90. Rotov, op. cit., p. 219.

91. Chessick, *How Psychiatry Heals,* p. 49.

Evidence of Effectiveness

92. For example, see John Leo, "Psychoanalysis Reaches a Crossroad," *New York Times,* August 4, 1968.

93. Interpretation of research which supports psychotherapy has been most enthusiastically voiced by Julian Meltzoff and Melvin Kornreich; see their *Research in Psychotherapy* (New York: Atherton Press, 1970).

A Final Note

94. Bergin and Strupp, op. cit., pp. 62–63.

95. See G. N. Braught, "The Deterioration Effect: A Reply to Bergin," *Journal of Abnormal Psychology,* Vol. 75 (1970).

96. Bergin and Strupp, op. cit., p. 61.

97. Florence Rush, "The Sexual Abuse of Children: A Feminist Point of View" (Pittsburgh: KNOW, 1971), p. 5.

III. SOMATOPSYCHIC ILLNESS

Types of Severe "Mental Disorders"

1. S. H. Kraines, "Neurological Theory of Depression," in William S. Sahakian, *Psychopathology Today* (Itasca, Illinois: F. E. Peacock Publishers, 1970), p. 415.

2. In general, the evidence for hereditary influence in depressive psychoses is very convincing, even more so than for schizophrenia. See Eliot Slater and Valerie Cowie, *The Genetics of Mental Disorders* (London: Oxford University Press, 1971), p. 263.

3. They seem ultimately to have failed, according to Sarbin and Mancuso.

4. "A New Old Treatment," *Newsweek* (July 9, 1973), p. 57.

5. "X Marks the Panic," *Newsweek* (August 28, 1972), p. 65.

6. The Professional Committee of the Schizophrenia Foundation of New Jersey, *The Schizophrenias: Yours and Mine* (New York: Pyramid Books, 1970), p. 11.

7. William T. Carpenter, Jr., John S. Strauss, and John J. Bartko, "Flexible System for the Diagnosis of Schizophrenia: Report From the WHO International Pilot Study of Schizophrenia," *Science*, Vol. 182 (December 1973).

8. See The Professional Committee of the Schizophrenia Foundation of New Jersey, op. cit.

9. Jack Ward, "Doctors Speak on the Ortho-Molecular Approach" (Saskatchewan: Canadian Schizophrenic Foundation, 1972).

10. Humphrey Osmond, "The Medical Model in Psychiatry," *Hospital & Community Psychiatry*, Vol. 21 (September 1970), pp. 275–281.

11. Ibid., p. 279.

12. Ibid., p. 278.

13. Allan Cott, *Ortho-Molecular Treatment: A Biochemical Approach to the Treatment of Schizophrenia* (New York: A Publication of the American Schizophrenia Association, 1970).

14. F. J. Kallmann, *Heredity in Mental Health and Disorder* (New York: W. W. Norton, 1953).

15. See John L. Fuller and William R. Thompson, *Behavior Genetics* (New York: John Wiley, 1960), and Slater and Cowie, op. cit.

16. Sarnoff A. Mednick, "Breakdown in Individuals at High Risk for Schizophrenia: Possible Predispositional Perinatal Factors," *Mental Hygiene*, Vol. 54 (1970).

17. See Carpenter, Strauss, and Bartko, op. cit. "Orthomolecular" psychiatrists A. Hoffer and H. Osmond have suggested that schizophrenia sufferers can be screened on the basis of reaction to certain vitamins.

18. A. F. Mirsky, "Neuropsychological Bases of Schizophrenia," *Annual Review of Psychology*, Vol. 20 (1969).

19. Light, "Psychiatry and Suicide: The Management of a Mistake," p. 829.

Does Psychotherapy Help Psychotic Patients?

20. Hale, *Freud and the Americans*, p. 349.

21. The Professional Committee of the Schizophrenia Foundation of New Jersey, op. cit., p. 126.

22. James A. Wechsler, *In A Darkness* (New York: W. W. Norton, 1972).

23. For example, see Don D. Jackson, "Psychotherapy for Schizophrenia," *Scientific American*, Vol. 189 (January 1953). According to Jackson, "There is nothing unique about the difficulties of schizophrenics except in degree."

24. See Charles B. Truax, "Effects of Client-Centered Psychotherapy With Schizophrenic Patients: Nine Years Pretherapy and Nine Years Posttherapy Hospitalization," *Journal of Consulting and Clinical Psychology*, Vol. 35 (1970); Bertram P. Karon and Gary R. VandenBos, "The Consequences of Psychotherapy for Schizophrenic Patients," Michigan State Psychotherapy Research Project, Bulletin No. 16 mimeographed; Michael Wogan, "Effect of Therapist-Patient Personality Variables on Therapeutic Outcome," *Journal of Consulting and Clinical Psychology*, Vol. 35 (1970); J. C. Whitehorn and B. J. Betz, "A Study of Psychotherapeutic Relationships Between Physicians and Schizophrenic Patients," *American Journal of Psychiatry*, Vol. 111 (1954); and J. C. Whitehorn and B. J. Betz, "Further

Studies of the Doctor as a Crucial Variable in the Outcome of Treatment with Schizophrenic Patients," *American Journal of Psychiatry*, Vol. 117 (1960).

25. See L. E. Hollister, "Choice of Antipsychotic Drugs," *American Journal of Psychiatry*, Vol. 127 (1970).

26. George E. Crane, "Clinical Psychopharmacology in Its 20th Year," *Science*, Vol. 181 (July 13, 1973).

27. See David R. Hawkins, *The Development of an Integrated Community System For the Effective Treatment of Schizophrenia* (New York: American Schizophrenia Association, 1972).

28. For example, Joshua Logan in an appearance on "Not For Women Only," NBC-TV (October 29, 1973).

29. Benjamin Kleinmuntz, "Greeting, Tributes, Speculation and Some Data," *Contemporary Psychology*, Vol. 12, No. 12 (1967).

The Mother of the Schizophrenic Patient

30. Gregory Bateson, Don D. Jackson, Jay Haley, and J. H. Weakland, "Toward a Theory of Schizophrenia," *Behavioral Science*, Vol. 1 (1956).

31. For example, as in Alfred B. Heilbrun, Jr., *Aversive Maternal Control: A Theory of Schizophrenic Development* (New York: Wiley-Interscience, 1973).

32. Lewis B. Hill, *Psychotherapeutic Intervention in Schizophrenia* (Chicago: University of Chicago Press, 1955).

33. Ibid., p. 108.
34. Ibid., p. 109.
35. Ibid., p. 111.
36. Ibid., p. 112.
37. Ibid., p. 115.
38. Ibid., p. 116.
39. Ibid., pp. 116–117.
40. Louise Wilson, *This Stranger, My Son* (London: John Murray, 1969), pp. 74–75.
41. Joan Huser Liem, "Effects of Verbal Communications of Parents and Children: A Comparison of Normal and Schizophrenic Families," *Journal of Consulting and Clinical Psychology*, Vol. 42, No. 3 (1974).

IV. PROFESSIONALISM

Sources of Psychotherapy

1. Ronald Leifer, *In the Name of Mental Health* (New York: Science House, 1969), p. 103.
2. Ibid.
3. Ibid., p. 155.
4. Ibid., p. 156.
5. Goldenberg, *Contemporary Clinical Psychology*, p. 304.
6. See Leifer, op. cit.
7. Kadushin, *Why People Go to Psychiatrists*, p. 324.
8. Ibid.
9. As reported in "Nader Report: Community Mental Health Centers," *Behavior Today*, Vol. 3, No. 30 (July 31, 1972), pp. 3–5.
10. Hurvitz, "Psychotherapy as a Means of Social Control," p. 236.
11. Ibid.
12. Ibid.

What Makes It a Profession

13. Nathan Roth, "The Strange Society of the Physician—Doctors Seek Each Other Out," *American Journal of Psychotherapy*, Vol. 24 (1970).
14. See William E. Henry, John H. Sims, and S. Lee Spray, *The Fifth Profession* (San Francisco: Jossey-Bass, 1971).
15. Tennov, "Women Evaluate and Describe Their Psychotherapy Outside the Clinical Setting."
16. Hunt, Corman, and Ormont, *The Talking Cure*, p. 88.
17. Tennov, "Women Evaluate and Describe Their Psychotherapy Outside the Clinical Setting."

Professional Imperialism

18. Dr. F. C. Redlich of Yale University, as quoted in John Leo, "Psychoanalysis Reaches a Crossroad," *New York Times* (August 4, 1968), p. 58.

How to Become a Professional Psychotherapist

19. Henry, Sims, and Spray, op. cit., p. 143.
20. Ibid., p. xi.
21. Ibid., pp. xi–xii.
22. Dorothy Tennov, "The Relationships Between Obstetrical Procedures and Perinatal Anoxia," *Journal of Clinical Child Psychology,* Vol. 2 (Fall 1973).
23. London, *The Modes and Morals of Psychotherapy,* p. 30.
24. Ibid., pp. 30–31.
25. Bergin and Strupp, *Changing Frontiers in the Science of Psychotherapy,* p. 414.
26. Hunt, Corman, and Ormont, op. cit., p. 91.
27. Viscott, *The Making of a Psychiatrist,* p. 312.
28. Glenn and Kunnes, "Repression or Revolution? Therapy in the United States Today," p. 23.
29. George Albee cited by Goldenberg, op. cit., pp. 73–74.
30. Bergin, op. cit., p. 237.
31. Charles B. Truax and Kevin M. Mitchell, "Research on Certain Therapist Interpersonal Skills in Relation to Process and Outcome," in Allen E. Bergin and Sol L. Garfield, *Handbook of Psychotherapy and Behavior Change: Empirical Analysis* (New York: John Wiley, 1971), p. 327.
32. Jeffrey G. Shapiro and T. Voog, "Effect of the Inherently Helpful Person on Student Academic Achievement," *Journal of Counseling Psychology,* Vol. 16 (1969), as cited by Truax and Mitchell, op. cit., p. 327.
33. Truax and Mitchell, op. cit., p. 337.

Clinical Psychology

34. Goldenberg, op. cit., p. 61.
35. American Psychological Association, "Ethical Standards of Psychologists," (Washington, D.C.: American Psychological Association, 1953).
36. See D. D. Bond, "Teaching Ethical Concepts to Medical Students and Psychiatric Residents," *American Journal of Psychiatry,* Vol. 126, 1969.

37. Goldenberg, *Clinical Psychology,* p. 63.
38. Ibid., pp. 63–64.
39. M. L. Goldschmid, D. D. Stein, H. Weissman, and J. Sorrells, "A Survey of the Training and Practices of Clinical Psychologists," *The Clinical Psychologist Newsletter,* Vol. 22 (1969).

Length of Treatment and Psychotherapy as a "Laboratory"

40. Frank, *Persuasion and Healing,* pp. 14–15.
41. Ibid., p. 15.
42. Joseph D. Matarazzo, "The Practice of Psychotherapy Is Art and Not Science," in Alvin R. Mahrer and Leonard Pearson, eds., *Creative Developments in Psychotherapy,* Vol. I (Cleveland: The Press of Case Western Reserve, 1971), p. 43.
43. Rogow, *The Psychiatrists,* p. 83.
44. See Schmideberg, "Psychotherapy with Failures of Psychoanalysis."
45. Viscott, op. cit., p. 309.
46. Kenneth I. Howard and David E. Orlinsky, "Psychotherapeutic Processes," *Annual Review of Psychology,* Vol. 23 (1972), p. 90.

Licensing, Certifying, and the Awarding of Diplomas

47. John A. Lazo, ed., *Biographical Directory of the American Psychological Association* (Washington, D.C.: American Psychological Association, 1973), p. xix.
48. Jules Asher, "Opposition Wins Latest Round in Fight Over New York Licensing Bill," *APA Monitor,* Vol. 4 (June 1973), p. 1.
49. Goldenberg, op. cit., p. 61.
50. Asher, op. cit., p. 1.
51. Michael C. Johnson, "The Age of Psychotherapy and 'Mental Health' is Over," *The Village Voice* (January 18, 1973), p. 35.
52. Harold Riegelman, "Letter to the Editor," *New York Times* (April 13, 1973).
53. William Sherman, "Probe Teacher on Psychotherapy," *New York Daily News* (July 20, 1972).

54. William Sherman, "Backing Grows for Controls in Mental Health," New York *Daily News* (July 26, 1972).
55. Allen Williams, director of the New York Psychological Association, as quoted, ibid.
56. Ibid.
57. George Frank, "More on Biondo," Letter to the Editor, *APA Monitor*, Vol. 4, No. 12 (December 1973).
58. Ibid.
59. Jim Warren, "Rogers Challenges Psychologists to Become Future Oriented," *APA Monitor*, Vol. 3, No. 11 (November 1972), p. 14.
60. Ibid.

Insurance

61. Constance Holden, "Psychology: Clinicians Seek Professional Autonomy," *Science*, Vol. 181, No. 2 (September 1973).
62. Jack Wiggins, "Should Psychotherapy Be Included in Health Insurance Programs? Yes!" *APA Monitor*, Vol. 4 (September–October 1973), p. 8.
63. Ibid.
64. Lloyd Humphreys, "Should Psychotherapy Be Included in Health Insurance Programs? No!" *APA Monitor*, Vol. 4 (September–October 1973), p. 8.
65. George Albee, "Who Gains?" Letter to the Editor, *APA Monitor*, Vol. 4, No. 1 (January 1973), p. 10.
66. Bill McChonochie, "Con Artists," Letter to the Editor, *APA Monitor*, Vol. 4, No. 11 (November 1973), p. 8.
67. Robert D. Weitz (Chairman, Ways and Means Committee, Council for the Advancement of the Psychological Professions and Sciences), in an open letter to psychologists (July 11, 1973).
68. *APA Guidelines for Psychiatric Services Covered Under Health Insurance Plans, Second Edition* (American Psychiatric Association, May 1973).

Fees

69. Tennov, "Women Evaluate and Describe Their Psychotherapy Outside the Clinical Setting," p. 1.

70. "Well over $10,000," according to Goldenberg, op. cit., p. 235.

71. Norbett L. Mintz, "Patient Fees and Psychotherapeutic Transactions," *Journal of Consulting and Clinical Psychology*, Vol. 36 (February 1971), pp. 2–3.

72. Kenneth M. Colby in a letter to Hans Strupp (January 9, 1968), cited in Bergin and Strupp, op. cit., pp. 162–163.

73. Hunt, Corman, and Ormont, op. cit., p. 92.

74. Ibid., p. 93.

75. George M. Burnell, "Financing Mental Health Care," *Archives of General Psychiatry*, Vol. 25 (July 1971), p. 49.

76. Chessick, op. cit., p. 117.

77. Ibid., p. 118.

78. Shapiro, "Placebo Effects in Medicine, Psychotherapy and Psychoanalysis," p. 453.

79. Viscott, op. cit., p. 351.

80. Ibid., p. 356.

81. William Schofield, "Psychotherapy: The Unknown Versus the Untold," *Journal of Consulting and Clinical Psychology*, Vol. 36 (February 1971), p. 10.

V. THE MAD RIDE

Professional Varieties

1. Roy R. Grinker, "Psychiatry Rides Madly in All Directions," *Archives of General Psychology*, Vol. 10 (1964).

2. Halleck, *The Politics of Therapy*, p. 35.

3. R. A. Harper, *Psychoanalysis and Psychotherapy: 36 Systems* (Englewood Cliffs, New Jersey: Prentice-Hall, 1959).

4. Goldenberg, *Contemporary Clinical Psychology*, p. 201.

5. London, *The Modes and Morals of Psychotherapy*, p. 220.

6. Goldenberg, op. cit., p. 268.

7. Max Hamilton, "Psychology in Society: Ends or End?" *Bulletin of the British Psychological Society,* Vol. 26 (1973), p. 188.
8. Carl R. Rogers, "In Retrospect: Forty-Six Years," *American Psychologist,* Vol. 29 (February 1974), p. 117.

Interactional Psychotherapy: An Example of a System

9. Sheldon Cashdan, *Interactional Psychotherapy: Stages and Strategies in Behavioral Change* (New York: Grune & Stratton, 1973).
10. Ibid., p. 63.
11. Ibid., p. 65.
12. Ibid., p. 67.
13. Ibid.
14. Ibid., p. 68.
15. Ibid., pp. 68–69.
16. Ibid., p. 69.
17. Ibid., p. 71.
18. Ibid., p. 73.
19. Ibid., p. 74.
20. Ibid., pp. 74–75.
21. Ibid., p. 77.
22. Ibid.
23. Ibid.
24. Ibid., p. 79.
25. Ibid., pp. 79–80.
26. Ibid., p. 83.
27. Ibid., p. 84.
28. Ibid.
29. Ibid., p. 85.
30. Ibid.
31. Ibid.
32. Ibid., p. 86.
33. Ibid.
34. Ibid.
35. Ibid., p. 94.
36. Ibid.
37. Ibid., p. 97.

38. For example, see Harrison and Carek, *A Guide to Psychotherapy.*

Group Therapy

39. George R. Bach and Yett M. Bernard, "Deserts and Oases," *Contemporary Psychology,* Vol. 12 (1967), p. 220.

40. Richard L. Bednar and G. Frank Lawlis, "Empirical Research in Group Psychotherapy," in Allen E. Bergin and Sol L. Garfield, eds., *Handbook of Psychotherapy and Behavior Change: An Empirical Analysis* (New York: John Wiley, 1971), p. 833.

41. Ibid., p. 820.

42. W. H. Coons, "Interaction and Insight in Group Therapy," *Canadian Journal of Psychology,* Vol. 11 (1957), pp. 1–8.

43. Donald M. Kaplan, "The Last Gasps of Pop Psychology," *The Village Voice* (August 31, 1972).

The Pop Group Movement

44. June Howard, "Encounter Groups: Emotional Striptease for Women?" *Vogue,* Vol. 155 (January 1970), pp. 10–11.

45. Goodwin Watson, "Growing Edges in Groups," *Contemporary Psychology,* Vol. 11, No. 5 (1966), p. 238.

46. Frederick H. Stoller, "The Long Weekend," *Psychology Today,* Vol. 1, No. 7 (December 1967).

47. Anonymous, "My Rat Feels Red," *Red Rat, The Journal of Abnormal Psychologists,* Vol. 3 (Summer 1971).

48. Rowan Bayne, "Psychology and Encounter Groups," *Bulletin of the British Psychological Society,* Vol. 25 (1972), p. 287.

49. William C. Schutz, *Joy: Expanding Human Awareness* (New York: Grove Press, 1967), p. 123.

50. Ibid., pp. 134–135.

51. Ibid., pp. 167–168.

52. Ibid., p. 169.

53. Ibid., p. 177.

54. Ibid., p. 222.
55. [Elaine Kepner and Lois Brien], American Academy of Psychotherapists, *Brochure on the 1973 Training Institute and Annual Conference* (Orlando, Florida: American Academy of Psychotherapists, 1973).
56. New Haven Center for Human Relations, *Brochure for Fall, 1973* (New Haven, Connecticut: New Haven Center for Human Relations, 1973).
57. Severin Peterson, *A Catalog of the Ways People Grow* (New York: Ballantine Books, 1971).
58. Frank H. Boring, "Ethical Perspectives on Growth Groups," *APA Monitor*, Vol. 3, No. 5 (May 1972), p. 3.
59. Ibid.
60. Ibid.
61. Yalom, *The Theory and Practice of Group Psychotherapy*.
62. Morton A. Lieberman, Irvin D. Yalom, and Matthew B. Miles, *Encounter Groups: First Facts* (New York: Basic Books, 1973).

Nonprofessional Independents

63. See Frank, *Persuasion and Healing*, and Arthur K. Shapiro, "Placebo Effects in Medicine, Psychotherapy and Psychoanalysis."

Paraprofessionals, Subprofessionals

64. Bergin and Strupp, *Changing Frontiers in the Science of Psychotherapy*, p. 115.
65. K. I. Pearce, "A Comparison of Care Given by Family Practitioners and Psychiatrists in a Teaching Hospital Unit," *American Journal of Psychiatry*, Vol. 127 (1970).
66. Franklin N. Arnhoff, Review of *Casebook in Psychopathology* by Frank J. Kobler, *Contemporary Psychology*, Vol. 11 (1966); see also Sarbin and Mancuso, "Failure of a Moral Enterprise. . . ."
67. The hostility encountered by nurse therapists is reported in Isaac Marks, "Conference on 'The Psychiatric Nurse As Therapist: Developments and Problems,'"

Bulletin of the British Psychological Society, Vol. 26 (1973); see also Gene Gary Gruver, "College Students as Therapeutic Agents," *Psychological Bulletin*, Vol. 76 (1971).

68. Hunt, Corman, and Ormont, *The Talking Cure*, p. 88.

69. Theodore H. Blau, "The Professional in the Community Views the Nonprofessional Helper: Psychology," *Professional Psychology* (Fall 1969), p. 25.

70. Robert Tyson, "Should M.A. Level Psychologists Have Full Membership?" *APA Monitor*, Vol. 3, No. 7 (July 1972), p. 2.

71. Ibid., p. 8.

72. See, for example, M. E. Reres, "A Survey of the Nurse's Role in Psychiatric Outpatient Clinics in America," *Community Mental Health Journal*, Vol. 5 (1969); Gary E. Stollak, "Undergraduates as Play Therapists: The Effects of Training and Personal Characteristics," paper presented at the Third Annual Meeting of the Society for Psychotherapy Research, Nashville, Tennessee (June 16, 1972); Arnold P. Goldstein, "Domains and Dilemmas," *International Journal of Psychiatry*, Vol. 7, No. 3 (March 1969); and Pearce, op. cit.

73. Goldenberg, op. cit., pp. 61–62.

74. See, for example, Stuart, *Trick or Treatment: How and When Psychotherapy Fails*.

75. Charles B. Truax and R. R. Carkhuff, *Toward Effective Counseling and Psychotherapy* (Chicago: Aldine, 1967).

76. Allen E. Bergin and S. Solomon, "Personality and Performance Correlates of Empathic Understanding in Psychotherapy," paper presented at the annual convention of the American Psychological Association, Philadelphia (1963).

77. Bergin and Strupp, op. cit., p. 235.

Feminist Therapy

78. *Bridgeport Post*, Bridgeport, Connecticut (May 3, 1973).

79. Dorothy Tennov, "Feminism, Psychotherapy, and Pro-

fessionalism," *Journal of Contemporary Psychotherapy*, Vol. 5 (1973).

80. Jean Ferson, "The Feminist Therapy Collective of Philadelphia," paper presented at the 81st Annual Convention of the American Psychological Association, Montreal, Canada (August 29, 1973).

81. Ibid.

82. Ibid.

83. Ibid.

"Radical Therapy" and "Antipsychiatry"

84. Thomas S. Szasz and George J. Alexander, "The American Association for the Abolition of Involuntary Mental Hospitalization," *The Abolitionist*, Vol. 1 (Summer 1971).

85. Thomas Szasz, *The Myth of Mental Illness* (New York: Harper & Row, 1961).

86. Jan B. Gordon, "The Meta-Journey of R. D. Laing," *Salmagundi*, Vol. 16 (Spring 1971).

87. Halleck, *The Politics of Therapy*, p. 34.

88. Ibid., p. 36.

89. Ibid., p. 251.

90. Claude M. Steiner, "Radical Psychiatry Manifesto," *The Radical Therapist*, Vol. 2, No. 3 (1971), p. 2.

91. Rick Kunnes, "How to be a Radical Therapist," *The Radical Therapist*, Vol. 2, No. 1 (April–May 1971), p. 3.

92. Ibid.

93. Hamilton, op. cit.

94. Ibid.

Self-Help

95. "Tyler Foresees New Era of Hope for Psychology," *APA Monitor*, Vol. 4, No. 11 (November 1973), p. 1.

96. Bergin and Strupp, op. cit., p. 20.

97. Nathan Hurvitz, "Peer Self-Help Psychotherapy Groups and the Implications for Psychotherapy," *Psychotherapy: Theory, Research and Practice*, Vol. 7 (Spring 1970), p. 48.

98. Ibid., p. 43.

99. Ibid., p. 46.

Behavior Therapy

100. Leonard Krasner and Leonard P. Ullman, *Behavior Influence and Personality* (New York: Holt, Rinehart and Winston, 1973), p. 261.
101. These comparisons are adapted from Hans J. Eysenck, "Learning Theory and Behavior Therapy," *Journal of Mental Science,* Vol. 105 (1959).
102. Ivan Wentworth-Rohr, "Symptoms, Insight and Behavior Therapies in Psychoanalytic Psychotherapy," *Psychoanalytic Review,* Vol. 57 (July 1970), p. 58.
103. See "Psychiatry Gives Behaviorism a Clean Bill of Health," *APA Monitor,* Vol. 4 (December 1973), p. 10.
104. See Joseph Wolpe, Andrew Salter, and L. J. Reyna, *The Conditioning Therapies* (New York: Holt, Rinehart and Winston, 1964), ch. 3.
105. Wentworth-Rohr, op. cit.
106. G. L. Paul, "Outcome of Systematic Desensitization. II. Controlled Investigations of Individual Treatment, Technique Variations, and Current Status," in Cyril M. Franks, ed., *Behavior Therapy: Appraisal and Status* (New York: McGraw-Hill, 1969).
107. Especially modeling; see Krasner and Ullman, op. cit., p. 289.
108. Hans Eysenck, personal communication to the author.
109. Krasner and Ullman, op. cit., p. 294.
110. See M. P. Feldman and M. J. MacCulloch, "The Application of Anticipatory Avoidance Learning to the Treatment of Homosexuality: 1. Theory, Technique and Preliminary Results," *Behavior Research and Therapy,* Vol. 2 (1965).
111. Albert Bandura, *Principles of Behavior Modification* (New York: Holt, Rinehart and Winston, 1969), p. 329.
112. Krasner and Ullman, op. cit., p. 294.
113. See R. Cautela, "Treatment of Compulsive Behavior by Covert Sensitization," *Psychological Record,* Vol. 16 (1966).
114. See Montrose Wolf, Todd Risley, and H. Mees, "Appli-

cation of Operant Conditioning Procedures to the Behavior Problems of an Autistic Child," *Behavior Research and Theory*, Vol. 1 (1964).

115. Bandura, *Principles of Behavior Modification*, p. 345.
116. Richard I. Evans, ed., *B. F. Skinner: The Man and His Ideas* (New York: E. P. Dutton, 1968), p. 34.
117. See Jack Sandler and Robert S. Davidson, *Psychopathology: Learning Theory, Research, and Applications* (New York: Harper & Row, 1973), pp. 257–260.
118. Ibid., p. 226.
119. Ibid., p. 227.
120. Bandura, *Principles of Behavior Modification*, p. 166.
121. Sandler and Davidson, *Psychopathology: Learning Theory, Research, and Applications*, p. 199.
122. Ibid., p. 198
123. See such books as Howard Lewis and Martha Lewis, *The Medical Offenders* (New York: Simon & Schuster, 1970); Anonymous, M.D., *The Healers: Confessions of a Successful Doctor* (New York: G. P. Putnam's Sons, 1967); and William Michelfelder, *It's Cheaper to Die* (New York: George Braziller, 1960).

VI. WOMEN AND THE PSYCHOTHERAPY PROFESSIONS

Images of Women in the Patriarchy

1. Dean D. Knudsen, "The Declining Status of Women: Popular Myths and the Failure of Functionalist Thought," *Social Forces*, Vol. 48, No. 2 (1969).
2. Dorothy Tennov, "The 'Seven Ages' of the Professional Woman," *Women Speaking*, Vol. 2, No. 4 (1972).
3. Interview with Simone de Beauvoir at her apartment in Paris (November 24, 1973).
4. Simone de Beauvoir, *The Second Sex*, translated and edited by H. M. Parshley (New York: Alfred A. Knopf, 1952; Bantam Books, 1961), p. 384.
5. For example, P. V. Olczak, E. H. Donnerstein, J. Thomas, and I. Kahn, "Group Hysteria and the MMPI," *Psychological Reports*, Vol. 28 (1971).

6. Walter R. Gove and Jeannette F. Tudor, "Adult Sex Roles and Mental Illness," *American Journal of Sociology*, Vol. 78 (January 1973).

7. Ibid., p. 827.

8. Inge K. Broverman, Donald M. Broverman, Frank E. Clarkson, Paul S. Rosenkrantz, and Susan R. Vogel, "Sex-Role Stereotypes and Clinical Judgments of Mental Health," *Journal of Consulting and Clinical Psychology*, Vol. 34, No. 1 (1970).

9. Ibid., p. 6.

10. Viscott, *The Making of a Psychiatrist*.

11. Krause, op. cit., p. 524.

12. William Schofield, *Psychotherapy: The Purchase of Friendship* (Englewood Cliffs, New Jersey: Prentice-Hall, 1964), p. 206.

13. Strupp, Wallach, and Wogan, "The Psychotherapy Experience in Retrospect. . . ."

14. "The most 'popular' patients with therapists were, in order of popularity, Caucasian women, Caucasian men, Mexican-American women, Negro women, and lastly Mexican-American and Negro men," see Rogow, *The Psychiatrists*, p. 75.

15. De Beauvoir, *The Second Sex*, p. 515.

16. Ibid.

17. Weisstein, "Psychology Constructs the Female . . ."

18. Ibid., p. 71.

19. Ibid., p. 71.

20. Ibid., p. 73.

21. That chapter, in Goodwin Watson, *Social Psychology: Issues and Insights* (New York: J. B. Lippincott, 1966), was a good one, too, for its time.

22. Kimball Young, *Social Psychology* (New York: F. S. Crofts, 1947).

23. R. Dewey and W. J. Humber, *An Introduction to Social Psychology* (New York: Macmillan, 1966), p. 461.

24. Millett, *Sexual Politics*, p. 194.

25. Ibid.

26. Alix Shulman, "Organs and Orgasms," in Vivian Gornick and Barbara K. Moran, eds., *Women in Sexist Society* (New York: Basic Books, 1971), p. 294.

27. William H. Masters and Virginia E. Johnson, "The Sexual Response Cycle of the Human Female. III. The Clitoris: Anatomic and Clinical Considerations," *Western Journal of Surgery, Obstetrics and Gynecology*, Vol. 70 (1962). Wilma Scott Heide has pointed out that the same observation was also made by "millions of honest women before them."

28. Shulman, op. cit., p. 296.

Psychotherapy Is a Male Enterprise

29. Ann Sutherland Harris, "The Second Sex in Academe," *American Association of University Professors Bulletin* (Fall 1970).

30. Betty M. Vetter, "Survey Paints Picture of Psychology Manpower," *APA Monitor*, Vol. 4, No. 11 (November 1973), p. 3.

31. C. Alan Boneau, "Psychologists Sized-Up at Last," *APA Monitor*, Vol. 5, No. 2 (February 1974), p. 14.

32. Dorothy T. Hoffman [Dorothy Tennov], Brian Scally, Andrew Deering, and Evelyn Kott, "Women in Psychology," paper presented at the American Psychological Convention, Miami Beach, Florida (September 7, 1970).

33. Martha Teghtsoonian, "Distribution by Sex of Authors and Editors of Psychological Journals, 1970–1972," *American Psychologist*, Vol. 29 (April 1974), p. 268.

34. Benjamin B. Wolman, ed., *Handbook in General Psychology* (Englewood Cliffs, New Jersey: Prentice-Hall, 1973).

35. Martha S. White, "Psychological and Social Barriers to Women in Science," *Science*, Vol. 170 (October 23, 1970).

Psychiatry Writes About Women

36. Matina S. Horner, "Toward an Understanding of Achievement-Related Conflicts in Women," *Journal of Social Issues*, Vol. 8 (1972).

37. The Code Napoleon asserted that a woman's "person

and her property were under rigorous marital control"
(de Beauvoir, op. cit., p. 102).

38. Gregory Zilboorg, "Masculine and Feminine: Some Biological and Cultural Aspects," in Jean Baker Miller, ed.,
Psychoanalysis and Women (Middlesex, England: Penguin Books, 1973), p. 100.

39. Ibid., p. 102.

40. Nathan K. Rickles, "The Angry Woman Syndrome,"
Archives of General Psychiatry, Vol. 24 (January 1971),
p. 91.

41. Ibid., p. 91.

42. Ibid., p. 93.

43. Ibid., p. 92.

44. Ibid., p. 93.

45. Ibid., p. 93.

46. Ibid., p. 94.

47. Ibid., p. 93.

48. Florence Rush, "Who's Afraid of Margaret Ribble?"
(Pittsburgh: KNOW, 1973).

49. John H. Houck, "The Intractable Female Patient,"
American Journal of Psychiatry, Vol. 129 (1972), p. 27.

50. Ibid., p. 27.

51. Ibid., p. 28.

52. Ibid., p. 30.

53. Ibid., p. 29.

54. Melitta Schmideberg, "Why Do Wives Put Up With
Violence?" *Social Worker* (January 17, 1974).

55. Ibid.

56. Ibid.

57. See Millon, *Modern Psychopathology*, p. 9.

58. William A. Browne, "A Psychiatric Study of the Life
and Work of Dorothea Dix," *American Journal of Psychiatry*, Vol. 126 (1969).

59. Ibid., p. 336.

60. Ibid., p. 336.

61. Ibid., p. 337.

62. Ibid., p. 337.

63. Ibid., p. 339.

64. Ibid., p. 339.

65. Ibid., p. 339.

66. Ibid.

67. Reuben Fine, "Psychoanalysis," in Raymond Corsini, *Current Therapies* (Itasca, Illinois: F. E. Peacock, 1973), p. 26.

68. Ibid., p. 28.

69. Ibid.

70. Ibid.

71. Harrison and Carek, *A Guide to Psychotherapy*, pp. 81ff.

72. Ibid., p. 217.

73. Erich Fromm, *The Art of Loving* (New York: Harper & Row, 1956), p. 45.

74. Theodore Lidz, Alice R. Cornelison, Stephen Fleck, and Dorothy Terry, "Marital Schism and Marital Skew," in William S. Sahakian, ed., *Psychopathology Today: Experimentation, Theory and Research* (Itasca, Illinois: F. E. Peacock, 1970), p. 299.

75. Jonathan Kellerman, "Sex-Role Stereotypes and Attitudes Toward Parental Blame for the Psychological Problems of Children" (Los Angeles: University of Southern California, 1973), p. 4.

76. Ibid., p. 2.

Woman Professionals Adopt the Male View

77. A discussion of the views of some of these women can be found in Mary Jane Lupton, with Emily Toth and Janice Deloney. "The First Pollution: Psychoanalysis and the Menarche," *Rough Times*, Vol. 4 (January–February 1974), pp. 9–11.

78. Editor Jean Baker Miller has compiled existing pro-women statements from within the psychoanalytic literature in *Psychoanalysis and Women* (Middlesex, England: Penguin Books, 1973).

79. Judith Bardwick, *Psychology of Women: A Study of Bio-Cultural Conflicts* (New York: Harper & Row, 1971).

80. Nancy Henley, "Tracking the Elusive Female Psyche: Recent Books on Psychology and Women," *Rough Times*, Vol. 3 (February–March 1973), pp. 16–17.

81. Corinne Hutt, *Males and Females* (Middlesex, England: Penguin Books, 1972).
82. Ibid., p. 18.
83. Ibid., p. 90.
84. Ibid., p. 119.
85. Ibid., p. 136.
86. Ibid., p. 138.
87. Ibid., p. 139.

Is It Changing?

88. Charlotte Wolff, *Love Between Women* (New York: Harper & Row, 1971), p. 79.
89. Ibid., p. 211.
90. Albert Ellis, "The Treatment of Love and Sex Problems in Women," in Violet Franks and Vasanti Burtle, eds., *Women in Therapy: New Psychotherapies for Changing Society* (New York: Brunner/Mazel, 1974).
91. Barbara Kirsch, "Consciousness-Raising Groups as Therapy for Women," in Violet Franks and Vasanti Burtle, eds., *Women in Therapy: New Psychotherapies for Changing Society* (New York: Brunner/Mazel, 1974).
92. Ibid., p. 351.
93. Elaine C. Pierson and William V. D'Antonio, *Female and Male: Dimensions of Human Sexuality* (Philadelphia: J. B. Lippincott, 1974), p. 13.

VII. ALTERNATIVES TO PSYCHODYNAMIC INSIGHT THERAPY

The Alternative Depends on the Function Served by Therapy

1. Harold E. McNelly and Norma Taylor Obele, *Psychotherapy: The Private and Very Personal Viewpoints of Doctor and Patient* (Chicago: Nelson-Hall, 1973).

Operant Behavior Principles

2. B. F. Skinner, *The Behavior of Organisms* (New York: Appleton-Century-Crofts, 1938).

3. B. F. Skinner, *Contingencies of Reinforcement, A Theoretical Analysis* (New York: Appleton-Century-Crofts, 1969).

4. See, for example, Roland G. Tharp and Ralph J. Wetzel, *Behavior Modification in the Natural Environment* (New York: Academic Press, 1969).

Operant Methods Applied in Individual Situations

5. The authors were, in addition to John C. Dollard, Leonard Doob, Neal Miller, O. Hobart Mowrer, and Robert Sears.

Controversy

6. Goldenberg, *Contemporary Clinical Psychology*, p. 284.

7. Rogers, "In Retrospect: Forty-Six Years," p. 119.

8. B. F. Skinner, "Behavior Modification," Letter to the editor, *Science*, Vol. 145 (September 6, 1974).

The Social Environment

9. Dorothy Tennov, "Mode of Control and Reinforcement Density as a Function of the Sex of the Behaver," *Women Speaking*, Vol. 3, No. 6 (July 1974), p. 7.

10. J. M. Joffe, R. A. Rawson, and J. A. Mulick, "Control of Their Environment Reduces Emotionality in Rats," *Science*, Vol. 180 (1973).

11. See Richard Winett, "Behavior Modification and Social Change," *Professional Psychology*, Vol. 5, No. 3 (August 1974).

12. For an excellent discussion of how analysis of consequences of behavior and operant technology would help solve many pressing societal problems, see Vitali Rozynko, Kenneth Swift, Josephine Swift, and Larney J. Boggs, "Controlled Environments for Social Change," in Harvey Wheeler, ed., *Beyond the Punitive Society* (San Francisco: W. H. Freeman, 1973). Also see B. F. Skinner, *Beyond Freedom and Dignity* (New York: Bantam Books, 1972).

Bibliography

Albee, George W. "The Uncertain Future of Clinical Psychology."
    American Psychologist, Vol. 25, No. 12 (1970), pp. 1071–
    1080.
——. "Who Gains?" Letter to the Editor. *APA Monitor*, Vol. 4
    (January 1973), p. 12.
Allport, Gordon W. *Letters from Jenny*. New York: Harcourt,
    Brace, Jovanovich, 1965.
American Academy of Psychotherapists. [Elaine Kepner and Lois
    Brien]. *Brochure on the 1973 Training Institute and Annual
    Conference*. Orlando, Florida, 1973.
American Psychological Association. *Ethical Standards of Psycholo-
    gists*. Washington, D.C.: American Psychological Association,
    1953.
Anonymous, M.D. *The Healers: Confessions of a Successful Doc-
    tor*. New York: G. P. Putnam's Sons, 1967.
*APA Guidelines for Psychiatric Services Covered Under Health In-
    surance Plans*. 2nd ed. American Psychiatric Association, May,
    1973.
Arnhoff, Franklyn N. Review of *Casebook in Psychopathology* by
    Frank J. Kobler. *Contemporary Psychology*, Vol. 11 (1966),
    pp. 230–231.

Asher, Jules. "Opposition Wins Latest Round in Fight Over New York Licensing Bill." *APA Monitor,* Vol. 4 (June 1973), pp. 1 and 12.

Astin, Alexander W. "The Functional Autonomy of Psychotherapy." In *The Investigation of Psychotherapy: Commentaries and Readings.* Edited by Arnold P. Goldstein and Sanford J. Dean. New York: John Wiley, 1966.

Ayllon, Teodoro, and Nathan H. Azrin. "The Measurement and Reinforcement of Behavior of Psychotics." *Journal of the Experimental Analysis of Behavior,* Vol. 8 (1965), pp. 357–383.

Bach, George R., and Yett M. Bernard. "Deserts and Oases." *Contemporary Psychology,* Vol. 12 (1967), pp. 200–221.

Bakan, David. *On Method: Toward a Reconstruction of Psychological Investigation.* San Francisco: Jossey-Bass, 1967.

Bandura, Albert. "Behavior Therapy and the Models of Man." Presidential Address, 82nd Annual Convention of the American Psychological Association. New Orleans, August 31, 1974.

—— —. *Principles of Behavior Modification.* New York: Holt, Rinehart and Winston, 1969.

——. "Psychotherapy as a Learning Process." *Psychological Bulletin,* No. 58 (1961), pp. 143–147.

Bardwick, Judith. *Psychology of Women: A Study of Bio-Cultural Conflicts.* New York: Harper & Row, 1971.

Barron, Frank, and Timothy F. Leary. "Changes in Psychoneurotic Patients With and Without Psychotherapy." *Journal of Consulting Psychology,* Vol. 19 (1955), pp. 239–245.

Bart, Pauline. "Social Structure and Vocabularies of Discomfort: What Happened to Female Hysteria?" *Journal of Health and Social Behavior,* Vol. 9 (September 1968), pp. 188–193.

Bateson, Gregory, Don D. Jackson, Jay Haley, and J. H. Weakland. "Toward a Theory of Schizophrenia." *Behavioral Science,* Vol. 1 (1956), pp. 251–264.

Bayne, Rowan. "Psychology and Encounter Groups." *Bulletin of the British Psychological Society,* Vol. 25 (1972), pp. 285–289.

de Beauvoir, Simone. *The Second Sex.* Translated and edited by H. M. Parshley. New York: Alfred A. Knopf, 1952; Bantam Books, 1961.

Bednar, Richard L., and G. Frank Lawlis. "Empirical Research in Group Psychotherapy." In *Handbook of Psychotherapy and Behavior Change: An Empirical Analysis.* Edited by Allen E. Bergin and Sol L. Garfield. New York: John Wiley, 1971.

———, and Jeffrey G. Shapiro. "Professional Research Commitment: A Symptom or a Syndrome." *Journal of Consulting and Clinical Psychology*, Vol. 34 (1970), pp. 323–326.

Beers, Clifford W. *A Mind That Found Itself*. New York: Longmans Green, 1908.

Bergin, Allen E. "The Evaluation of Therapeutic Outcomes." In *Handbook of Psychotherapy and Behavior Change: An Empirical Analysis*. Edited by Allen E. Bergin and Sol L. Garfield. New York: John Wiley, 1971.

——— and Sol L. Garfield. "Personality and Performance Correlates of Empathetic Understanding in Psychotherapy." *American Psychologist*, Vol. 18 (1963).

———, and S. Solomon. "Personality and Performance Correlates of Empathic Understanding in Psychotherapy." Paper presented at the Annual Convention of the American Psychological Association. Philadelphia, 1963.

———, and Hans S. Strupp. *Changing Frontiers in the Science of Psychotherapy*. Chicago: Aldine, 1972.

Berne, Eric. *Games People Play*. New York: Grove Press, 1964.

Blau, Theodore H. "The Professional in the Community Views the Nonprofessional Helper: Psychology." *Professional Psychology* (Fall 1969), pp. 25–31.

Bond, D. D. "Teaching Ethical Concepts to Medical Students and Psychiatric Residents." *American Journal of Psychiatry*, Vol. 126 (1969).

Boneau, C. Alan. "Private Practice Pays Handsomely." *APA Monitor*, Vol. 5 (May 1974), p. 3.

———. "Psychologists Sized-Up at Last." *APA Monitor*, Vol. 5, No. 2 (February 1974), p. 14.

Boring, Frank H. "Ethical Perspectives on Growth Groups." *APA Monitor* (May 1972), pp. 3, 11.

Braucht, G. N. "The Deterioration Effect: A Reply to Bergin." *Journal of Abnormal Psychology*, Vol. 75 (1970), pp. 293–299.

Brodsky, Stanley L. "Shared Results and Open Files With the Client." *Professional Psychologist*, Vol. 4 (1972), pp. 362–364.

Brockbank, R. "On the Analyst's Silence in Psychoanalysis: A Synthesis of Intrapsychic Content and Interpersonal Manifestations." *International Journal of Psycho-Analysis*, Vol. 51 (1970), pp. 457–464.

Bromberg, Walter. *The Mind of Man: A History of Psychotherapy and Psychoanalysis*. New York: Harper & Row, 1959.

Broverman, Inge K., Donald M. Broverman, Frank E. Clarkson, Paul S. Rosenkrantz, and Susan R. Vogel. "Sex-Role Stereotypes and Clinical Judgments of Mental Health." *Journal of Consulting and Clinical Psychology*, Vol. 34, No. 1 (1970), pp. 1–7.

Browne, William A. "A Psychiatric Study of the Life and Work of Dorothea Dix." *American Journal of Psychiatry*, Vol. 126 (1969), pp. 335–341.

Budzilek, Nora. "Women and Psychotherapy." Unpublished independent research project, University of Bridgeport, Conn., 1973.

Bugental, James F. T. "The Person Who Is the Psychotherapist." In *Creative Developments in Psychotherapy*: Vol. 1. Edited by Alvin R. Mahrer and Leonard Pearson. Cleveland: Press of Case Western Reserve University, 1971.

Burnell, George M. "Financing Mental Health Care." *Archives of General Psychiatry*, Vol. 25 (July 1971), pp. 49–55.

Carnegie, Dale. *How to Win Friends and Influence People*. New York: Simon & Schuster, 1936.

Carpenter, William T., Jr., John S. Strauss, and John J. Bartko. "Flexible System for the Diagnosis of Schizophrenia: Report From the WHO International Pilot Study of Schizophrenia." *Science*, Vol. 182 (December 1973), pp. 1275–1278.

Cashdan, Sheldon. *Interactional Psychotherapy, Stages and Strategies in Behavioral Change*. New York: Grune & Stratton, 1973.

Cates, Judith N. "Sex and Salary." *American Psychologist*, Vol. 28, No. 10 (October 1973), p. 929.

Cautela, J. R. "Treatment of Compulsive Behavior by Covert Sensitization." *Psychological Record*, Vol. 16 (1966), pp. 33–41.

Chesler, Phyllis. *Women and Madness*. Garden City, New York: Doubleday, 1972.

Chessick, Richard D. *How Psychotherapy Heals*. New York: Science House, 1969.

Cochrane, Raymond, and John Duffy. "Psychology and Scientific Method." *Bulletin of the British Psychological Society*, No. 27 (1974), pp. 117–121.

Colby, Kenneth Mark. "Researchers Are Weeded Out." *International Journal of Psychiatry*, Vol. 7 (March 1969), pp. 116–117.

Coons, W. H. "Interaction and Insight in Group Therapy." *Canadian Journal of Psychology*, Vol. 11 (1957), pp. 1–8.

Corsini, Raymond. *Current Psychotherapies*. Itasca, Illinois: F. E. Peacock, 1973.

Cott, Alan. *Ortho-Molecular Treatment: A Biochemical Approach to the Treatment of Schizophrenia.* New York: American Schizophrenia Association, 1970.

Crane, George E. "Clinical Psychopharmacology in Its 20th Year." *Science,* Vol. 181 (July 1973), pp. 124–128.

Curran, William J., Eugene M. Laska, Honora Kaplan, and Rheta Bank. "Protection of Privacy and Confidentiality." *Science,* Vol. 182 (November 1973), pp. 797–802.

Dewey, R., and W. J. Humber. *An Introduction to Social Psychology.* New York: Macmillan, 1966.

Didato, Salvatore V. "Therapy Failure: Pride and/or Prejudice of the Therapist?" *Mental Hygiene,* Vol. 55 (1971), pp. 219–220.

Dollard, John C., Leonard Doob, Neal Miller, O. Hobart Mowrer, and Robert Sears. *Frustration and Aggression.* New Haven: Yale University Press, 1939.

Dolliver, Robert H. "Concerning the Potential Parallels Between Psychotherapy and Brainwashing." *Psychotherapy: Theory, Research and Practice,* Vol. 8 (1971), pp. 289–318.

Donofrio, Anthony F. "Child Psychotherapy—Help or Hindrance?" *Mental Hygiene,* Vol. 4 (1970), pp. 510–515.

Draguns, Juris C., and Leslie Phillips. *Psychiatric Classification and Diagnosis: An Overview and Critique.* Morristown, New Jersey: General Learning Press, 1971.

Ellis, Albert. "The Treatment of Love and Sex Problems in Women." In *Women in Therapy: New Psychotherapies for Changing Society.* Edited by Violet Franks and Vasanti Burtle. New York: Brunner/Mazel, 1974.

Evans, Richard I. *B. F. Skinner: The Man and His Ideas.* New York: E. P. Dutton, 1968.

Eysenck, Hans J. "The effects of Psychotherapy: An Evaluation." *Journal of Consulting Psychology,* Vol. 16 (1952), pp. 319–324.

———. "Learning Theory and Behavior Therapy." *Journal of Mental Science,* Vol. 105 (1959), pp. 61–75.

Fancher, Raymond E., and Robert F. Strahan. "Galvanic Skin Response and the Secondary Revision of Dreams: A Partial Disconfirmation of Freud's Dream Theory." *Journal of Abnormal Psychology,* Vol. 77 (1971), pp. 308–312.

Farina, A., D. Gliha, L. A. Boudreau, J. G. Allen, and M. Sherman. "Mental Illness and the Impact of Believing Others Know About It." *Journal of Abnormal Psychology,* Vol. 77 (1971), p. 1–5.

——, C. H. Holland, and K. Ring. "The Role of Stigma and Set in Interpersonal Interaction." *Journal of Abnormal Psychology*, Vol. 71 (1966), pp. 421–428.

Feifel, Herman, and Janet Eells. "Patients and Therapists Assess the Same Psychotherapy." *Journal of Consulting Psychology*, Vol. 27 (1963), pp. 310–318.

Feldman, M. P., and M. J. MacCulloch. "The Application of Anticipatory Avoidance Learning to the Treatment of Homosexuality: 1. Theory, Technique and Preliminary Results." *Behavior Research and Therapy*, Vol. 2 (1965), pp. 165–183.

Ferson, Jean. "The Feminist Therapy Collective of Philadelphia." Paper presented at the 81st Annual Convention of the American Psychological Association. Montreal, Canada, August 29, 1973.

Fine, Reuben. "Psychoanalysis." In *Current Therapies*. Edited by Raymond Corsini. Itasca, Illinois: F. E. Peacock, 1973.

Fischer, E. H., and J. L. Turner. "Factors in Attitudes Toward Seeking Professional Help." *Proceedings of the 77th Annual Convention of The American Psychological Association*, Vol. 4 (1969).

Foulkes, D. and A. Rechtschaffer. "Presleep Determinants of Dream Content: Effects of Two Films." *Perceptual and Motor Skills*, Vol. 19 (1964), pp. 983–1005.

Frank, George. "More on Biondo." Letter to the Editor. *APA Monitor*, Vol. 4 (December 1973), p. 15.

Frank, Jerome D. "Common Features Account for Effectiveness." In *Changing Frontiers in the Science of Psychotherapy*. Edited by Allen E. Bergin and Hans S. Strupp. Chicago: Aldine, 1972.

——. *Persuasion and Healing*. Baltimore: The Johns Hopkins University Press, 1961.

Franks, Violet, and Vasanti Burtle, eds. *Women in Therapy: New Psychotherapies for a Changing Society*. New York: Brunner/Mazel, 1974.

Freud, Anna. *The Ego and the Mechanisms of Defense*. New York: International Universities, 1948.

Freud, Sigmund. *A General Introduction to Psychoanalysis*. New York: Simon & Schuster, 1969.

Fromm, Erich. *The Art of Loving*. New York: Harper & Row, 1956.

Fuller, John L., and William R. Thompson. *Behavior Genetics*. New York: John Wiley, 1960.

Glenn, Michael, and Richard Kunnes. *Repression or Revolution? Therapy in the United States Today*. New York: Harper & Row, 1973.

Goldenberg, Herbert. *Contemporary Clinical Psychology*. Monterey, California: Brooks/Cole, 1973.

Goldschmid, M. L., D. D. Stein, H. Weissman, and J. Sorrells. "A Survey of the Training and Practices of Clinical Psychologists." *The Clinical Psychologist Newsletter*, No. 22 (1969), pp. 89–107.

Goldstein, Arnold P. "Domains and Dilemmas." *International Journal of Psychiatry*, Vol. 7, No. 3 (March 1969), pp. 128–134.

Gordon, Jan B. "The Meta-Journey of R. D. Laing." *Salmagundi*, Vol. 16 (Spring 1971), pp. 38–63.

Gorer, Geoffrey. "Psychoanalysis in the World." In *Psychoanalysis Observed*. Edited by Charles Rycroft. New York: Coward, McCann & Geoghegan, 1967.

Gove, Walter R., and Jeannette F. Tudor. "Adult Sex Roles and Mental Illness." *American Journal of Sociology*, Vol. 78 (January 1973), pp. 812–835.

Green, Hannah. *I Never Promised You A Rose Garden*. New York: Holt, Rinehart and Winston, 1964.

Grinker, Roy R. "Psychiatry Rides Madly in All Directions." *Archives of General Psychology*, Vol. 10 (1964), pp. 228–237.

Grove, Carl and John Radford. "Dear Colleague: A Replication." *Bulletin of the British Psychological Society*, No. 26 (1973), pp. 129–130.

Gruver, Gene Gary. "College Students as Therapeutic Agents." *Psychological Bulletin*, No. 76 (1971), pp. 111–127.

Hagebak, Robert W., and George V. C. Parker. "Therapist Directiveness, Client Dominance, and Therapy Resistance." *Journal of Consulting and Clinical Psychology*, Vol. 33 (1969), pp. 536–540.

Hale, Nathan G., Jr., *Freud and the Americans: The Beginnings of Psychoanalysis in the United States, 1876–1917*. New York: Oxford University Press, 1971.

Haley, Jay. *Strategies of Psychotherapy*. New York: Grune & Stratton, 1972.

Halleck, Seymour L. *The Politics of Therapy*. New York: Science House, 1971.

Hamilton, Max. "Psychology in Society: Ends or End?" *Bulletin of the British Psychological Society*, No. 26 (1973), pp. 185–189.

Harper, R. A. *Psychoanalysis and Psychotherapy: 36 Systems.* Englewood Cliffs, New Jersey: Prentice-Hall, 1959.

Harris, Ann Sutherland. "The Second Sex in Academe." *American Association of University Professors Bulletin.* (Fall 1970), pp. 283–295.

Harris, Thomas A. *I'm OK, You're OK.* New York: Harper & Row, 1969.

Harrison, Saul I., and Donald J. Carek. *A Guide to Psychotherapy.* Boston: Little, Brown, 1966.

Hawkins, David R. *The Development of an Integrated Community System For the Effective Treatment of Schizophrenia.* New York: American Schizophrenia Association, 1972.

Heilbrun, Alfred B., Jr., *Aversive Maternal Control: A Theory of Schizophrenic Development.* New York: Wiley-Interscience, 1973.

Henley, Nancy. "Tracking the Elusive Female Psyche: Recent Books on Psychology and Women." *Rough Times,* Vol. 3 (February–March 1973), pp. 16–17.

Henry, William E., John H. Sims, and S. Lee Spray. *The Fifth Profession.* San Francisco: Jossey-Bass, 1971.

Hill, Lewis B. *Psychotherapeutic Intervention in Schizophrenia.* Chicago: University of Chicago Press, 1955.

Hoffman, Dorothy T. [Tennov], Brian Scally, Andrew Deering, and Evelyn Kott. "Women in Psychology." Paper presented at the American Psychological Convention. Miami Beach, Florida, September 7, 1970.

Holden, Constance. "Psychology; Clinicians Seek Professional Autonomy." *Science,* Vol. 181, No. 2 (September 1973), pp. 1147–1150.

Holland, Viki. "The Tyranny of Grimping." *Human Behavior* (October 1973), pp. 32–33.

Hollingshead, A. B., and F. C. Redlich. *Social Class and Mental Illness: A Community Study.* New York: John Wiley, 1958.

Hollister, L. E. "Choice of Antipsychotic Drugs." *American Journal of Psychiatry,* Vol. 127 (1970), pp. 186–190.

Holt, Edwin. *The Freudian Wish and Its Place in Ethics.* New York: B. W. Huebsch, 1915.
As cited in Nathan G. Hale, Jr., *Freud and the Americans: The Beginnings of Psychoanalysis in the United States, 1876–1917.* New York: Oxford University Press, 1971, p. 429.

Holt, Robert R. "Forcible Indoctrination and Personality Change." In *Personality Change.* Edited by P. Worchel and D. Byrne. New York: John Wiley, 1964.

———. *Methods of Research in Clinical Psychology.* A University Programs Modular Study. Morristown, New Jersey: General Learning Press, 1973.

Horner, Matina S. "Toward an Understanding of Achievement—Related Conflicts in Women." *Journal of Social Issues,* Vol. 8 (1972), pp. 157–175.

Houck, John H. "The Intractable Female Patient." *American Journal of Psychiatry,* Vol. 129 (1972), pp. 27–31.

Howard, June. "Encounter Groups: Emotional Striptease for Women?" *Vogue* (January 1970), pp. 10–11.

Howard, Kenneth I., and David E. Orlinsky. "Psychotherapeutic Processes." *Annual Review of Psychology,* Vol. 23 (1972), pp. 615–668.

Humphreys, Lloyd. "Should Psychotherapy Be Included in Health Insurance Programs? No!" *APA Monitor,* Vol. 4 (September–October 1973), p. 8.

Hunt, Morton M., and Rena Corman, with Louis R. Ormont. *The Talking Cure.* New York: Harper & Row, 1964.

Hurvitz, Nathan. "Peer Self Help Psychotherapy Groups and the Implications for Psychotherapy." *Psychotherapy: Theory, Research and Practice,* Vol. 7 (Spring 1970), pp. 41–48.

———. "Psychotherapy as a Means of Social Control." *Journal of Consulting and Clinical Psychology,* Vol. 40 (1973), pp. 232–239.

Hutt, Corinne. *Males and Females.* Middlesex, England: Penguin Books, 1972.

Jackson, Don D. "Psychotherapy for Schizophrenia." *Scientific American,* Vol. 189 (January 1953), pp. 55–58.

Joffe, J. M., R. A. Rawson, and J. A. Mulick. "Control of Their Environment Reduces Emotionality in Rats." *Science,* Vol. 180 (1973), pp. 1383–1384.

Johnson, Michael C. "The Age of Psychotherapy and 'Mental Health' Is Over." *The Village Voice,* January 18, 1973, p. 35.

Kadushin, Charles. *Why People Go to Psychiatrists.* New York: Aldine, 1969.

Kahne, Merton J. "Suicide Among Patients in Mental Hospitals: A Study of the Psychiatrists Who Conducted Their Therapy." *Psychiatry,* Vol. 31 (1968), pp. 32–43.

Kallman, F. J. *Heredity in Mental Health and Disorder.* New York: W. W. Norton, 1953.

Kaplan, Donald M. "The Last Gasps of Pop Psychology." *The Village Voice,* August 31, 1972, pp. 25–28.

Kaplan, Donald M. "Comments on the Screening Function of a 'Technical Effect,' With Reference to Depression and Jealousy." *International Journal of Psycho-Analysis*, Vol. 51 (1970), pp. 489–502.

Karon, Bertram P., and Gary R. VandenBos. "The Consequences of Psychotherapy for Schizophrenic Patients." Mimeographed. Michigan State Psychotherapy Research Project, Bulletin No. 16.

Kellerman, Jonathan. "Sex-Role Stereotypes and Attitudes Toward Parental Blame for the Psychological Problems of Children." Mimeographed. Los Angeles: The University of Southern California, 1973.

Kirsch, Barbara. "Consciousness-Raising Groups as Therapy for Women." *Women in Therapy: New Psychotherapies for Changing Society*. Edited by Violet Franks and Vasanti Burtle. New York: Brunner/Mazel, 1974.

Kleinmuntz, Benjamin. "Greetings, Tributes, Speculations and Some Data." *Contemporary Psychology*, Vol. 12, No. 12 (1967), pp. 596–598.

Knoff, W. F. "A History of the Concept of Neurosis With a Memoir of William Cullen." *American Journal of Psychiatry*, Vol. 127 (1970), pp. 80–84.

Knudsen, Dean D. "The Declining Status of Women: Popular Myths and the Failure of Functionalist Thought." *Social Forces*, Vol. 48, No. 2 (1969), pp. 183–193.

Kraines, S. H. "Neurological Theory of Depression." In *Psychopathology Today*. Edited by William S. Sahakian. Itasca, Illinois: F. E. Peacock, 1970.

Kramer, Ernest. *A Beginning Manual for Psychotherapists*. New York: Grune & Stratton, 1970.

Krasner, Leonard. "The Therapist As a Social Reinforcer: Man or Machine." Paper presented at the Annual Meetings of the American Psychological Association. Philadelphia, 1963.

——, and Leonard P. Ullman. *Behavior Influence and Personality*. New York: Holt, Rinehart and Winston, 1973.

Krause, Merton S. "Construct Validity for the Evaluation of Therapy Outcomes." *Journal of Abnormal Psychology*, Vol. 74 (1969), pp. 524–530.

Kubie, Lawrence S. "The Destructive Potential of Humor in Psychotherapy." *American Journal of Psychiatry*, Vol. 127, No. 7 (January 1971), pp. 861–866.

Kunnes, Rick. "How to be a Radical Therapist." *The Radical Therapist*, Vol. 2, No. 1 (April–May 1971), pp. 3–4.

Kysar, John E. "The Two Camps in Child Psychiatry: A Report from a Psychiatrist-Father of an Autistic and Retarded Child." *American Journal of Psychiatry*, Vol. 125 (July 1968), pp. 103–109.

Laidlow, James. "Is 'Real Self' a Useful Topic for First-Year Psychology Courses?" *Bulletin of the British Psychological Society*, No. 27 (1974), pp. 129–131.

Landis, C. "A Statistical Evaluation of Psychotherapeutic Methods." In *Concepts and Problems of Psychotherapy*. Edited by L. E. Hinsie. New York: Columbia University Press, 1937.

Lazo, John A., ed. *Biographical Directory of the American Psychological Association*. Washington, D.C.: American Psychological Association, 1973.

Leifer, Ronald. *In the Name of Mental Health*. New York: Science House, 1969.

Lemkau, Paul V. and Guido M. Crocett. "An Urban Population's Opinion and Knowledge About Mental Illness." *American Journal of Psychiatry*, Vol. 118 (1962), pp. 692–700.

Leo, John. "Psychoanalysis Reaches a Crossroad." *New York Times*, August 4, 1968.

Lewis, Howard, and Martha Lewis. *The Medical Offenders*. New York: Simon & Schuster, 1970.

Lidz, Theodore, Alice R. Cornelison, Stephen Fleck, and Dorothy Terry. "Marital Schism and Marital Skew." In *Psychopathology Today: Experimentation, Theory and Research*. Edited by William S. Sahakian. Itasca, Illinois: F. E. Peacock, 1970.

Lieberman, Morton A., Irvin D. Yalom, and Matthew B. Miles. *Encounter Groups: First Facts*. New York: Basic Books, 1973.

Liem, Joan Huser. "Effects of Verbal Communications of Parents and Children: A Comparison of Normal and Schizophrenic Families." *Journal of Consulting and Clinical Psychology*, Vol. 42, No. 3 (1974), pp. 438–450.

Lifton, Robert. *Thought Reform and the Psychology of Totalism*. New York: W. W. Norton, 1961.

Light, Donald W., Jr. "Psychiatry and Suicide: The Management of a Mistake." *American Journal of Sociology*, Vol. 77 (1972), pp. 821–837.

Little, Kenneth B. "Problems in the Validation of Projective Techniques." *Journal of Projective Techniques*, Vol. 23 (1959), pp. 287–290.

———. "Symposium on Current Aspects of the Problem of Validity: Problems in the Validation of Projective Techniques." *Journal of Projective Techniques*, Vol. 23 (1959), pp. 287–290.

London, Perry. *Behavior Control.* New York: Harper & Row, 1969.
——. *The Modes and Morals of Psychotherapy.* New York: Holt, Rinehart and Winston, 1964.

Lowe, C. M. *Value Orientations in Counseling and Psychotherapy.* San Francisco: Chandler, 1970.

Luborsky, Lester, Arthur Auerbach, Michael Chandler, Jacob Cohen, and Henry M. Bachrach. "Factors Influencing the Outcome of Psychotherapy: A Review of Quantitative Research." *Psychological Bulletin,* No. 75 (1971), pp. 145–182.

Lupton, Mary Jane, with Emily Toth and Janice Deloney. "The First Pollution: Psychoanalysis and the Menarche." *Rough Times,* Vol. 4 (January–February 1974), pp. 9–11.

Mahrer, Alvin R., and Leonard Pearson. *Creative Developments in Psychotherapy.* Cleveland: Press of Case Western Reserve University, 1971.

Marks, Isaac. "Conference on 'The Psychiatric Nurse As Therapist: Developments and Problems.'" *Bulletin of the British Psychological Society,* No. 26 (1973), pp. 299–301.

Marks, Isaac M. "Empiricism Is Accepted." In *Changing Frontiers in the Science of Psychotherapy.* Edited by Allen E. Bergin and Hans S. Strupp. New York: Aldine, 1972.

Martin, David G. *Introduction to Psychotherapy.* Monterey, California: Brooks/Cole, 1971.

Masters, William H., and Virginia E. Johnson. "The Sexual Response Cycle of the Human Female. III. The Clitoris: Anatomic and Clinical Considerations." *Western Journal of Surgery, Obstetrics, and Gynecology,* Vol. 70 (1962), pp. 248–257.

Matarazzo, Joseph D. "The Practice of Psychotherapy Is Art and Not Science." In *Creative Developments in Psychotherapy,* Vol. I. Edited by Alvin R. Mahrer and Leonard Pearson. Cleveland: Press of Case Western Reserve University, 1971.
——. "Psychotherapeutic Processes." In *Annual Review of Psychology,* Vol. 16. Edited by P. R. Farnsworth and Q. McNemar. Palo Alto: Annual Reviews, 1965, pp. 181–224.
——. "Some Psychotherapists Make Patients Worse!" *International Journal of Psychiatry,* Vol. 3, No. 3 (1967), pp. 156–157.

May, Philip R. A. *Treatment of Schizophrenia.* New York: Science House, 1968.

May, Rollo. "Contributions of Existential Philosophy." In *Creative Developments in Psychotherapy.* Edited by Alvin R. Mahrer and Leonard Pearson. Cleveland: Press of Case Western Reserve University, 1971.

McChonochie, Bill. "Con Artists." Letter to the Editor. *APA Monitor* (December 1972), p. 80.

McGuire, William, ed., and Ralph Manheim and R. F. C. Hull, trans. *The Freud/Jung Letters: The Correspondence Between Sigmund Freud and C. J. Jung*. Princeton: Princeton University Press, 1974.

McNeely, Harold E., and Norma Taylor Obele. *Psychotherapy: The Private and Very Personal Viewpoints of Doctor and Patient*. Chicago: Nelson-Hall, 1973.

Mednick, Sarnoff A. "Breakdown in Individuals at High Risk for Schizophrenia: Possible Predispositional Perinatal Factors." *Mental Hygiene*, Vol. 54 (1970), pp. 50–63.

Meltzoff, Julian, and Melvin Kornreich. *Research in Psychotherapy*. New York: Aldine, 1970.

Menninger, Karl. *Theory of Psychoanalytic Technique*. New York: Basic Books, 1958.

Michelfelder, William. *It's Cheaper to Die*. New York: George Braziller, 1960.

Miller, Jean Baker, ed. *Psychoanalysis and Women*. Middlesex, England: Penguin Books, 1973.

Millett, Kate. *Sexual Politics*. Garden City, New York: Doubleday, 1970.

Millon, Theodore. *Modern Psychopathology*. Philadelphia: W. B. Saunders, 1969.

Mintz, Jim. "What is 'Success' in Psychotherapy?" *Journal of Abnormal Psychology*, Vol. 80 (1972), pp. 11–19.

Mintz, Norbett L. "Patient Fees and Psychotherapeutic Transactions." *Journal of Consulting and Clinical Psychology*, Vol. 36 (February 1971), pp. 1–8.

Mirsky, A. F. "Neuropsychological Bases of Schizophrenia." *Annual Review of Psychology*, Vol. 20 (1969), pp. 321–348.

"My Rat Feels Red." *Red Rat, the Journal of Abnormal Psychologists*, Vol. 3 (Summer 1971), pp. 18–20.

"Nader Report: Community Mental Health Centers." *Behavior Today*, Vol. 3, No. 30 (July 31, 1972), pp. 3–5.

New Haven Center for Human Relations. Brochure for Fall, 1973. New Haven: Center for Human Relations, 1973.

"A New Old Treatment." *Newsweek*, July 9, 1973, p. 57.

Noll, John O. "Needed—A Bill of Rights for Clients." *Professional Psychology*, Vol. 5, No. 1 (1974), pp. 3–12.

Olczak, P. V., E. H. Donnerstein, J. Thomas, and I. Kahn. "Group Hysteria and the MMPI." *Psychological Reports*, Vol. 28 (1971), pp. 413–414.

Orr, Douglas. "Transference and Countertransference: A Historical Survey." *Journal of the American Psychoanalytic Association,* Vol. 2 (1954), pp. 621–670.

Osmond, Humphrey. "The Medical Model in Psychiatry." *Hospital & Community Psychiatry,* Vol. 21 (September 1970), pp. 275–281.

Patterson, C. H. *Theories of Counseling and Psychotherapy.* New York: Harper & Row, 1966.

Paul, G. L. "Outcome of Systematic Desensitization. II. Controlled Investigations of Individual Treatment, Technique Variations, and Current Status." In *Behavior Therapy: Appraisal and Status.* Edited by Cyril M. Franks. New York: McGraw-Hill, 1969.

———. "Strategy of Outcome Research in Psychotherapy." *Journal of Consulting Psychology,* Vol. 31 (1967), pp. 109–118.

Pearce, K. I. "A Comparison of Care Given by Family Practitioners and Psychiatrists in a Teaching Hospital Unit." *American Journal of Psychiatry,* Vol. 127 (1970), pp. 835–840.

Peterson, Severin. *A Catalog of the Ways People Grow.* New York: Ballantine Books, 1971.

Pierson, Elaine C., and William V. D'Antonio. *Female and Male: Dimensions of Human Sexuality.* Philadelphia: J. B. Lippincott, 1974.

Pivnicki, D. "The Beginnings of Psychotherapy." *Journal of the History of Behavioral Science,* Vol. 5 (1969), pp. 238–247.

Professional Committee of the Schizophrenia Foundation of New Jersey. *The Schizophrenias: Yours and Mine.* New York: Pyramid Books, 1970.

"Psychiatry Gives Behaviorism a Clean Bill of Health." *APA Monitor,* Vol. 4 (December 1973), p. 10.

Reres, M. E. "A Survey of the Nurse's Role in Psychiatric Outpatient Clinics in America." *Community Mental Health Journal,* Vol. 5 (1969), pp. 382–385.

Richter, Anne. *Lay Analyst.* New York: Richard W. Baron, 1971.

Rickles, Nathan K. "The Angry Woman Syndrome." *Archives of General Psychiatry,* Vol. 24 (January 1971), pp. 91–94.

Riegelman, Harold. Letter to the Editor. *New York Times,* April 13, 1973.

Roback, Howard B., Alfred Webersinn, and Harry Guion. "Effects of the Psychotherapeutic Experience on Emerging Psychotherapists." *Mental Hygiene,* Vol. 55 (April 1971), pp. 228–229.

Rogers, Carl R. *Counseling and Psychotherapy*. Cambridge, Massachusetts: Houghton Mifflin, 1942.

——. "In Retrospect: Forty-Six Years." *American Psychologist*, Vol. 29 (February 1974), pp. 115–123.

Rogow, Arnold A. *The Psychiatrists*. New York: Dell, 1970.

Roth, Nathan. "The Strange Society of the Physician—Doctors Seek Each Other Out." *American Journal of Psychotherapy*, Vol. 24 (1970), pp. 494–498.

Rotov, Michael. "Death by Suicide in the Hospital: An Analysis of 20 Therapeutic Failures." *American Journal of Psychotherapy*, Vol. 25 (April 1970), pp. 216–227.

Rotter, Julian. "Psychotherapy." *Annual Review of Psychology*, Vol. 11 (1960), pp. 381–414.

Rozynko, Vitali, Kenneth Swift, Josephine Swift, and Larney J. Boggs. "Controlled Environments for Social Change." In *Beyond the Punitive Society*. Edited by Harvey Wheeler. San Francisco: W. H. Freeman, 1973, pp. 71–100.

Rubin, Jerome. "Master's Level—Con." Letter to the Editor. *APA Monitor* (July 1972), p. 8.

Ruesch, Jurgen. *Therapeutic Community*. New York: W. W. Norton, 1961.

Rush, Florence. "Notes From a Social Worker." *The Radical Therapist*, Vol. 2, No. 2 (September 1971), pp. 13–14.

——. "The Sexual Abuse of Children: A Feminist Point of View." Pittsburgh: KNOW, 1971.

——. "Who's Afraid of Margaret Ribble?" Pittsburgh: KNOW, 1973.

Saenger, Gerhart. "Patterns of Change Among 'Treated' and 'Untreated' Patients Seen in Psychiatric Community Mental Health Clinics." *Journal of Nervous and Mental Diseases*, Vol. 150, No. 1 (1970), pp. 37–50.

Salzman-Webb, Marilyn. "Women as Secretary, Sexpot, Spender, Sow, Civic Actor, Sickie." In *Roles Women Play: Readings Toward Women's Liberation*. Edited by Michele Hoffnung Garskof. Belmont, California: Wadsworth, 1971, pp. 7–24.

Sandler, J., C. Dare, and A. Holden. "Basic Psychoanalytic Concepts: X. Interpretations and other Interventions." *British Journal of Psychiatry*, Vol. 11 (1971), pp. 53–59.

Sandler, Jack, and Robert S. Davidson. *Psychopathology: Learning Theory, Research, and Applications*. New York: Harper & Row, 1973.

Sarbin, Theodore R. "On the Futility of the Proposition That Some

People Be Labeled 'Mentally Ill.'" *Journal of Consulting Psychology*, Vol. 31 (1967), pp. 447–453.

——, and James C. Mancuso. "Failure of a Moral Enterprise: Attitudes of the Public Toward Mental Illness." *Journal of Consulting and Clinical Psychology*, Vol. 35 (1970), pp. 159–173.

Scheff, Thomas J. "Users and Nonusers of a Student Psychiatric Clinic." *Journal of Health and Human Behavior*, Vol. 7 (1966), pp. 114–141.

Schmideberg, Melitta. "A Contribution to the History of the Psycho-Analytic Movement in Britain." *British Journal of Psychiatry*, Vol. 118, No. 542 (January 1971), pp. 61–68.

——. "Principles of Psychotherapy." *Comprehensive Psychiatry*, Vol. 1 (June 1960), pp. 186–193.

——. "Psychotherapy with Failures of Psychoanalysis." *British Journal of Psychiatry*, Vol. 116 (1970), pp. 195–200.

——. "Sociolegal Consequences of Psychiatric Diagnoses in U.S.A. and Britain." *International Journal of Offender Therapy*, Vol. 14, No. 3 (1972), pp. 157–172.

——. "Why Do Wives Put Up With Violence?" *Social Worker*, Vol. 17 (January 1974).

Schofield, William. *Psychotherapy: The Purchase of Friendship.* Englewood Cliffs, New Jersey: Prentice-Hall, 1964.

——. "Psychotherapy: The Unknown Versus the Untold." *Journal of Consulting and Clinical Psychology*, Vol. 36 (February 1971), pp. 9–11.

Schutz, William C. *Joy: Expanding Human Awareness.* New York: Grove Press, 1967.

Shapiro, Arthur K. "The Curative Waters and Warm Poultices of Psychotherapy." *Psychosomatics*, Vol. 7 (February 1966), pp. 21–23.

——. "Placebo Effects in Medicine, Psychotherapy and Psychoanalysis." In *Handbook of Psychotherapy and Behavior Change: Empirical Analysis.* Edited by Allen E. Bergin and Sol L. Garfield. New York: John Wiley, 1971.

Shapiro, Jeffrey G. and T. Voog. "Effect of the Inherently Helpful Person on Student Academic Achievement." *Journal of Counseling Psychology*, Vol. 16 (1969).

Shepard, Martin, and Marjorie Lee. *Games Analysts Play.* New York: Berkley, 1972.

Sheridan, Charles L. *Fundamentals of Experimental Psychology.* New York: Holt, Rinehart and Winston, 1971.

Sherman, William. "Backing Crows for Controls in Mental Health." New York *Daily News*, July 26, 1972.

——. "Probe Teacher on Psychotherapy." *Daily News,* July 20, 1972.

Shulman, Alix. "Organs and Orgasms." In *Women in Sexist Society.* Edited by Vivian Gornick and Barbara K. Moran. New York: Basic Books, 1971.

Skinner, B. F. "Behavior Modification." Letter to the Editor. *Science,* Vol. 145 (September 1974), p. 813.

——. *The Behavior of Organisms.* New York: Appleton-Century-Crofts, 1938.

——. *Beyond Freedom and Dignity.* New York: Bantam Books, 1972.

——. *Contingencies of Reinforcement: A Theoretical Analysis.* New York: Appleton-Century-Crofts, 1969.

Slater, Eliot, and Valerie Cowie. *The Genetics of Mental Disorders.* London: Oxford University Press, 1971.

Snyder, William V. *The Psychotherapy Relationship.* New York: Macmillan, 1961.

Star, Shirley. "The Public's Ideas About Mental Illness." Paper presented to the Annual Meeting of the National Association for Mental Health, Indianapolis, Indiana, November 5, 1955. As cited by Paul V. Lemkau and Guido M. Crockett, "An Urban Population's Opinion and Knowledge About Mental Illness." *American Journal of Psychiatry,* Vol. 118 (1962), pp. 692–700.

Steiner, Claude M. "Radical Psychiatry Manifesto." *The Radical Therapist,* Vol. 2, No. 3 (1971), p. 2.

Stengel, Erwin. *Suicide and Attempted Suicide.* Baltimore: Penguin Books, 1965.

Stieper, Donald R., and Daniel N. Wiener. *Dimensions of Psychotherapy.* Chicago: Aldine, 1965.

Stollak, Gary E. "Undergraduates as Play Therapists: The Effects of Training and Personal Characteristics." Paper presented at the 3rd Annual Meeting of the Society for Psychotherapy Research. Nashville, Tennessee, June 16, 1972.

Stoller, Frederick II. "The Long Weekend." *Psychology Today,* Vol. 1, No. 7 (December 1967), pp. 28–33.

Stone, Alan A. "Suicide Precipitated by Psychotherapy, A Clinical Contribution." *American Journal of Psychotherapy,* Vol. 25 (1971), pp. 18–26.

Storr, Anthony. "The Concept of Cure." In *Psychoanalysis Observed.* Edited by Charles Rycroft. New York: Coward, McCann & Geoghegan, 1967.

Stream, H. S., and A. Blatt. "Long or Short Term Therapy: Some Selected Issues." *Journal of Contemporary Psychology,* Vol. 2 (1969), pp. 115–122.

Strupp, Hans S. "Psychotherapy." *Annual Review of Psychology,* Vol. 13 (1962), pp. 460–471.

——, M. S. Wallach, and M. Wogan. "The Psychotherapy Experience in Retrospect: A Questionnaire Survey of Former Patients and Their Therapists." *Psychological Monographs,* Vol. 78 (1964), pp. 1–45.

Stuart, Richard B. *Trick or Treatment: How and When Psychotherapy Fails.* Champaign, Illinois: Research Press, 1970.

Szasz, Thomas. *The Myth of Mental Illness.* New York: Harper & Row, 1961.

——, and George J. Alexander. "The American Association for the Abolition of Involuntary Mental Hospitalization." *The Abolitionist,* Vol. 1 (Summer 1971), p. 1.

Taylor, Robert L., and E. Fuller Torrey. "Mental Health Coverage Under a National Health Insurance Plan." Pamphlet of the National Institutes of Mental Health, Rockville, Maryland, 1973.

Teghtsoonian, Martha. "Distribution by Sex of Authors and Editors of Psychological Journals, 1970–1972." *American Psychologist,* Vol. 29 (April 1974), pp. 262–269.

Tennov, Dorothy. "Feminism, Psychotherapy, and Professionalism." *Journal of Contemporary Psychotherapy,* Vol. 5 (1973), pp. 107–111.

——. "Mode of Control and Reinforcement Density as a Function of the Sex of the Behaver." *Women Speaking,* Vol. 3, No. 6 (July 1974), pp. 7–8.

——. "Psychotherapy, Women, and the Women's Movement." Paper presented at the Annual Meetings of the Society for Psychotherapy Research, Philadelphia, Pennsylvania, June 1973.

——. "The Relationship Between Obstetrical Procedures and Perinatal Anoxia." *Journal of Clinical Child Psychology,* Vol. 2 (Fall 1973), pp. 20–22.

——. "The 'Seven Ages' of the Professional Woman." *Women Speaking,* Vol. 2, No. 4 (1972), pp. 7–8.

——. "Women Evaluate and Describe Their Psychotherapy Outside the Clinical Setting." Paper prepared for presentation at the Annual Meetings of the Society for Psychotherapy Research. Denver, Colorado, June 1974.

See also Hoffman, Dorothy T. [Tennov], *et al.*

Tharp, Roland G., and Ralph J. Wetzel. *Behavior Modification in the Natural Environment*. New York: Academic Press, 1969.

Truax, Charles B. "Effective Ingredients in Psychotherapy." *Journal of Counseling Psychology*, Vol. 10 (1963), pp. 256–263.

——. "Effects of Client-Centered Psychotherapy With Schizophrenic Patients: Nine Years Pretherapy and Nine Years Posttherapy Hospitalization." *Journal of Consulting and Clinical Psychology*, Vol. 35 (1970), pp. 417–422.

——, and R. R. Carkhuff. *Toward Effective Counseling and Psychotherapy*. Chicago: Aldine, 1967.

——, and Kevin M. Mitchell. "Research on Certain Therapist Interpersonal Skills in Relation to Process and Outcome." In *Handbook of Psychotherapy and Behavior Change: Empirical Analysis*. Edited by Allen E. Bergin and Sol L. Garfield. New York: John Wiley, 1971.

"Tyler Foresees New Era of Hope for Psychology." *APA Monitor*, Vol. 4 (November 1973), pp. 1, 6.

Tyson, Robert. "Should M. A. Level Psychologists Have Full Membership?" *APA Monitor*, Vol. 3, No. 7 (July 1972), p. 2.

Ullman, Leonard P., and Leonard Krasner. *Case Studies in Behavior Modification*. New York: Holt, Rinehart and Winston, 1965.

Vetter, Betty M. "Survey Paints Picture of Psychology Manpower." *APA Monitor*, Vol. 4, No. 11 (November 1973), pp. 3, 7.

Viscott, David S. *The Making of a Psychiatrist*. New York: Fawcett, 1973.

Wallace, Harold E. R., and Marion B. H. Whyte. "Natural History of Psychoneuroses." *British Medical Journal*, Vol. 1 (January 1959), pp. 144–148.

Ward, Jack. "Doctors Speak on the Ortho-Molecular Approach." Saskatchewan: Canadian Schizophrenic Foundation, 1972.

Warren, Jim. "Rogers Challenges Psychologists to Become Future Oriented." *APA Monitor* (November 1972), pp. 1, 7, 14.

Watson, Goodwin. "Growing Edges in Groups." *Contemporary Psychology*, Vol. 11, No. 5 (1966), p. 238.

——. *Social Psychology: Issues and Insights*. Philadelphia: J. B. Lippincott, 1966.

Wechsler, James A. *In A Darkness*. New York: W. W. Norton, 1972.

Weinberg, George. *Society and the Healthy Homosexual*. Garden City, New York: Doubleday, 1973.

Weiss, Steven Lee. "Perceived Effectiveness of Psychotherapy."

Journal of Consulting and Clinical Psychology, Vol. 39 (1972), pp. 156–159.

Weisstein, Naomi. "Psychology Constructs the Female, or the Fantasy Life of the Male Psychologist." In *Roles Women Play: Readings Toward Women's Liberation.* Edited by Michele Hoffnung Garskof. Monterey, California: Brooks/Cole, 1971.

Weitz, Robert D. [Chairman, Ways and Means Committee, CAPPS]. An open letter to psychologists. Council for the Advancement of the Psychological Professions and Sciences, July 11, 1973.

Wells, Harry K. *The Failure of Psychoanalysis: From Freud to Fromm.* New York: International, 1963.

Wentworth-Rohr, Ivan. "Symptoms, Insight and Behavior Therapies in Psychoanalytic Psychotherapy." *Psychoanalytic Review*, Vol. 57 (July 1970), pp. 47–59.

White, Martha S. "Psychological and Social Barriers to Women in Science." *Science*, Vol. 170 (October 1970), pp. 413–416.

Whitehorn, J. C., and B. J. Betz. "Further Studies of the Doctor as a Crucial Variable in the Outcome of Treatment with Schizophrenic Patients." *American Journal of Psychiatry*, Vol. 117 (1960), pp. 215–223.

———. "A Study of Psychotherapeutic Relationships Between Physicians and Schizophrenic Patients." *American Journal of Psychiatry*, Vol. 111 (1954), pp. 321–331.

Wiggins, Jack. "Should Psychotherapy Be Included in Health Insurance Programs? Yes!" *APA Monitor*, Vol. 4 (September–October 1973), p. 8.

Wildman, Robert W., and Robert W. Wildman, III. "The Practice of Clinical Psychologists in the United States." *Journal of Clinical Psychology*, Vol. 23, No. 3 (1967), pp. 292–295.

Wilson, Louise. *This Stranger, My Son.* London: John Murray, 1969.

Winett, Richard. "Behavior Modification and Social Change." *Professional Psychology*, Vol. 5, No. 3 (August 1974), pp. 239–248.

Wogan, Michael. "Effect of Therapist-Patient Personality Variables on Therapeutic Outcome." *Journal of Consulting and Clinical Psychology*, Vol. 35 (1970), pp. 356–361.

Wolf, Montrose, Todd Risley, and H. Mees. "Application of Operant Conditioning Procedures to the Behavior Problems of an Autistic Child." *Behavior Research and Theory*, Vol. 1 (1964), pp. 305–312.

Wolff, Charlotte. *Love Between Women.* New York: Harper & Row, 1971.

Wolman, Benjamin B., ed. *Handbook in General Psychology.* Englewood Cliffs, New Jersey: Prentice-Hall, 1973.

Wolpe, Joseph. "Psychotherapeutic Efficacy and Objective Research." In *Changing Frontiers in the Science of Psychotherapy Research.* Edited by Allen E. Bergin and Hans S. Strupp. Chicago: Aldine, 1972.

———, Andrew Salter, and L. J. Reyna. *The Conditioning Therapies.* New York: Holt, Rinehart and Winston, 1964, chapter 3.

"X Marks the Panic." *Newsweek,* August 28, 1972, p. 65.

Yalom, I. D. *The Theory and Practice of Group Psychotherapy.* New York: Basic Books, 1970.

Young, Kimball. *Social Psychology.* New York: F. S. Crofts, 1947.

Zeligs, Rose. "Do Therapists Play God?" *Mental Hygiene,* Vol. 54 (1970), p. 161.

Zilboorg, Gregory. "Masculine and Feminine: Some Biological and Cultural Aspects." In *Psychoanalysis and Women.* Edited by Jean Baker Miller. Middlesex, England: Penguin Books, 1973.

Index